SPECTRAL SPAIN

SERIES PREFACE

Gothic Literary Studies is dedicated to publishing groundbreaking scholarship on Gothic in literature and film. The Gothic, which has been subjected to a variety of critical and theoretical approaches, is a form which plays an important role in our understanding of literary, intellectual and cultural histories. The series seeks to promote challenging and innovative approaches to Gothic which question any aspect of the Gothic tradition or perceived critical orthodoxy. Volumes in the series explore how issues such as gender, religion, nation and sexuality have shaped our view of the Gothic tradition. Both academically rigorous and informed by the latest developments in critical theory, the series provides an important focus for scholarly developments in Gothic studies, literary studies, cultural studies and critical theory. The series will be of interest to students of all levels and to scholars and teachers of the Gothic and literary and cultural histories.

SERIES EDITORS
Andrew Smith, University of Sheffield
Benjamin F. Fisher, University of Mississippi

EDITORIAL BOARD
Kent Ljungquist, Worcester Polytechnic Institute Massachusetts
Richard Fusco, St Joseph's University, Philadelphia
David Punter, University of Bristol
Chris Baldick, University of London
Angela Wright, University of Sheffield
Jerrold E. Hogle, University of Arizona

For all titles in the Gothic Literary Studies series visit *www.uwp.co.uk*

Spectral Spain
Haunted Houses, Silent Spaces and Traumatic Memories in Post-Franco Gothic Fiction

Heidi Backes

UNIVERSITY OF WALES PRESS
2024

© Heidi Backes, 2024

All rights reserved. No part of this book may be reproduced in any material form (including photocopying or storing it in any medium by electronic means and whether or not transiently or incidentally to some other use of this publication) without the written permission of the copyright owner except in accordance with the provisions of the Copyright, Designs and Patents Act. Applications for the copyright owner's written permission to reproduce any part of this publication should be addressed to the University of Wales Press, University Registry, King Edward VII Avenue, Cardiff CF10 3NS.

www.uwp.co.uk

British Library Cataloguing-in-Publication Data
A catalogue record for this book is available from the British Library.

ISBN 978-1-83772-126-9
eISBN 978-1-83772-127-6

The right of Heidi Backes to be identified as author of this work has been asserted in accordance with sections 77 and 79 of the Copyright, Designs and Patents Act 1988.

Typeset by Marie Doherty
Printed by CPI Antony Rowe, Melksham, United Kingdom

*To my daughter, who has inherited
my love of books and Spain.*

Contents

Acknowledgements — ix

Introduction: Spectral Spain — 1

Part I: Haunted Houses

Introduction — 19

1 A Ghost in the Looking Glass: Reflections on Women's Autonomy and Catalan Independence in Mercè Rodoreda's *A Broken Mirror* — 23

2 Shifting Borders: Race, Class and the Phantasmagoric Other in *Bene* by Adelaida García Morales — 40

3 A (Haunted) Room of One's Own: The Evolution of Gender Roles and Female Sexuality in Adelaida García Morales's *Aunt Águeda* and *Elisa's Secret* — 60

4 War at Home: The Haunted House as Battlefield in Ana María Matute's *Family Demons* — 87

Part II: Silent Spaces

Introduction — 107

5 The Ghost Howls at Night: Silence, Death and the Politics of Fear in Julio Llamazares's *Wolf Moon* — 111

6   Life in a Ghost Town: Gothic Landscapes, Rural   125
    Memory and the Silence of Loss in Julio Llamazares's
    The Yellow Rain

7   Unspeakable Truths: Silence, Spectrality and the   141
    Artefacts of Memory in Cristina Fernández Cubas's
    The Swing

Part III: Traumatic Memories

Introduction   157

8   Violent Childhood: Dark Imagination and the Trauma   160
    of Progress in Espido Freire's *Irlanda*

9   The End of Innocence: Childhood Fantasy and   175
    Monstrous Reality in Ana María Matute's
    Uninhabited Paradise

10 As the Ghost Speaks: Bearing Witness to Fascist   190
    Horror in Carlos Ruiz Zafón's *The Prisoner of Heaven*

Conclusion   205

Notes   211
Bibliography   235
Index   253

Acknowledgements

I first began my research on Spanish Gothic literature as a master's student in 2006, at a time when very little had been published about the Gothic in Spain and when the field of literary Hispanism itself still seemed rather resistant to considering it a valid area of study. I was lucky to have two incredibly supportive advisors during my graduate career – Will Risley and Jeffrey Oxford – who encouraged my pursuit of Gothic fiction as my main concentration during my master's work and, later, for my doctoral thesis. Without their early mentorship, this book would not have been possible.

I am also grateful to my many wonderful colleagues in the International Gothic Association, the Gothic Association of New Zealand and Australia, and the Gothic Spaces conference at the University of Tokyo, whose feedback and conversations over the past several years have been both helpful and highly motivational, contributing immensely to the central arguments of this book. I extend special thanks to the editorial board of the University of Wales Press and particularly to Sarah Lewis for her communication and support throughout the writing and editorial process.

Finally, a most heartfelt thanks to my beloved father, David James Backes, who passed away unexpectedly just two days after I finished writing this manuscript. He was a retired professor of mass communication at the University of Wisconsin-Milwaukee, an environmentalist, an author of numerous books, and the kindest, gentlest soul I have ever known. His love and support throughout my life and career were unwavering, and the countless conversations we had during the writing of this book were invaluable to me in the framing of history and human nature. He was my first and greatest teacher, the best mentor I could have asked for, and the best friend I will ever have. To him I am eternally grateful.

Introduction
Spectral Spain

※

In his book *Tomorrow in the Battle Think on Me* (1994), Spanish novelist Javier Marías notes the rather remarkable fact that there is no Spanish-language equivalent of the verb 'to haunt', pointing instead to the English and the French (*hanter*) as verbs that 'both describe what ghosts do to the places and people they frequent or watch over or revisit' or, simply, as words that act as 'another name for the curse of memory'.[1] Perhaps ironically, this leaves Spanish authors without a specific word that signifies the effects of these spectral returns of memory – an extraordinarily relevant topic in a contemporary era that is defined by the increasingly persistent ghosts of the past. In Europe and elsewhere, as memory and trauma scholars have noted for many years, the vestiges of twentieth-century genocide and its aftermath continue to serve as reminders of the devastating effects of collective trauma and as warnings of the potential monstrosity that exists within humankind. In Spain, memory and history converge in the present at a contentious intersection between the need for meaningful acknowledgement of their own national trauma – the civil war (1936–9) and resulting dictatorship of Francisco Franco – and the compulsion to remain silent.

Among literary and cultural scholars of Spain, the now nearly fifty-year period from 20 November 1975 (the date of Franco's death) until the present is typically referred to as the 'post-Franco era', despite the multitude of political, social and cultural events that have occurred in the five decades the term references. The continued use of this blanket term points to the fact that our language for the contemporary era in Spain inherently evokes present absences, lending it a spectral quality that is impossible to ignore.[2] The concept of the ghosts of the past still lingering in the present is, of course, highly relevant in Spain, where the death of the dictator and the subsequent burial of his body in the Valley of the Fallen (a massive monument towering over the countryside outside of Madrid, its stone cross visible from the main highway) became an immediate point of contention between those who mourned the loss of the dictator and those who were glad to see him go. This has resulted in a decades-long obsession with Franco's physical body and political legacy, as Sebastiaan Faber has recently examined in *Exhuming Franco*.[3] In Spain, the metaphorical ghosts of the past are also accompanied by the quite literal corporeal remains of the more than 100,000 estimated victims of the civil war who have yet to be exhumed from mass graves.[4] Thus, the idea of exhuming the past is not just figurative speech in Spanish culture, but quite a literal situation of the (un)dead, physical corpse of memory that lingers in Spain still in the twenty-first century. Beyond these graves, the existence of the Francisco Franco Foundation (created in 1976 to promote the legacy of the dictator) and the use of Francoist symbols and titles have, until the passing of the Democratic Memory Law in October 2022, continued to favour the historical narrative of the regime. The tangible presence of the past is even witnessed in the prevalence of streets throughout the country that still retain their names in honour of Franco's military officers and government officials nearly fifty years after the regime ended, and more than eighty years after the civil war.[5] Memorialising the past through the act of naming – recalling those who supported the dictator and his regime – is yet another reminder of the power of memory and its pervasive presence not just in the context of artistic production but in the very spaces that we inhabit, spaces in Spain that are inevitably palimpsests of trauma itself.

    These haunted spaces also manifest themselves in the literary realm, where contemporary Spanish authors frequently portray individual and collective trauma through a Gothic lens, giving absence, silence and mourning a place for recognition. What we see in the literature of the post-Franco era is not only an acknowledgement of the injustices and inequities that lasted throughout the dictatorship, but also a reflection on the disillusionment of the Transition,[6] a period that promised to modernise Spain by ushering in a new democracy that would rid the nation of its most pernicious ghosts. In the decades since Franco's death, Spanish authors have continued to draw attention to the lack of reparations and the inherited silence about the dictatorship – in part a result of the 1977 Amnesty Law, which forged the act of forgetting into national policy. The direct result of this authoritative stance was the creation of a new national memory about the past that purposefully tried to erase any trauma stemming from the civil war era; consequently, as numerous authors of fiction have shown in their post-Franco narratives, the following generation inherited not just the trauma, but also the silence – and the ghosts – that came with it.

The spectral presence of the past in contemporary Spanish cultural production has been a recurring theme in scholarship since Jacques Derrida's theory of hauntology[7] provided a critical framework for understanding how present absences infiltrate, influence and, indeed, disrupt modern life. The first Hispanist to apply Derrida's theory to Spanish culture was Jo Labanyi, who very clearly argued that 'the whole of modern Spanish culture – its study and its practice – can be read as one big ghost story'[8] and, later, that 'an aesthetics of haunting' is perhaps the most appropriate lens through which to examine Spanish history.[9] In their volume on Franco's legacy in contemporary Spain, Eloy Merino and H. Rosi Song consider 'the dictatorship as a distressing conditioner of the present', noting 'a focus on how the past haunts and produces victims'.[10] José Colmeiro, in turn, points to the physical evidence of victimhood found in the mass graves that the Association for the Recovery of Historical Memory is currently excavating: 'Thousands of unmarked burial sites in ditches along the roads still remain in the Spanish landscape, invisible but ever present, just like ghosts still awaiting their day of justice.'[11] The landscape itself becomes the focal point of Patricia Keller's study of the aesthetics of haunting in Spanish film and photography, in which she notes: 'Ghosts are everywhere in contemporary Spain and hold a pervasive and profoundly palpable place in the country's cultural landscape.'[12] Most recently, Antonio Córdoba and Daniel García-Donoso have explored death as a common theme in Spanish culture and, emphasising the deeply divisive nature of the large cross atop the monument at the Valley of the Fallen, assert: 'Spectrality provides a fundamental language to disarm the Valley's hostile memory and highlight the contours of the historical trauma of Francoism.'[13]

Although these critics all agree that contemporary Spanish culture is best understood through an aesthetics of haunting, they most frequently focus their studies on visual culture and film media; moreover, none have examined the manifestation of spectrality in Spain from a Gothic literary perspective. Cinema has been a common focal point for nearly all of the studies of haunting and the Gothic in contemporary Spanish cultural production, with critical works dedicated to films like *The Spirit of the Beehive* (Victor Erice, 1973), *Raise Ravens* (Carlos Saura, 1976), *The Devil's Backbone* (Guillermo del Toro, 2001), *The Others* (Alejandro Amenábar, 2001), *Pan's Labyrinth* (del Toro, 2006) and *The Orphanage* (J. A. Bayona, 2007).[14] It is important to note that this frequent focus on Spanish film has perhaps unintentionally led to an area of study that is almost entirely dominated by the work of male cinema directors, leaving women's voices out of much of contemporary Spanish Gothic scholarship. Among the studies on Spanish Gothic that do include literature, the majority of the primary texts are written by men, likely due in part to the fact that male-authored Spanish texts tend to have more accessible English translations than those written by their female peers. There is a need to amplify these still-marginalised voices in order to better understand the ramifications of twentieth-century trauma from a variety of perspectives within a field (Spanish Gothic studies) that is, itself, still relatively marginalised from mainstream Gothic scholarship and from the study of European literature more broadly, where Spain frequently features as an exoticised Other.

In his discussion of the Gothic, Fred Botting notes: 'Gothic atmospheres – gloomy and mysterious – have repeatedly signalled the disturbing return of pasts upon presents and evoked emotions of terror and laughter'.[15] Spain's turbulent past makes it a prime setting for the formation of a Gothic literary perspective: it provides a natural *locus terribilis*, since the Spanish present is a space of anxiety in which the dark and violent past meets widespread uncertainty about the future. And yet, despite this natural inclination toward the Gothic, the study of Spanish Gothic literature has only just begun to be accepted in academic circles within the past decade. For the better part of the last century, Hispanists largely ignored the vast contributions of Spanish authors to the Gothic literary corpus, instead returning to the long-held belief that realism is the country's true literary form. Labanyi has pointed to the steadfast insistence of Peninsularists on the study of high culture, noting that such preference 'has systematically made invisible – ghostly – whole areas of culture which are seen as non-legitimate objects of study because they are consumed by subaltern groups'.[16] She explains that, in part, this lack of academic consideration is due to the residual effects of Francoism's 'co-option of popular and mass culture'.[17] For Spanish academics in the Transition era, popular forms of culture were inevitably tainted with the memory of the dictatorship, and thus the focus on high culture was a trend in the field of Peninsular Studies for decades. When this stigma against popular literature is combined with the common over-application of the term 'fantastic' to describe what is, in reality, Gothic fiction, it is easy to see why the study of Spanish Gothic literature has been slower to gain traction.

Xavier Aldana Reyes, in his book *Spanish Gothic*, includes a detailed summary of the trajectory of the field up to the book's publication in 2017;[18] in order to avoid an exhaustive repetition of these textual references, I would like to briefly highlight a few main texts and concepts that serve as points of departure for the present study. In the early 2000s, essays by Jo Labanyi and Janet Pérez provided a critical framework for an approach to haunting[19] and the feminine neo-Gothic[20] in late-twentieth-century Spanish cultural production. Miriam López Santos's 2010 monograph on the early Gothic narrative in Spain was the first book-length survey of early Spanish Gothic fiction, featuring an extensive examination of primary texts that can be classified as Gothic.[21] Abigail Lee Six has also been a foundational figure in highlighting many of the more common Gothic themes as they appear in works by various Spanish authors from the nineteenth century to the present, whose narratives she compares to earlier forms of northern European Gothic. Her work on Adelaida García Morales[22] is highly influential to my own scholarship on that author included in Part I of the present book, and her subsequent work on Gothic terror and Spanish vampires[23] has added tremendously to the extant research on Peninsular Gothic. Ann Davies's *Contemporary Spanish Gothic* (2016) studies Gothic production in art, cinema and bestselling fiction, concluding that '[c]ontemporary Spanish culture, then, functions as a Gothic nexus'.[24] Davies considers Spanish Gothic to have always been transnational, although it does on occasion draw on Spanish narratives and cultural concerns to greater or lesser degrees. In his own survey of Spanish Gothic, Aldana Reyes examines both literature and film in an era spanning from 1785 to the present, building upon the canon initially established by López Santos and adding to it the visual media of the twentieth and twenty-first centuries. His book considers Spanish Gothic as less of a regional and more of a general, national product based on external influences that Spanish authors have adapted to their own particular uses; to this extent, he explains that his interest lies more in 'the synergies between Spain and the Gothic as a transnational mode to which the Spanish have consistently turned since the late-eighteenth century'.[25] In viewing the Gothic as a national cultural product with transnational influences and appeal, Aldana Reyes points to various trends in Spanish Gothic production that follow certain historical and political timelines and which demonstrate clearly the British and American cultural influences in the peninsula.

If the Spanish Gothic (and particularly Spanish Gothic cinema) is transnational in form, as Aldana Reyes and Davies have argued, to the Spanish literary community its themes are profoundly specific, touching upon regional and national concerns that reflect a twentieth-century experience that is also uniquely Spanish: living in Europe under a dictatorship for nearly four decades, and then transitioning to a democracy that was built around structures and figures from the regime, mandating silence about the past through a national law that would not be overturned for three more decades. While Spanish cinema, because of its international audience, relies on a certain transnational appeal that moves its Gothic forms and themes

Introduction

beyond the regional, here I will argue that Spanish literature – with few exceptions – does the opposite: most of the authors included in this book write for a Spanish audience, taking advantage of the condition of shared experience in their portrayals and recollections of the past. Many of these texts employ elements of the literary realism typical of Spanish fiction (where *costumbrismo*, a focus on regional customs, is a national form). These Gothic texts are often less concerned with the creation of fictitious monsters and more with the portrayal of reality itself as the ultimate source of terror. Because of their treatment of the past, rooted primarily in the need to recover marginalised voices that have been silenced in official narratives, these works of Gothic fiction may also be considered part of the literary 'Memory Boom' in the 1990s and early 2000s, in which Spanish authors frequently turned their attention to historical memory and trauma resulting from the dictatorship. For women authors especially, the representation of the nation and their role in it is an overwhelming feature of their Gothic literary production; through the haunted house motif and explorations of dark childhood fantasy, they speak to individual and collective trauma resulting from a culture of violence and fear, reflecting their own regional experiences in the development of their Gothic narratives. These voices, commonly left out of discussions of Spanish cultural studies precisely because of the contemporary academic focus on cinema, could perhaps be described as always already Gothicised: speaking from the margins, their literary works inherently subvert traditional memory discourse, questioning the very structures of Spanish democracy during and after the Transition era, and highlighting the spectral traces of the past that continue to haunt the present.

Spectral Spain will therefore establish the Gothic as an especially apt mode for Spanish authors to express notions of trauma, historical memory and the fractured self in the years after the dictatorship. If spectrality is, as Derrida suggests, the always-already returning ghosts of the past in the present, in Spain it is emblematic of the continued tension between modernity and the imposition of a monocultural, nationalised tradition throughout the twentieth century. Haunting is a symptom of not just the past trauma of the civil war and resulting dictatorship continuing to work its way into the present, but also of the disenchantment – particularly prevalent during the 1980s and 90s, with another notable resurgence in the past ten years – of a large part of the population who saw that the transition to democracy did not erase the injustices of the recent past. Some of these authors focus directly on the civil war and the immediate post-war era; others take on broader contexts of haunting and its implications in an array of socio-political issues, especially emphasising gender, class and race; still others use haunting as a trope to comment on the loss of cultural tradition in the remote Spanish countryside, where the advent of modern technology and the contemporary urban-centred lifestyle have left scores of ghost towns, whose dilapidated structures have transformed into symbolic cemeteries in memory of traditional ways of life that will never return. The texts studied in this book serve as not only popular entertainment with all the trappings of the Gothic, but also as markers of memory in post-Franco Spain; the Gothic, in this historical moment, is a tool that is perfectly conditioned to address notions of trauma, loss and mourning, gender roles, race, class, regional identity politics and more in a period defined by socio-political anxiety and a fear of the return of the not-so-distant past. Spectrality in all its forms is inevitably a defining feature of post-Franco Spanish cultural production.

By focusing the present study on literature, I aim to highlight in particular the voices of several canonical women authors who have been mostly left out of contemporary Spanish Gothic scholarship due to the frequent focus on cinema and the issues with accessibility of translations noted above. Works by Mercè Rodoreda, Adelaida García Morales, Ana María Matute, Cristina Fernández Cubas and Espido Freire – several of which have not yet been translated into English and are thus mostly unknown to scholars and readers outside of literary Hispanism – along with novels by Julio Llamazares and Carlos Ruiz Zafón will form the basis of my analysis of Gothic haunting in post-Franco Spanish literature. The mix of regional backgrounds represented in the chosen works allows me to be more inclusive of voices from a variety of geographical and cultural regions in Spain, facilitating commentary on urban and rural areas in the north and the south, resulting in a less monolithic understanding of Spanish cultural history than is often the case in Hispanic Studies.

Introduction

In the following sections, I will elaborate on the relationship between memory and spectrality in Spain, and briefly outline the main themes of the chapters to come. An important part of this project is establishing these authors and texts within the Spanish Gothic canon to which they rightfully belong (an ongoing issue in literary Hispanism, where the common over-application of the term 'fantastic' has led to the under-recognition of Gothic texts); moving forward, the translation of these texts into English would be an invaluable contribution to the field of Gothic Studies. Given that the target audience of this book is English-speaking, I have used English translations of the primary texts where available; where these are not available, I have provided my own translations. In every chapter, I have also included biographical information about each author and summaries of the novels studied in the hope of encouraging international scholars to consider these authors and texts as a starting point for future work on regional and transnational forms of the Gothic.

Haunting and Memory in Contemporary Spain

In her seminal text on the Spanish Transition era, *El mono del desencanto* [*The Monkey of Disenchantment*], Teresa Vilarós describes the transition to democracy as a site of rupture from which the monstrous body of the past arises, only to be quickly buried due to the political insistence on silencing memory. Using rather Gothic terminology to depict this monstrous creation, she states:

> Ambas, las purgas sociales de la dictadura y las reformas políticas de la transición, esconden inevitablemente una ruptura, una fisura inscrita en lo más profundo, hábitat del monstruo en que se ha convertido nuestro pasado histórico. Monstruo, Cosa, fantasma, cadáver o vampiro, el espacio fisural es el espacio de su retirada.

> [Both, the social purges of the dictatorship and the political reforms of the transition, inevitably hide a rupture, a fissure inscribed in the furthest recesses, habitat of the monster into which our historical past has transformed. Monster, Thing, ghost, cadaver or vampire, the fissure space is the space of its retreat.][26]

With this extended metaphor, Vilarós emphasises the unspeakable nature of the recent Spanish past, pointing to disillusionment with the political processes that essentially continued Francoist policies under the guise of democracy. It is no coincidence that the term 'historical memory' has come to be associated with the liberal Spanish demand for recognition of the traumatic past (as noted in the Historical Memory Law of 2007); although seemingly redundant – memory and history are always inherently intertwined – , 'memory' itself is, in post-Franco Spain, increasingly reminiscent of the problematic rendering of the past that was part of the pact to forget injustices in order to rebuild the nation as a whole. For Michael Richards, historical memory is 'situated *between* history and memory',[27] occupying a liminal space that, for our purposes here, is inevitably spectral in nature. By asserting that the new democracy was based on a mythologised, hegemonic version of the past that relied on propagandistic fabrications and denials of historical truths, Vilarós and other cultural historians of contemporary Spain have paved the way for an examination of Spanish historical memory as a Derridean revenant (or what Paul Ricouer has called a 'trace of the past'[28]) that is always already returning to the present, reminding us of the collective inheritance of trauma.

Memory and history are thus inextricably linked in Spain as two sides of a contentious coin that constantly shifts between an institutionalised version of the past that suppresses difference and one that recognises the victims' voices as equally valid in the curation of social memory. Censorship, fundamental to the project of fascism, has survived the Franco dictatorship in the form of the ongoing push for silence, part of a conservative political ideology that treats the historical past as an unspeakable secret in a process that inevitably invokes Nicholas Abraham and Maria Torok's transgenerational phantom.[29] Indeed, the concept of fascism itself is imbued with spectral potentiality, as Richard Golsan explains when he claims that 'the debate over fascism becomes implicitly a debate over fascism's return, or perhaps its continuing and continuous presence in contemporary life'.[30] For Joan Ramon Resina, the ghosts of post-Franco Spain are the 'residue of the past in the emotions of the living',[31] a profound connection to memory that becomes an integral part of the Spanish being. From a sociological perspective, as Avery Gordon notes, '[h]aunting is a constituent element of modern social life. It is neither pre-modern supposition nor individual psychosis; it is a generalizable social phenomenon of great import. To study social life one must confront the ghostly aspects of it.'[32]

Recognising the traces of fascist politics in the policies and practices of the Transition era, Spanish authors saw the structure of the new democratic nation as a house haunted by the lingering ghosts of the recent past. A literal cemetery populated with the mass graves of the civil war's victims – the bodies of whom Carlos Jerez Farrán and Samuel Amago have called 'some of the most "alive" dead bodies in contemporary Spain'[33] – the Spanish landscape becomes, in these Gothic texts, a liminal space in which the past and present endlessly converge, creating ghosts from the fragmented pieces of collective memory. We will see that the authors studied here have sought to answer George Haggerty's question – 'What manner of prose narrative most effectively embodies a nightmare vision?'[34] – with their own form of the Gothic, employing some techniques of literary realism within an ominous, terror-inducing Gothic atmosphere that speaks to present concerns about the unresolved past. With the exception of Mercè Rodoreda and Ana María Matute, the other authors included in this book were born after the civil war and, thus, grew up during the dictatorship; as Carmen Moreno-Nuño notes, 'Although this generation was not part of the fighting, it has in fact lived through its painful consequences; its members were raised on an oral tradition that rehashed the horror of the conflict.'[35] These authors – survivors or inheritors of the initial trauma stemming from the civil war – became important voices in the memory landscape of Spanish literature in the aftermath of the dictatorship, speaking directly to the Spanish public about the need to acknowledge the recent past. In his discussion of this Transition era, Resina has said:

> Histories proliferate according to the need to countenance a society's ghosts. The historian gives a face to the faceless dead, the unknown, silent, or silenced ones. During the Transition new histories seemed to emerge from the great zones of amnesia, histories that were not grounded in the accepted historical discourse. Such histories were

not just other but were often unreconcilable with those bequeathed by state-oriented historiography. Their emergence amounted to a deregulation of memory, lifting the state monopoly on the past.[36]

Here we must note the important double meaning of the Spanish word 'historia', which signifies both history and story; the 'histories' to which Resina refers might, therefore, be equally understood as historical or fictional narratives that seek to recover memory. Not surprisingly, the subsequent literary 'Memory Boom' of the 1990s and 2000s is, as Fiona Schouten has suggested, 'not a phenomenon that Spain feels fully comfortable with'[37] because of the ongoing urge to maintain the silence of the Transition era, repressing these histories in accordance with the political pact to forget. The spectral traces in these narratives are, then, an inevitable feature of contemporary Spanish literature that demands further examination; as María del Pilar Blanco and Esther Peeren have asserted, 'studies of ghosts and haunting can do more than obsessively recall a fixed past; in an active, dynamic engagement, they may reveal the insufficiency of the present moment, as well as the disconsolations and erasures of the past, and a tentative hopefulness for future resolutions'.[38] Through their representations of the spectral returns of the past, these Spanish authors address not just the injustices of the past, but also the disillusionment with the present (in which reparations have yet to be made) and the fear that these histories may be repeated in the future.

Spectral Spain

Taking into consideration the ongoing political struggles over the memory narrative in contemporary Spain, what interests me here are the specific ways in which Spanish Gothic literature interacts with and reflects historical memory during the Transition era and into the present. The first part of this book, titled 'Haunted Houses', focuses specifically on multiple issues related to gender, in combination with class and race, illuminating women's reactions to the gendered expectations of the dictatorship and the sexual revolution of the Transition era. The haunted house motif

Introduction

in general provides ample scope for addressing the Female Gothic, and I draw on the work of scholars such as Ellen Moers, Juliann Fleenor, Donna Heiland, Julia Kristeva, Sandra Gilbert and Susan Gubar, among others, in the four chapters included in this section. Chapter 1 studies the only novel in this book that was published just prior to Franco's death: *The Broken Mirror* by Mercè Rodoreda (1974). This chapter examines the Gothic haunted house as a marker of social class and placeholder of regional memory, through a study of objects within the house and their relation to trauma and differences in socioeconomic status in metropolitan Barcelona. Rodoreda's focus on mirrors and glass denotes visions of the Catalan past, and ghosts – as spectres of the past – reflect anxieties about the as-yet uncertain national and regional future. Despite the fact that this novel was published prior to Franco's death, it holds tremendous value as one of the first narratives to address the beginning of the civil war from a Gothic perspective, and its symbolic reflections and fragmentations illuminate the continued projection of instability and fear onto the imminent future. Chapter 2 focuses on boundaries and phantasmagoric transgression associated with race, class, and otherness in *Bene*, by Adelaida García Morales (1985), applying Kristeva's theory of abjection to provide critical commentary on the treatment of the Roma people and perceptions of difference in post-war southern Spain. In Chapter 3, *Aunt Águeda* and *Elisa's Secret* by García Morales (1995, 1999) are the basis for a feminist analysis of the shifting expectations of women throughout twentieth-century Spain and the modernising role of sexuality in the Transition era, examining the roles of the 'Angel in the House' and the monstrous Other in relation to the spectral masculine gaze. Chapter 4 is dedicated to a study of Ana María Matute's very last novel, *Family Demons*, which she left unfinished at the time of her death in 2014. This text portrays the haunted house as a battlefield in which the protagonist's deceased grandmother wages war on those who live inside it, paralleling the civil war that is beginning just beyond the property line and invoking the ghosts of the war in Morocco that augment the Colonel's desire for a return of the mythologised past.

Part II, 'Silent Spaces', focuses on various manifestations of silence and spectrality, with critical commentary on rural Spain as a site of memory and extended mourning, taking into consideration Sergio del Molino's notion of the 'Great Trauma' of twentieth-century rural exodus, alongside theoretical approaches to spectrality and mourning by Jacques Derrida, Nicolas Abraham and Maria Torok, Sigmund Freud and others. Chapter 5 studies the representation of *maquis* as spectral monsters in Julio Llamazares's *Wolf Moon* (1985), in which the politics of terror combines with a Gothic atmosphere of silence, darkness and death to portray the impossibility of hope and the inevitability of loss in the immediate post-war era. The central role of mourning in this text provides a fascinating commentary on the role of the recent historical past in the collective memory of rural Asturias and Cantabria. In Chapter 6, a study of Llamazares's *The Yellow Rain* (1988) examines silence, fear, and mental degeneration derived from complete isolation in a ghost town in Aragón, painting a critical portrait of the effects of rural exodus in twentieth-century Spain, leaving behind a spectral landscape that encourages oblivion. Chapter 7 references Alison Landsberg's theory of prosthetic memory in a study of silence and the artefacts of memory in Cristina Fernández Cubas's *The Swing* (1995), in which the re-creation of the past – or forced continuation of it through denial of the present (seen in the uncles' melancholia) – leads to ghostly apparitions of the protagonist's mother and fear associated with reliving trauma, all within a rural Catalan landscape that intensifies tradition and alters the passage of time.

Part III, 'Traumatic Memories', focuses on individual and collective trauma, particularly from the perspective of children. These chapters draw on theoretical work in memory and trauma studies by authors like Cathy Caruth, Roger Luckhurst and Dominick LaCapra, along with critical studies in Gothic trauma and spectrality. Chapter 8 studies Espido Freire's *Irlanda* (1998), in which folk tales and the natural landscape of the rural north blend with the spirits of the dead that haunt the young narrator, Natalia. Compelled to acts of violence because of the tension between the desire for stasis and the pressure to mature according to tradition, Natalia's transgression is rooted in the trauma of progress, a notion that speaks to the transitional era in which the novel was written. Chapter 9 focuses on Ana María Matute's *Uninhabited Paradise* (2009), in which protagonist Adriana's childhood is structured around the patriarchal expectations of girls and women. In this text, monstrosity combines with the phantasmagoric to create competing worlds of fantasy and transgression from the perspective of a young girl whose childhood is marked by absence, isolation and traumatic loss. The abrupt end to Adriana's magical realm coincides with the beginning of the civil war and the devastating realisation that fantasy never returns. Chapter 10 studies Carlos Ruiz Zafón's *The Prisoner of Heaven* (2011) as a testimonial of horror in which protagonist Fermín Romero de Torres details the unspeakable acts of violence in Barcelona's Montjüic Prison after the war, describing himself and his fellow survivors as ghostly presences in a newly-formed regime that seeks to destroy all evidence of its own wrongdoing. This text, notably different from the first two novels in Ruiz Zafón's *Cemetery of Forgotten Books* series, focuses specifically on the brutality of the Franco dictatorship, acknowledging the need to bear witness to the horrors of fascism in a contemporary era that continues to be defined by the spectral returns of the traumatic past.

Through the study of these novels, it becomes clear that haunting is a motif that Spanish authors have used to engage with a variety of social, economic and political issues related to the war, the resulting dictatorship and the disenchantment of the post-Franco era. The contemporary period from the Transition through to the subsequent 'Memory Boom' of the 1990s and 2000s is noted here as a prime literary moment for an elaboration of anxieties in spectral, Gothic form, given its focus on the return of the past in the present and aided by the simultaneous work of the Association for the Recovery of Historical Memory and its ongoing mission to recover the bodies of the victims of the war whose stories have yet to be told. Despite the repeated and ongoing attempts to preserve the institutionalised narrative of the twentieth-century dictatorship, these encounters with the past are, as Teresa Vilarós notes, an inevitable aspect of the Spanish present and future: 'Lo queramos o no, cuando muramos todos aquellos que vivimos la etapa franquista, los gusanos encontrarán en nuestro cuerpo el sabor del pasado, este mismo pasado que se nos ha quedado incorporado ahora como cáncer destructor y como una deuda que hay que pagar' ['Whether we want it or not, when all of us who lived through the Francoist era die, the worms will find in our bodies the taste of the past, that same past that has now become incorporated into us like a destructive cancer and like a debt that must be paid'].[39] Recognising the role of memory as a primary problematic in post-Franco narratives, *Spectral Spain* addresses the present absences at the root of contemporary Spanish Gothic fiction, highlighting the inherent tensions between modernity and the recent past, and contemplating haunting as a mode of expression that grapples with an array of cultural traditions, regional identities, and individual and collective traumas.

Part I

Haunted Houses

Introduction

Ellen Moers, in her seminal feminist study *Literary Women*, famously coined the term 'Female Gothic' to describe Gothic texts written by women authors for whom 'the terrors, the restraints, the dangers of the Gothic novel were not the fantasies but the realities of a woman's life'.[1] As a literary genre that originated primarily for a female audience, the Gothic has quite naturally evolved around the themes central to women's lived experiences, frequently problematising traditional perceptions of womanhood by converting the domestic space – the home – into a site of anxiety and terror. In these texts, the idealised image of the 'angel in the house' contrasts sharply with the monstrous feminine, which arises as a result of (and as a reaction to) the limitations placed on women in the patriarchal systems in which they live and write. In fact, Sandra Gilbert and Susan Gubar see this dichotomous relationship as central to the project of women's authorship, asserting that 'a woman writer must examine, assimilate, and transcend the extreme images of "angel" and "monster" which male authors have generated for her'.[2]

The symbolic nature of the house, which inherently evokes images of maternal comfort and security, makes it a preferred space for female Gothic authors to disrupt and challenge these societal norms, portraying the domestic sphere as one in which warmth and benevolence cede to entrapment, claustrophobia and fear. Indeed, as Maggie Kilgour notes, the female Gothic 'enables us to see that the home *is* a prison, in which the helpless female is at the mercy of ominous patriarchal authorities'.[3] Likewise, Kate Ferguson Ellis considers the house to be one of the foremost Gothic motifs, noting that the genre 'is a discourse about the home, about women's inscription into that space' and about 'the power of women that they [men] have erased, or which women have surrendered as the price of integration into a culture that "placed" them in the home'.[4] In the female Gothic, the physical boundaries of the home transform into liminal spaces with the entrance of the phantasmagoric;

the haunted house thus becomes a prime setting for an elaboration of women's anxieties related to the separate spheres of gendered tradition.

In *Contemporary Women's Gothic Fiction*, Gina Wisker states that female Gothic authors 'are always dealing with ghosts and hauntings'.[5] Given the focus on the home as a preferred setting for many women writers of the Gothic, it is perhaps inevitable that the domestic space is one in which hauntings of many kinds become paramount to the female inhabitants' experience therein. As Diana Wallace notes, 'Possession, confinement, penetration, loss of identity are all shadows which haunt the home for women, particularly those who inhabit – or fear inhabiting – the roles of housewife and mother.'[6] Dara Downey also references the haunting quality of the house, a space which she sees as 'a gothic locus of dread . . . in which women, in Wharton's words, become "domesticated with the Horror, accepting its perpetual presence as one of the fixed conditions of life"'.[7]

The perpetual horror of domesticity is especially relevant to twentieth-century Spain, in which women under Franco's regime (and under the guidance of the fascist Women's Section led by Pilar Primo de Rivera) were subjected to oppressive regulations regarding their relationships, labour and bodies. In order to carry out the mission of National Catholicism, Franco centred women's bodies as vital to the growth of the nation, portraying motherhood as a fundamental patriotic duty. The Women's Section started a massive re-education campaign for women and young girls that focused on the ideals of domesticity and maternal affection, stating explicitly in their propaganda pamphlets: 'Hay que formar en las niñas lo que debería ser la ambición básica de toda mujer: el hacer de la casa la extensión de su persona' ['It is necessary to teach girls what should be the basic ambition of every woman: to make the house an extension of her body'].[8] Here, the official narrative conflating the woman's body with the house is a perfect invitation to Gothic horror: incapable of escaping the domestic confines mandated by the authoritarian regime, Spanish women inevitably saw the nation write itself on and through their bodies, stripping them of autonomy and relegating them to their perceived 'natural space' in the home.

Through the intense national focus on idealised womanhood, twentieth-century Spanish women continued to be perceived (and to perceive themselves) in accordance with the dichotomous angel/monster images of Victorian tradition. As Rosa Isabel Galdona Pérez explains, 'Aquel panorama social propició que la mujer quedase encerrada, en aquella España de hambre y represión, en el sempiterno y estrecho dualismo de ángel o diablo, de casta o prostituta, de *mujer privada* o de *mujer pública*' ['That social panorama encouraged women to stay locked up, in that Spain of hunger and repression, in the never-ending and narrow dualism of angel or devil, of chaste or prostitute, of *private woman* or *public woman*'].[9] That the house itself was supposed to be a space that ensured women's purity through confinement (already a noteworthy feature of Spain's treatment of women beginning in the Golden Age), becomes in the Gothic an inherent fallacy; trapped inside the house, the female protagonists are subjected to the penetrating masculine gaze in spectral form, which denies them bodily autonomy while also stripping the domestic space of its promised safety. Thus, for Spanish women living during the Franco era, the house is always already Gothicised; it is a haunted space that emphasises entrapment and threatens retaliation for those who do not comply.

Part I of *Spectral Spain* considers these matters of domesticity and ideal womanhood as central to the fascist project of twentieth-century Spain. The following four chapters seek to highlight the Gothic haunted house narrative as an especially apt mode through which Spanish women writers elaborate on fears and anxieties related to motherhood, race, class and the nation from their perspectives at the end of the dictatorship, and during and after the Transition era. If, as Galdona Pérez asserts, '[l]a mujer ha sido durante demasiado tiempo lo que podemos denominar una *ausencia histórica*' ['woman has been for too long what we could call a *historical absence*'][10] – implying the spectral nature of women in our very retelling and remembering of history – then the authors studied in this section attempt to shift the historical narrative through their purposeful focus on women's experiences as an important aspect of Spanish cultural memory. Novels by Mercè Rodoreda (*A Broken Mirror*, 1974), Adelaida García Morales (*Bene*, 1985; *Aunt Águeda*, 1995; *Elisa's Secret*, 1999) and Ana María Matute (*Family Demons*,

2014) form the basis for an examination of social norms and the politicised female body within the Gothic setting of the haunted house. Through close readings of these novels, we will come to better understand Spanish women's role in the (de)construction of the nation and the preservation (or destruction) of borders, the repudiation of tradition, and the progress toward female sexual liberation. Hélène Cixous famously emphasised the importance of the act of writing in (re)establishing women's place in history, urging female authors to '[w]rite your self. Your body must be heard.'[11] In the case of the Gothic, as Donna Heiland has asserted, '[t]o inhabit a woman's body is to be a gothic heroine'.[12] For the authors featured in the present section, the Gothic is a perfect mode for the writing of the self, clearly showcasing the threatening spaces that women inhabit while also allowing for the possibility of recovering their bodies – and, thus, their voices – by preserving memory through the act of writing.

1

A Ghost in the Looking Glass: Reflections on Women's Autonomy and Catalan Independence in Mercè Rodoreda's A Broken Mirror

༄

Mercè Rodoreda (1908–83) is considered one of Spain's most influential twentieth-century authors and one of the most widely recognised writers in the Catalan language. As a child growing up in Barcelona, Rodoreda received little formal education but developed an early love of literature. She married her uncle at age twenty and together they had one son, whom Rodoreda gave to her mother to raise upon separating from her husband. She worked for the Institute of Catalan Letters during the early 1930s, a period that Kathleen McNerney describes as 'a stimulating time for her and for Catalonia, a brief period of Catalan autonomy between the repressive dictatorships' of Miguel Primo de Rivera and Francisco Franco.[1] When Franco declared victory in 1939, Rodoreda and others working for the Institute crossed the border into France, where she would live as an exiled author until after Franco's death. For Catalan authors like Rodoreda who was 'a *catalanista* and a supporter of the Republic',[2] the newly-minted Franco regime represented a complete loss of political, cultural and linguistic autonomy. Joan Ramon Resina explains the significance of this exile when he states: 'Unlike the other Spanish exiles, this group could not rely on the continuity of its language or its nation. Publication venues, libraries, the transmission of literacy in schools, everything necessary for the existence of cultural memory had been wiped out after the fall of Catalonia.'[3]

Rodoreda's Catalanist political stance has been well documented in biographies and in numerous studies of her literary work. Many scholars have pointed to her self-proclaimed lack of allegiance to the feminist movement as a seemingly incongruent aspect of her personal politics, especially when considered alongside her female-centric narratives. Lisa Vollendorf, for instance, asserts that despite this stance, 'many of the author's critiques of the patriarchy were also being explored by feminist theorists of the same period'.[4] Likewise, Eva Bru also notes that although 'Rodoreda would remain distant from the feminist cause throughout her entire life . . . it is clear that the majority of her texts give voice, shape and form to the female experience'.[5] Women's autonomy and the unstable political situation of the civil war era are two of Rodoreda's common themes, undoubtedly due to her own experience during that historical period. Resina explains sombrely that the author 'saw her lifetime marked by an overabundance of corpses' and that she 'saw herself in the maelstrom as unintentional witness to the vast mid-century tragedy. That tragedy certainly included the Spanish Civil War, but also the massive exodus and inhumane treatment in French concentration camps.'[6] It is due to this experience that Rodoreda would later write her 1947 short story 'Nit i boira' ['Night and Fog'], one of the first literary texts about the concentration camps to be published shortly after World War II.

Rodoreda's personal experience with this tumultuous political history and women's role in society clearly informs her novel *Mirall trencat* [*A Broken Mirror*], published in 1974. This text follows working-class Teresa Valldaura as she marries into wealth and oversees the next two generations of the family in their large estate outside Barcelona, during a period roughly spanning the 1870s or 1880s into the 1940s. Rodoreda writes the first two parts of the novel in the style of literary realism, describing the upper-class Catalan society of the Valldauras in contrast with the servants who help to manage the household. As Teresa's daughter, Sofia, grows up, she also marries for wealth, and her husband has numerous affairs with the servants and showgirls in town, eventually having a daughter with one of them. Sofia decides to adopt this girl, Maria, and they bring her to the house, where she grows up with Sofia's two sons. Jaume, the youngest, is continually tortured and teased by his two older siblings, who eventually kill him by drowning him in a pond behind the house. Maria and Ramon, Sofia's oldest son, grow very close and, believing that Maria is adopted (as they have heard from the servants), they fall in love. Once they discover that they are, in fact, siblings, Ramon flees the estate and Maria commits suicide by jumping from the roof of the house onto a broken limb of a laurel tree. As each generation grows older and as tragedy continues to strike the family, matriarch Teresa becomes absorbed by her memories of the past. At this point in the novel, the narrative shifts from literary realism to the Gothic mode, with frequent mentions of hauntings and supernatural events occurring in the house. Not long after Teresa's death, the civil war begins and Sofia hides the family's jewels and goes into exile in France. After the war is over, she returns to Barcelona and the estate once more, this time planning to tear down the old mansion and replace it with modern apartment buildings. As workers begin to remove the remaining possessions from the house, Maria's ghost pleads with them to leave her things alone, and Armanda (the long-time cook) prays for her soul to be released. The final chapter is narrated from the perspective of a rat, as he searches the dilapidated mansion for food and shelter, with the workers ultimately discovering him dead several days later.

A Broken Mirror is a tremendously ambitious novel written in multiple narrative styles that allow the reader a broad view of the society of the era while also giving a glimpse of the characters' psychology through dream sequences and episodes of supernatural apparitions. Because of its complexity and due to Rodoreda's significance as a Catalan writer during the Franco regime, numerous scholars have studied the author and this novel in the decades since its publication. In her book on Rodoreda's literary works, Christine Arkinstall considers *A Broken Mirror* to be an example of the author's postmodernist style and a vivid portrayal of Catalonia in the pre-war era, noting:

> Rodoreda uses symbols, structures, characters, settings, and literary techniques to graph a cultural history essential for understanding contemporary Catalunya: a history dependent on valuing the heritage of the past to elaborate a novel and society of the future. Contrary to many scholarly studies, I will argue that Rodoreda does not eschew realism but deploys it self-consciously in her elaboration of a metaliterary universe and cultural history of modern Catalunya. For her, realism and modernism are not antagonistic events but intersecting elements vital to the construction of the modern novel.[7]

Gonzalo Navajas also reads this novel as a postmodernist narrative, studying the notion of *Heimat* (the ideal space) in Rodoreda's depictions of Barcelona and Catalonia as a whole, asserting that there is a clear gap 'between the actual Catalan national reality and the ideal *Heimat*'.[8] Eva Bru examines the physical descriptions of women in the novel in relation to Catalan art from the early twentieth century, arguing that 'Rodoreda creates a tension within the boundaries of corporeal representability insofar as the surface of the female body is constructed as porous and excessive, ultimately shattering the borders that shape the body into idealized and normative constructions of femininity'.[9] Similarly, Elizabeth Scarlett focuses on the representation of women's bodies through her study of the relationship 'between the heroine's body, a flower, and feminine folklore of Catalonia',[10] noting the strong presence of plants and flowers in all of Rodoreda's post-war narratives.

Many scholars have examined the undeniable autobiographical elements of *A Broken Mirror*, highlighting Rodoreda's political inclinations and personal experiences as a constant undertone in her work. Josefina González has noted the many parallels between the novel and Rodoreda's own life, including 'el abandono del hijo, el poco instinto maternal, el incesto y el triángulo amoroso en conjunto con el adulterio. También convergen los espacios narrativos: Viena, París y Barcelona' ['the abandonment of the son, the little maternal instinct, incest and the love triangle in conjunction with adultery. The narratives spaces also converge: Vienna, Paris and Barcelona'].[11] Arkinstall makes note of Rodoreda's political posturing throughout her literary oeuvre, explaining that the author 'establishes her own Catalanist position that fuses the strengths of both *modernisme* and *noucentisme* to advocate a modern society and culture based on the inclusivity of others and the recognition of their differences'.[12]

Despite the numerous studies of this novel, very few scholars have focused exclusively on the role of the supernatural elements in *A Broken Mirror*, and just one has commented on the Gothic nature of the narrative. Vollendorf considers the novel to be an example of the 'feminist fantastic', and she argues that '[t]he use of the fantastic in the novel, which coincides with the definitive decline of the matriarchy, can thus be read as an attempt to liberate the feminine subject, to deterritorialize the feminine from the patriarchy'.[13] Like many literary Hispanists, Vollendorf limits her reading of the supernatural elements in the novel to the fantastic, and does not take into account the Gothic genre. Janet Pérez is the only scholar to examine the Gothic elements in Rodoreda's novel (and, given the publication date of 1994, we might in fact consider her chapter to be one of the first essays ever written on the Spanish Gothic). Pérez studies the author's use of many Gothic tropes and focuses especially on the description of the setting, leading her to assert that '*Mirall trencat* might most accurately be described as the chronicle of how a Gothic space came to be'.[14] Pérez's categorisation of *A Broken Mirror* as a Gothic narrative is one that deserves more elaboration, and the elements she considers in her essay – alongside the other authors' studies of the socio-political aspects of the text – greatly inform my own reading of the novel.

In the present chapter, I will propose a reading of *A Broken Mirror* as a Gothic haunted house narrative in which the fraught relationships between legacy and economy manifest themselves in the women's generational fight for ownership of the domestic space and the fortune therein. By acknowledging the Valldaura house as an always already transgressive environment cloaked in Gothic trappings, we can better come to understand the women's actions as responses to the patriarchal systems around them, and the struggles within the house as a microcosm of the ongoing fight for Catalan autonomy amid the threat of civil war. The protagonist's villa in the middle of an ivy-choked wood is the perfect backdrop for Rodoreda's Gothic narrative, in which an emphasis on mirrors and glass denotes memories and visions of the past, and ghosts – as spectres of the past – reflect anxieties about the as-yet uncertain future. As Derrida notes, spectres are always already returning; in *A Broken Mirror*, Rodoreda portrays the traumatic past as an inherent spectral presence, compounded by physical reminders of the dead that haunt every member of the family. The emphasis on physical possessions through Teresa's transformation into a woman of high society makes the house itself irrevocably haunted by the past, and the objects within it – along with the women themselves – become placeholders of memory that continue to haunt Teresa and each subsequent generation of the family.

Despite the literary realism that defines the first two parts of the narrative, Rodoreda includes very clear Gothic markers from the beginning of her novel that denote the Valldaura estate as a prime location for the development of the haunted house motif. Rodoreda dedicates a considerable amount of space in her text to the description of the setting of the Valldaura mansion, which is surrounded by untamed wilderness in which the trees themselves become a focal point for Teresa's sublime fear of the property. The garden, a typical *locus amoenus* in literary Romanticism, is envisioned here as a *locus terribilis*; the order of the Romantic setting gives in to the disorder of Gothic nature, which appears dark and foreboding throughout the text. The grounds, which Teresa considers 'beautiful, but scary',[15] are rendered especially ominous in a thunderstorm in chapter five, in which winds rip through the towers of the house, slamming doors and blowing out the candlelight, terrifying Teresa, new-born Sofia and the female servants. During this storm a bolt of lightning strikes the laurel tree next to the wall of the house, and half of the tree falls to the ground. This same tree, slightly later in the text, appears monstrous when Jaume sees it through the glass windowpanes: 'The laurel tree, with branches groaning in the wind, was darker; full of arms, full of voices, a shudder of light on each leaf. Its trunk, if he scratched it with a sharp stone, oozed a sap' (p. 81). This sap, portrayed here as arboreal blood, foreshadows the moment near the end of the second part of the novel when Armanda notices that the trunk is stained with a shiny red liquid, only to discover that it is blood from Maria's lifeless body hanging in the limbs above (p. 147). The trees surrounding the house play a pivotal role in the evocation of fear in the text, which González recognises when she states: 'Este temor que inspira la personificación de los árboles, es consistente en *Mirall trencat* en donde los personajes viven constantemente bajo la sombra de castaños que crean el ambiente siempre inminente de misterio y tragedia' ['This fear that the personification of the trees inspires is consistent in *A Broken Mirror*, where the characters live constantly under the shadow of the chestnut trees that create an environment of always imminent fear and tragedy'].[16] It is on these wild grounds that the children's games become increasingly dark and violent. Ramon tortures and kills lizards, gouges out birds' eyes and talks of killing witches. He and Maria frequently take knives from the kitchen to dig holes in the trunks of the trees and to fashion spears out of branches (one of which ends up instrumental in Jaume's death, as Ramon uses it to push the young boy backwards into the pond while their sister stabs his neck with a needle). The property on which the estate rests is thus a primed Gothic site of constant aggression and violence and, ultimately, a space that invites haunting and death.

Surrounded by this ominous wilderness, the massive villa with its labyrinth of rooms and multiple towers acquires a Gothic castle-like image that, according to Pérez, assists in establishing the supernatural aspect of the narrative:

> An air of ruin and decay combines with the physical isolation, predisposing readers to accept the uncanny, the marvelous, the supernatural, paranormal, and fantastic. Although the house at Sant Gervasi lacks the Gothic network of dark tunnels underneath, it has its seldom-used stairways, rooms with locked doors, half-abandoned upper floors and turrets, the narrow, winding staircase to the roof associated from the outset with fear . . . and with death.[17]

Aside from the architecture of the house itself, Rodoreda continues to emphasise the Gothic character of the villa through its relationship with nature: not only is it located in the middle of the imposing woods, but the walls of the house are covered with creeping ivy that 'turned the color of blood in the fall and climbed the smooth walls because it had little hands' (p. 74). The continuous personification of nature in the text assists Rodoreda in establishing her Gothic setting and gives the entire house – inside and out – an air of monstrosity and death.

Inside the house, Rodoreda repeatedly draws our attention to the numerous objects lining the walls and filling every room. Indeed, there are so many items decorating the interior of the villa that when Jesús Masdéu first steps inside, we are told that he 'didn't have enough eyes to look' at everything surrounding him (p. 38). Among the possessions that Rodoreda most frequently mentions are a handful of peacock feathers with their 'eyes' at the tip (which are a constant source of fascination for young Jaume) and an antique Japanese armoire. Furniture of a variety of styles and colour patterns fills the living space, the walls are adorned with paintings, wreaths and other art, and the ceilings themselves are made of inlaid wood mosaics. The overabundance of objects in the home converts it into a site that overwhelms and seeks to absorb those within it, adding to the monstrous quality of the space – far from Scarlett's assertion that the mansion's interior is 'stable and uniting';[18] when read as a Gothic narrative, we can understand the home as a site of subversion and transgression, the opposite of an ideal domestic space though still attempting to maintain an ideal façade. Dara Downey, in her study of American women's ghost stories, clearly notes the role that interior objects play in Gothic narratives: 'while domesticity and home life are the agents of oppression, domestic furnishings, commodities and interior decoration function as vehicles for memory, bearing witness to the oppression in which they participate'.[19] In fact, Downey highlights decorative objects and inherited items as the medium through which possession often occurs in these narratives, demonstrating the intimate connection between the domestic space and women's oppression and haunting. As Arkinstall notes, in *A Broken Mirror* the majority of the events take place inside the villa and its grounds, which she considers 'an enclosed scenario that connotes the ultimately stagnant nature of the Catalan upper-class world depicted'.[20]

The oppressive and stagnant bourgeois setting of Rodoreda's novel manifests itself not only in the physical space of the house, but also in the female characters living within it. Bru, who considers Teresa to be 'clearly linked to *Modernista* models of ideal femininity',[21] points to the symbolic meaning of the title of the opening chapter: 'A Jewel of Value'. It is no coincidence that Rodoreda decides to begin her novel with a scene in a jewellery store, in which Teresa convinces her husband to buy her an ostentatious brooch (which she quickly pawns for money to maintain her secret son). Through the chapter's title, Rodoreda purposefully positions her female protagonist – the eventual matriarch of the Valldaura family – as an object of value herself, signified by her adornment in precious jewels. The hasty sale of the brooch in the first few pages of the text also immediately establishes the idea of Teresa's inherent economic value: if the brooch is representative of the woman, the transaction in the jewellery store implies the trade and sale of the female body within the capitalist society of late-nineteenth-century Barcelona. This assertion is further corroborated by the knowledge that Teresa has only married this older man for his fortune, clearly becoming part of 'an exchange economy in which women's worth can only be defined in terms of men's money and power'.[22]

As Teresa evolves from a working-class single mother into a bourgeois matriarch, possessions and clothing become an integral part of her strategy toward acceptance and belonging in upper-class Catalan society. Rodoreda repeatedly draws our attention to Teresa's luxurious dresses and jewels, which seem to multiply in volume and number as she grows older, always attracting the eye of attentive male suitors despite her status as a married woman. Just as she fills the house with countless objects that denote her status and wealth, Teresa also adorns herself in what appears to be an overzealous attempt to blend in to her physical and societal surroundings. As Downey notes, in the traditional upper-class home,

> the wife herself had to *become* pure surface, by allowing the house to absorb her and conceal her as a visual object. The respectable nineteenth-century wife must all but vanish into the furniture, even to the point of wearing chintz patterns all but identical to those covering her sofas, armchairs, walls, and floors; contemporary fashion also worked hard to effect this absorption by confining and restricting the body.[23]

Although Teresa's use of jewellery and fashion is not an attempt to make herself invisible within the home, it is nonetheless an attempt to blend in to a society to which she does not, by blood or upbringing, belong. The result is that visitors to the house experience an onslaught of visual and sensory stimuli that are undeniably marked by Teresa, whose body itself is the focal point of this domestic economy. Altogether, the protagonist's accessories and home décor highlight yet another incongruent aspect of the house that detracts from its function as an ideal, comfortable space.

Female sexuality – an often-fraught theme in Gothic narratives – underscores much of Rodoreda's novel, in which the women in the Valldaura mansion appear either hyper-sexualised (Teresa and many of the maids) or sexually defiant (Sofia). Pérez has stated that '[s]exuality, one of the "dark secrets" of Gothic fictions, is the secret *par excellence* of Rodoreda's longest and most complex novel'[24] and, likewise, Vollendorf asserts that in *A Broken Mirror*, 'women's sexuality poses a threat to the status quo, and women constantly struggle to sublimate tautological signs of desire'.[25] Teresa's need to maintain the appearance of belonging to the bourgeois class into which she has married has the direct effect of stifling her access to true love and affection; in compensation for the oppressive atmosphere around her, she seeks love and sexual satisfaction in the form of several affairs throughout her lifetime. In contrast, Sofia – Teresa's daughter – renounces her mother's lavish style and overt sexuality, instead choosing to dress in plain outfits that seek to minimise her appeal, purposefully rejecting or ignoring potential suitors. After postponing her marriage for two years due to her father's death, Sofia's first acts of intimacy with her new husband, Eladi, are marked with violence after he admits that he has a daughter with another woman: 'She got up, finished undressing, almost tearing off her clothes, and, naked, went to him, hugged him hard, and struck her knee between his thighs, pushing all the way up' (p. 68). Whereas the matriarch, Teresa, is a symbol of male desire and sexual economy, Sofia takes on the role of the monstrous female: she is, from the beginning, full of rage and spite, renouncing her mother's femininity through adornments and instead focusing her ambition on economic independence through ownership of the home and rejection of male desire.

Both Teresa and Sofia, whose lives unfold almost entirely inside the villa, are caught in the patriarchal, capitalist structure of turn-of-the-century Barcelona; the economic privilege that they acquire is strictly achieved through marriage and inheritance. Within this system, they also share another trait: a near total lack of maternal instinct and affection. Both women, trapped in this stagnant bourgeois atmosphere, stifle their own children in a continuation of the very system that denies the women their autonomy. Rodoreda emphasises this lack of motherly affection from the beginning of the novel, when she tells us that Teresa 'didn't quite like' her firstborn son because she finds his nose ugly (p. 8). Once she marries Valldaura and gives birth to Sofia, her husband's wealth allows her to pay a nursemaid to take care of the child, and – like many upper-class women of her era – she has little to do with the upbringing of her daughter. Sofia, who 'never loved her mother much' (p. 57), finds Teresa's bedazzled body a constant source of embarrassment, and even has thoughts of killing her – a matricidal urge that is repeated years later in Maria, when she tells Armanda that she is taking a knife from the kitchen '[t]o kill Mama' (p. 149). During her own first pregnancy, Sofia is terribly ill and refuses to let her husband touch her; Rodoreda portrays this rejection of intimacy as the catalyst of Eladi's sexual escapades with numerous women over the course of his marriage. When she becomes pregnant for a second time, Sofia's only excitement is the thought that if the child is a girl, she can use her as a tool to separate Eladi from Maria, who is clearly her husband's favourite. Indeed, Sofia has only allowed Maria to stay in the house because she sees the child as a pawn in her revenge against Eladi; as Rodoreda tells us, 'the girl stimulated her spiteful sense of dominion' (p. 124). That Sofia's second child will not serve her intended purpose is made obvious not only by the fact that he is a boy, but that he is born prematurely and is, for the remainder of his short life, sickly and malformed; consequently, despite Sofia's strategy to use her child to purchase power in her household, it is, in the end, a futile prospect, and she remains emotionally distant from her children throughout the novel. As Vollendorf notes:

> these examples of unhappy pregnancies, difficult births, maternal apathy and disdain, and the repulsion for the maternally marked body abound in the novel, suggesting that both the body and the spirit resist the maternal. Such negative ideology of motherhood betrays a fundamental problematic within a system that seeks to secure power through matrilineage, as Teresa's does.[26]

In this manner, Rodoreda again centres the house as a site of subversion of the domestic order, imbuing it with Gothic potentiality. The imposing villa becomes the birthplace of maternal disaffection and the dual host of idealised matricide (Sofia and Maria wish to kill their mothers) and realised fratricide (Ramon and Maria kill Jaume).

Despite the clearly malignant atmosphere of the house, the women of each generation seek sole ownership of the estate in what becomes an inherited obsession with the notion of autonomy through economic independence and self-reliance. This is, of course, a flawed concept from the beginning; as Rodoreda demonstrates, complete autonomy is impossible in an environment that favours the stability of tradition over progress. Nevertheless, the Valldaura women continue to strive for control of the home as a way to gain power over their lives. Therefore, when Sofia discovers that her father has left the estate to Teresa, she cries 'tears of rage and shame until the wee hours' (p. 58). Sofia will later become enraged when she finds out that her mother, prior to her death, has decided to leave the property to Maria in a surprising subversion of the typical bourgeois emphasis on bloodlines (a move which is only possible because Teresa, herself, has rejected all traditions associated with maternity). Sofia's ownership of the house is only official after Maria's death, a scene that once again highlights Sofia's lack of motherly affection when she visits the girl's bedroom: 'Sofia smiled as she raised her head and smelled her perfumed fingers. Whenever she was alone, she pulled her head up as much as possible to avoid having a wrinkled neck. Good-bye, Maria' (p. 150). Sofia's rare smile in the context of the death of her step-daughter – combined with her vane awareness of her flawless neck – is a further indication of her monstrosity and utter lack of empathy associated with ideal femininity. Sofia is not just anti-maternal; she is the anti-mother. Navajas asserts that in this novel, the 'collective national entity finds a replica in the family. The intimate family nucleus constitutes a stable world where the individual can find a refuge from external aggression.'[27] The home, in the scenario he portrays here, is clearly central to the project of stabilising its inhabitants in a safe space in tradition and the past; the problem is that the Valldaura home is neither stable, nor safe – it is a site in which the domestic tradition is inherently and problematically subverted. The estate and those who live in it are inevitably haunted by the memories of the past and, eventually, by the literal ghosts of the departed.

To this extent, the numerous references to windows and glass panes throughout the novel serve as a medium through which memories – as reflections of the past – and distorted realities combine and invite the supernatural into the home. This is nowhere more evident than in chapter five of part three, when Armanda trips on the stairs while holding Sofia's looking glass, which shatters as it hits the floor. Armanda, in her attempt to fit the pieces back together, wonders: 'Did the pieces of the mirror, having lost their level, reflect things as they were? Suddenly, in each piece of the mirror she saw years of her life spent in that house. Fascinated, crouching on the floor, she could not make sense of it. Everything passed, stopped, disappeared' (p. 188). In the shards of broken glass, Armanda suddenly has visions of the past that flash before her eyes in full colour, illuminating fragmented moments that seem impossibly distant. This reflective state is, itself, shattered at the sound of gunshots in the distance, bringing Armanda back to the present reality of the outbreak of the civil war. The maid quickly heads to the kitchen to dull her growing fear with champagne, and then, staring into the mirror once more, she begins to see skeletons reflected back at her through the pieces of glass: 'three skeletons were laughing with convulsed jaws . . . Where did all those bones, so nicely held together, with no flesh or skin to cover them, come from?' (p. 189). Armanda sees four skeletons in all, each of which belongs to one of the deceased members of the family: Teresa, Valldaura, Eladi and Maria. This episode is a pivotal moment in the text not only because of its admission of the supernatural into the house, but also because of the symbolic nature of the broken shards of the mirror, which evoke spectral images of the past and project them onto the imminent future. Notably, Rodoreda's entire narrative serves a similar function, by presenting us with fragmented chapters that – like shards of glass – give us glimpses into moments in the life of the family and, therefore, the nation.

Part three of *A Broken Mirror* purposefully employs haunting as a marker of memory, stressing the importance of how we view the past from our present perspective. Navajas considers this an example of the distorting lens of nostalgia, which he says 'transforms the essence of reality and makes of the past the context where the creations of the imagination and reality seem to coincide and the objective world yields to desire'.[28] It is this yearning for an idealised version of the past that traps Maria as a spectral presence on the grounds of the estate. Chapter nine of part three is entirely narrated by Maria's ghost in a revealing stream-of-consciousness that treats memories in much the same way as Teresa once decorated her house: collections of varying meaning, keepsakes of times gone by, and illusions of a reality that was destined to be shattered. Here again we see physical objects inextricably linked to memory and identity as Maria begs the workers not to take her memorial plaque at the base of the laurel tree because '[t]his stone is me' (p. 201) and '[o]nce they have taken me, everything will be erased. Without time. Without memory' (p. 203). Her profound desire to continue to exist in the present leads Maria to purposefully interact with the visitors to the property, caressing their cheeks in a ghostly touch that they feel as cobwebs brushing against their skin. The child who once played violent games in the shadow of the trees now fully exists within the comfort of her own idealised past.

The ghosts of the dead are not the only spectral presence in Rodoreda's text. The narrative is populated with memories of fragmented moments in nearly every adult character's life that render them unable to cope with their present realities. Valldaura is haunted by his tragic memory of Barbara, the first and only woman he truly loved, who killed herself years before his marriage to Teresa. Teresa is likewise haunted by memories of Miquel, the father of her firstborn son whom she gave up prior to her first marriage, just as Riera is tortured by his feelings of guilt for leaving Teresa. Ramon, for his part, tries desperately not to think of the estate and the memories he associates with it because 'memory would mean perdition' (p. 209). In every case, memory itself is a marker of disruptions that shatter the characters' ability to view and understand life as a whole, undistorted image. Memory is, therefore, an inherently spectral presence in this novel because of its always already returning state; illusions of the past, understood without context, are destined to create distorted realities.

Rodoreda's ending to *A Broken Mirror* presents us with a stark reminder of the historical reality of Catalonia reflected in the

Valldaura estate. The women's unending struggle for ownership of the house abruptly ends as the war begins, when Sofia flees the country and soldiers commandeer the property. After the war has ended, Sofia returns to reclaim the estate, which has been left in shambles and nearly emptied of its decorations and furniture. Seeing herself in control of her family's fortune at last, Sofia decides to have the house razed to build modern apartment buildings on the lot. With the destruction of the home and the final removal of Maria's plaque and all other possessions that remain on the property, Sofia has effectively given permission for the haunting voices of the past to be silenced. This act is reminiscent of Teresa's desire years earlier to destroy the estate before her death, when Rodoreda tells us that 'she felt like setting fire to everything: all she had loved, furniture, trees, house. All to die in flames. Purified. No more memories!' (p. 97). Thus, when Sofia tells the workers to 'drop all the office furniture, and, instead of moving it, set it on fire' (p. 204), she is, in fact, acting parallel to her mother's unspoken wishes. The destruction of the house, if symbolic of the repression of memory, is therefore a catalyst of haunting in and of itself because it presupposes the eradication of the trauma of the past through the removal of its physical signs in the present. When read as a metaphor for Catalan identity in the nation under Franco, Rodoreda's novel juxtaposes the fragmented, idealised past with the disillusioned whole. The abrupt silencing of memory becomes an inevitable metaphor for dictatorial censorship, which Resina has portrayed as cultural genocide: 'For it was this region's stubborn persistence in its historical personality that Spanish nationalists considered a threat to the state; therefore, they were determined to eradicate not only its representative institutions but the Catalan personality itself.'[29] With the end of Catalan autonomy represented in the final destruction of the house, Rodoreda implies that Sofia's true inheritance – the legacy of the past – is too painful to acknowledge and impossible to restore.

By reading this novel as a Gothic haunted house narrative, we can better understand the inherent connections between women – around whom the novel is centred – and the regional struggle for autonomy. Because the Valldaura women are limited to acting within the strict confines of the patriarchal structure around them (a structure whose notion of legacy relies on the treatment of women as commodities), they seem destined to uphold the system they have inherited. According to Vollendorf, 'Rather than opposing or challenging patriarchal cultural codes, Teresa's matriarchy assimilates and expresses them in the dynamics surrounding women's sexual and maternal identities throughout the novel.'[30] In this manner, the female-centred home replicates the male-dominated structure of the outside world, reinforcing the stagnant qualities of turn-of-the-century Barcelona while being entirely unable to capitalise on the prospect of modernity. The haunted house, as a reflection of the fears and anxieties of the tumultuous era, positions women in an unstable domestic space in which maternal instincts and inherited traditions are actively subverted, and where the present absences invoked in the act of remembering guarantee the impossibility of progress.

Interestingly, the only character in the novel who acknowledges the spectral presences on the property is Armanda, the Valldaura's longtime cook, who also happens to be the sole protector of the estate in the interim years between the start of the war and Sofia's return. After seeing skeletons in the broken fragments of the looking glass, Armanda begins a habit of throwing flowers into the yard on each visit to the property in a sign of respect for Maria's spirit. Not surprisingly, when she feels Maria's ghostly hand on her cheek, she is the only person to recognise this touch for what it is and, instead of being afraid, she speaks out loud into the trees: 'If it is a dead one from this household who now thinks of me, may God help him and give him the repose he needs' (p. 214). Upon saying this, she sees what appears to be mist in the form of a wing materialise in front of her and then vanish, an indication that Maria is no longer trapped in the torturous returns of the past. Arkinstall and Vollendorf read this as evidence that the supernatural is a venue for women to reclaim their voices; indeed, Downey has similarly noted that in women's ghost stories, 'it is only after the disappearance of the body that the feminine author or narrative voice can speak – or rather write – at all, the "death space" acting as a source of power because it denies the spectacle of the female body to the patriarchal, masculine gaze that seeks to reify and codify it' (86). Thus, Vollendorf sees this moment as 'a reconciliation with the past and a liberation from patriarchal constraints'.[31] If this is true, then the final scenes of the novel – which set up the destruction of the house and maintain its inescapable link to death in the form of a rat who is the protagonist of the last chapter and is ultimately found bloated and decaying by the workers days later – are inconsistent with the possibility of reclaiming the female voice that other scholars have noted in their interpretations of the ending.

Perhaps, in this sense, Rodoreda extends the Valldaura women's generational fight for power beyond the pages of her novel, by implying the brute, overwhelming force of seeing reality reflected through an intact mirror. As an author who 'never lost her preoccupation with economic independence',[32] Rodoreda, writing this text during the final years of the Franco dictatorship, inevitably saw her own image as a reflection of Catalan women in general, whose autonomy was doubly challenged through the prohibition of their language and cultural traditions, and through the separate standards that restricted women's freedom during much of her lifetime. As Pérez notes, 'Whether rich or poor, the women in *Mirall trencat* are disadvantaged, especially those who are young, motherless, and vulnerable.'[33] In 1974, when *A Broken Mirror* was published, the nation was still under control of the dictatorship and women continued to live under the oppressive rules that were thrust upon them nearly four decades earlier. Unlike Sofia, however, who decides to reduce the past to embers in a sign of the futility of hope, Rodoreda pieces together the broken shards of personal and collective memory, ultimately portraying the past as an always returning ghost unless, and until, society is able to look upon its own reflection as a whole, undistorted image, projected equally onto the past, present and future.

2

Shifting Borders: Race, Class and the Phantasmagoric Other in Bene by Adelaida García Morales

As one of the more prominent female Spanish authors to receive critical acclaim in the post-Franco period, Adelaida García Morales (1945–2014) highlighted many of the contemporary concerns of Spanish citizens and intellectuals regarding Spain's turbulent transition from dictatorship to democracy. Born in Badajoz, Spain in 1945, she spent most of her childhood in Seville, a city that later would become the setting for many of her literary works. She obtained a degree in philosophy from the University of Madrid in 1970 and worked numerous jobs, including teaching Spanish language, literature and philosophy at the high school level, translating for OPEC nations in Algiers, and even acting and modelling in the Esperpento theatre of Seville. Her first publication, *The South and Bene* (1985), was an immediate success, inspiring a film of the same name directed by her partner, Victor Erice. These accomplishments, along with the publication of her first novel (*The Silence of the Sirens*) also in 1985, brought García Morales instant recognition as an important author of Spanish fiction and earned her the Icaro Prize and the Herralde Prize, demonstrating her rising influence in literary and academic circles. Her works underscore the political nature of the Gothic genre, demonstrating clearly how Spain's recent past is perhaps best viewed through a Gothic lens.

Although *Bene*, the second novella in the 1985 volume *The South and Bene*, has received less critical attention than *The South* since the time of its publication, some scholars have noted the many similarities between the two novellas and have included *Bene* in their studies of García Morales's literature. The plots and the style of narration are in many ways strikingly similar: in both novellas, the female narrator relates episodes from her childhood in which the fantastic and the monstrous appear to be an almost natural part of a secluded and strictly conservative environment. When Bene, a Roma girl, comes to work as a housekeeper for narrator Angela's father, Angela at first tries to befriend her, delighted to have the teenager in her house. After several incidents in which Bene appears to become overtaken by a supernatural force – which Angela attributes to the ghost of her deceased Roma boyfriend – Angela becomes afraid of Bene and worries that the girl is taking control of Santiago. Once the family expels Bene from their home, Santiago runs away with her, only to return two weeks later, at which point he locks himself in the house's tower and eventually dies. Angela learns from her friend Juana – Bene's half-sister – that Bene has also died, and these traumatic losses lead Angela herself to accept death and to allow Bene's phantom boyfriend to quite mysteriously take control of her with his supernatural powers. This final scene has been interpreted in many ways, but readers most frequently understand it to imply the narrator's spiritual (not physical) death.

Among the critics who have studied *Bene*, Currie Thompson provides the most distinct interpretation, focusing her attention solely on this novella through a psychoanalytic perspective. Although Thompson does briefly acknowledge the Gothic aspect of the text, she chooses to emphasise the negative masculine presence in *Bene*, stating:

> If on its most superficial level this text is a macabre example of Gothic horror, it is also the narrative of a twelve-year-old girl's awareness of inner space and of the transformation of that space from a secure sanctuary into a besieged area which is eventually invaded by a sinister masculine force.[1]

Elizabeth Ordóñez also notes the masculine presence in both *The South* and *Bene*, depicting it as 'the lingering ghosts of patriarchy or the insinuating presence of the paternal sacrificial contract'.[2] In her book about García Morales's Gothic literature, Abigail Lee Six compares *The South* and *Bene* with Oscar Wilde's novel *The Picture of Dorian Gray*, partially aligning herself with Thompson and Ordóñez in her view of the strongly sexualised nature of the text when she writes: 'from Angela's perspective, sexual desire is linked with the devil and death, joining up with the gypsy ghost as its personification in her imagination'.[3] Epicteto José Díaz chooses to focus on images of solitude and isolation in both novellas, also commenting on the Gothic character of *Bene* in particular: '*Bene* presenta una serie de elementos comunes con el relato que le precede, pero también importantes diferencias, que en parte tienen que ver con el tipo de relato utilizado, el de las "ghost story"' ['*Bene* presents a series of common elements with the tale that precedes it, but also important differences, which in part have to do with the type of tale utilised, that of the "ghost story"'].[4] Similarly, Thomas Deveny highlights the '[i]ntense emotions and Gothic elements' of the novella and states: 'The preoccupation with death and its relationship to love also links these narratives to the tradition of Gothic and fantastic literature.'[5] Although all the above-mentioned critics have at least briefly noted Gothic elements in *Bene*, none of them focus on the Gothic as an important aspect of García Morales's socio-political commentary. Without acknowledging the relationship between the Gothic and the abject other as a major component of the author's narrative strategy, one cannot fully comprehend the symbolic significance of both the characters and the supernatural events that take place.

In this chapter, I will examine the interplay within *Bene* between the phantasmagoric, physical boundaries, and the other, studying Bene as the representation of the monster figure in this text in accordance with Julia Kristeva's notion of the abject. Through her version of the haunted house, García Morales employs the Gothic motifs of entrapment and haunting to highlight her socio-political consciousness, focusing on the image of the Roma people as the Gothic other within post-war Spanish society. Bene's familial relation to this marginalised group and her highly sexualised nature are at the root of her monstrous conversion, leading to her portrayal as a *belle dame sans merci* by the other women in the novella. The racial undertones combine with the phantasmagoric to create a commentary on the treatment of the Roma people in Franco's Spain, implying the existence of borders beyond the physical realm.

In order to understand the portrayal of race and class in *Bene*, we must first recognise the long history of discrimination and marginalisation of the Roma people – called 'gypsies' (a despective colloquial term) in this novella – within Spanish society. Carolina García Sanz explains that the Franco regime was not the first to issue wide-reaching policies against the Roma; in fact, as she notes, Miguel de Cervantes's story 'The Little Gypsy Girl' (1613) serves as evidence of the long-held negative view of the Roma population in Spain when he writes: 'Parece que los gitanos y gitanas solamente nacieron en el mundo para ser ladrones' ['It seems that gypsies were born into the world solely to be thieves'].[6] She then points to the Royal Spanish Academy's definition of 'gypsy' as yet another example of this pervasive mentality still present in the Spanish language four hundred years later: 'Una de sus acepciones para "gitano," aun admitiendo su uso denigratorio, es "trapacero" (quien realiza "artificio engañoso e ilícito con que se perjudica y defrauda a alguien en alguna compra, venta o cambio")' ['One of their entries for "gypsy," even admitting its denigratory use, is "swindler" (a person who does "deceitful and illicit tricks with which to harm or defraud someone in a purchase, sale, or exchange")'].[7] Throughout the early twentieth century, Spanish law specifically targeted the Roma people as suspect in accordance with this Cervantine perspective. Under Franco, the push for a monocultural national identity exacerbated what was already a systemic discriminatory practice. David Corkill, in his discussion on the treatment of the Spanish Roma population, notes:

> There has been a gypsy population in Spain since the early fifteenth century. Long the butt of prejudice, official persecution and legal action under the Vagrancy and Social Dangerousness Laws, gypsies have been seen as social outcasts and linked to criminal behaviour. During the 1940s the Franco regime ordered the *Guardia Civil* to monitor and investigate gypsy behaviour. This clearly indicates that the regime regarded them as different from mainstream society, forming part of that realm of "otherness" of popular discourse.[8]

Likewise, Jo Labanyi highlights the regime's insistence on mandating sameness when she states: 'The Franco regime tried to unify the nation by projecting difference outside its borders, or confining it to internal exclusion zones, in the form of otherness: *la anti-España*, necessarily equated with foreign influence.'[9] The centuries-old image of the 'gypsy' as other in Spanish cultural discourse assisted the regime's calculated effort to further marginalise the Roma people and continued to play a role in the definition of cultural and socio-political borders in the decades after Franco's death. In his study of contemporary Spanish culture, Paul Julian Smith asserts that in modern cultural production 'the gypsy is presented as a new, hybrid subject, both strange and familiar, who is at once a response to and a displacement of Spaniards' confrontation with a more radical otherness: that of global immigration to the Spain that was for so long a nation of net emigration'.[10] Thus, in Spain, the image of the 'gypsy' has for centuries represented both intrinsic Spanishness and the exoticised, cast-off other. In the 1960s, the conflation of this image with southern flamenco culture led to the exaltation of Andalusia as a premier tourist destination (with Franco knowingly capitalising on its unique cultural flair under the now-famous slogan 'Spain is different'), all while continuing to marginalise and target the Roma population through prejudicial legal practices.

This process of identity-building through mandated repression and delegitimisation of perceived otherness is perhaps best explored through Kristeva's notion of the abject, in which the self is at once diametrically opposed to and paradoxically reliant on the other, which it attempts to cast off. Kristeva describes the process in terms of borders: 'The border has become an object. How can I be without border? . . . It is something rejected from which one does not part, from which one cannot protect oneself as from an object.'[11] According to Kristeva, abjection is caused by that which 'disturbs identity, system, order. What does not respect borders, positions, rules. The in-between, the ambiguous, the composite.'[12] The subconscious struggle, then, is often manifested in terms of 'I/Other' or 'Inside/Outside'.[13] In twentieth-century Spain, the nation under Franco was construed as a body whose cultural boundaries were its defining feature: the Spanish self, dependent on the supremacy of the Castilian language and culture, was at war with all other groups whose practices did not align with this restrictive identity. Barbara Creed, in *The Monstrous Feminine*, points to the fear associated with identity formation within the context of monstrosity, noting: 'Fear of losing oneself and one's boundaries is made more acute in a society which values boundaries over continuity, and separateness over sameness.'[14] As Franco outlawed the use of other languages in regions like Galicia, the Basque Country and Catalonia, the regime looked increasingly inward for signs of anti-Spanishness, fortifying the nation's self-perception with symbolic borders that served to amplify difference.

Gothic literature is incredibly reliant on the construction of borders because it is a genre that is highly focused on the body and the definition of the self. Indeed, Eugenia DeLamotte has suggested that 'All the major Gothic conventions involve either literal or metaphorical boundaries, and sometimes both.'[15] In her study of the Gothic corporeal, Marie Mulvey-Roberts asserts: 'Corporeality has been used by the Gothic to express horror of the Other . . . The construct of the monster is a declaration of war on individuals, who are demonised for their marginality and whose bodies are overlaid with fear and danger.'[16] Borders and bodies are interdependent notions in Gothic texts, and race is frequently a primary feature in the classification of monstrosity and otherness. As Maisha Wester notes, 'Race has long been a haunting discourse in Gothic literature. Often masked by a monstrous visage, racial minorities appear throughout traditional Gothic texts as figures around which authors spin debates about civilisation, enlightenment, freedom and human nature.'[17] In García Morales's *Bene*, race and class serve as markers of otherness and catalysts of monstrosity. The author employs the Spanish notion of the 'gypsy' to comment on the construction (and deconstruction) of national identity during the dictatorship of Francisco Franco, emphasising the interplay between physical boundaries and phantasmagoric threats.

George Haggerty has stated that 'space is always threatening and never comfortable in the Gothic novel'.[18] In *Bene*, García Morales demonstrates this Gothic perspective of space by subverting the typical image of the home as a safe haven, choosing instead to depict it as a prison in which the inhabitants are continually threatened by evil, menacing forces. The physical space surrounding the narrator is delineated in terms of seclusion, obstruction, prohibition and imprisonment: Angela describes her world as one in which she is 'shut forever in the house', noting that their estate in Extremadura is a 'large, isolated house miles from town'.[19] Her limited experience of the outside world is immediately obvious: 'I never missed any chance of going out, as I was weary of stationing myself at the gate and watching the road, which was almost always empty, through the bars. Out there where the world began, I imagined that the most extraordinary things could happen' (p. 60). Unable to cross the boundaries of her family's property line, Angela is confined to her house and gardens. Her observation that the road itself – the one path that connects her own limited world to the rest of society – almost always is empty, emphasises the isolated nature of Angela's family and forces her to envision the world without ever having experienced it. In this manner, the highway becomes an entirely imagined space – one that Angela must create and recreate in her own mind in order to envision the possibility of difference and the unknown.

The repeated mention of the physical barriers that prohibit Angela's access to the outside world is one technique that García Morales employs in defining the Gothic setting of the novella. Ordóñez notes: 'Something unspeakable lies always beyond the boundaries of the household gates.'[20] Díaz considers the gate at the edge of the property to be 'un espacio poco delimitado, siempre entrevisto, en donde se producen las "apariciones" de un gitano que había sido novio de Bene, y que será el umbral entre dos mundos, el material y el espiritual' ['a barely delimited space, always glimpsed, in which the "apparitions" of a gypsy who had been Bene's boyfriend are produced, and which will be the threshold between two worlds, the material and the spiritual'].[21] Thompson also mentions the 'undefined evil which is outside the walls'[22] and notes the gate as one of the key barriers to these diabolical forces. García Morales explicitly defines the setting of *Bene* in terms of barriers that separate not only two spaces within the physical world (the house and property from the highway and beyond) but also two different realms (the known from the unknown, or the natural from the supernatural). The existence of the unknown and its close proximity to Angela make its inaccessibility to her even more frustrating, thereby heightening her fixation on the closed space around her as the text progresses. However, as the aforementioned critics have noted, this space is not entirely restrictive, since the phantasmagoric appears to reside precisely on the border between the known and the unknown in this text, and ultimately enters Angela's home without permission.

By emphasising the restrictive physical boundaries and barriers within this space, García Morales paradoxically opens her novella to the entrance of the phantasmagoric. The author intentionally contrasts her use of these exaggeratedly tense physical boundaries with her depiction of the fluctuating border between the natural and the supernatural to expose the effects of these spaces on the characters who reside within them. Katherine Henry cites Eve Kosofsky Sedgwick's notion of Gothic space when she states: 'the Gothic derives its "most characteristic energies" . . . from its capacity to turn boundaries into sites of anxiety, to bring "what's inside, what's outside, and what separates them" into a disruptive tension'.[23] García Morales's depiction of the house as a markedly tense location in the novella takes advantage of what Sedgwick considers to be a trademark of Gothic narrative space: the inherent ability to transform physical boundaries into sites of fear and anxiety. For this reason, we can highlight Angela's aunt Elisa and her tutor Rosaura as two characters who are incredibly influenced by the Gothic tension of their surroundings. Both women illustrate the negative psychological effects of the oppressive space around them as they continuously refer to the dangers that lie just beyond the property line, and even police the comings and goings of every person who crosses the border and enters the home. Angela's friend Juana, for instance, is not allowed access to the property, and the narrator claims that 'Aunt Elisa would tell me off if I let her come in or if I went out to play with her' (p. 61). The aunt's violent response to Angela's association with Juana is based largely on another kind of barrier: the separation of classes. Juana, a young beggar, is restricted to both the literal and figurative space that pertains to those of her social class. Ironically, though, it is the aunt (under the command of Angela's father) who physically brings Bene – the eventual representation of the threatening other – into their home. This rupture of the pre-established boundaries that separate the home from the rest of society is the first step toward the admission of the phantasmagoric into the otherwise restricted space.

One of the first mentions of the supernatural occurs in connection with the tower, where Angela and her brother have spent much of their childhood. The tower structure itself is a frequent motif in Gothic fiction, acting as a space of entrapment and/or seclusion in which the characters (generally the protagonists) attempt to escape from humanity and the supernatural events that haunt them. The tower in *Bene* appears to have a similar function in the sense that it is yet another place of limited access (in this case reserved for the children only), but – in contrast with the classic tower motif – the children paradoxically encourage the supernatural events in the tower as a way to forge an emotional and spiritual bond with one another. In this space, the narrator and her brother are free from the scrutinising eye of their aunt and other adult figures. Angela explains the significance of this place to Bene:

> I used to hide up there if I was unhappy or annoyed, and . . . Santiago and I used to meet in this room when we had something secret to tell each other or we wanted to be far away from everybody . . . On calm nights we often heard strange noises. Sometimes they were like groans and sometimes quiet murmurings which my brother, deliberately trying to scare me, said came from unknown beings, dwellers in another dimension, or disembodied spirits who were lost and wandered the earth. (pp. 65–6)

The tower, then, is not simply a separate area of the house reserved for the self-imposed isolation into which the children escape, but it is also the space in which Angela and her brother first allow the supernatural to enter their world. In this case, the children's perspective of the tower subverts the typical notion of entrapment by taking advantage of the space's Gothic inclination in order to provide them with a refuge from the closed house as well as with entertainment through sublime fear. Their association of the physical environment of the tower (particularly the wind, rain and lightning) with the phantasmagoric is significant because it underscores their willingness to believe in – and to give life to – the unknown. The seemingly supernatural events that take place in the tower serve to open the children to the power of otherworldly forces at work around them. While Angela and Santiago sequester themselves in a tower room to which the adult characters do not have access, they foster a fluid sense of space that will later allow phantasmagoric events to infiltrate their otherwise barricaded lives.

Due to the fluctuating boundaries between the real and the unknown that the children have created within the tower, it is not surprising that this space is also the location of Bene's first supernatural transformation. Attempting to win Bene's affection, Angela takes her up to the tower room, hoping to share this special spot with her. Shortly after she enters the room, however, Bene's facial expression changes abruptly, and she tells Angela that they need to leave the tower immediately. Angela explains Bene's reaction in direct correlation with the spatial surroundings: 'For an instant I was afraid of the chill in her eyes. Suddenly, that room, which in spite of its untidiness had always been a welcoming place, became hostile, and the light from its single lamp seemed gloomy' (p. 66). Shortly after, when the two girls descend from the tower, Angela says that Bene 'was lively again, without that awful expression on her face. It seemed to me as though life had left her for an instant, filling her with the void of death' (p. 67). When Bene is introduced to the tower – the Gothic space typically denoting seclusion, entrapment, and even claustrophobia – she suddenly becomes somehow less than human, as though death itself has taken control of her body. It is significant that Bene's transformation seems to propel her into a state like that of the living dead: the 'void of death' that Angela describes foreshadows the impending supernatural events which will lead to the physical deaths of both Bene and Santiago. This imagery also alludes to death as a Gothic presence that underscores García Morales's narrative and provides further reason for the increasing level of anxiety and fear as the text progresses. Bene's latent monstrosity particularly scares Angela and impels her to keep a closer eye on Bene during the rest of the girl's time as a maid in the family's home.

The barriers separating Bene from the rest of the family are established from her very first moment in the house and are due largely to Bene's familial connections to the Roma – an aspect of her past that has already marked her as other within this upper-class

Spanish home. The lack of specific knowledge about Bene's past bothers Angela, but it also heightens her interest, as she believes that there is something sinister about the teenager that her aunt knows but that she does not. Angela's need to uncover this grave secret illustrates the typical Gothic portrayal of the fear of the unknown, and García Morales develops the narrator's anxiety in connection with Bene's ethnicity. As Angela learns more about Bene's past and her Roma boyfriend, the image she maintains of Bene gradually grows more complex, to the point of actually frightening her: 'The word "gypsy" awakened in me dreadful images. I was haunted by the idea of suffering and danger . . . And this horror, which I never witnessed, became one of the most constant nightmares in my life' (pp. 72–3). Later in the novella, when discussing Bene's boyfriend, Angela states: 'he was the nearest thing to the devil I had ever seen in my life' (p. 104). Here we can see that it is not just the diabolical, supernatural aspect of these characters that scares the young narrator, but their lives as Roma people. In fact, it is this relation to the marginalised group that, in many ways, gives Bene power over the young girl. Although Angela's depiction of Bene's alterity in diabolical form is her attempt to separate herself from the teenager by transforming her into a Gothic monster, Angela does not seem to anticipate her own attraction toward the monstrous image projected by Bene. Despite the horror that these people – and Bene, by association – inspire in her, Angela also admits that the girl's connection to the Roma foments her curiosity. This rather dark fascination with Bene is an excellent example of the Gothic's ability to turn the other into not just a site of terror but also an object of interest; Ruth Bienstock Anolik and Douglas L. Howard write: 'The Gothic is marked by an anxious encounter with otherness, with the dark and mysterious unknown.'[24] Once again we note the power of abjection and its relationship to the sublime: this unknown – Bene's past life and association with the Roma – is what simultaneously attracts and repels Angela, leading to the young narrator's eventual belief that Bene is, without a doubt, a being from another world.

Perhaps partly due to Angela's need for a female companion and role model, as well as her keen interest in and partial distrust of Bene's distinct character, Angela begins to narrate with more precision the family's reactions to Bene, as well as her own personal, supernatural experiences with her after the incident in the tower. Through Angela's descriptions of the family's collective experiences with Bene, we can begin to define the controversial teenager as the monster figure within this text in two distinct ways, depending on the perspective adopted. According to the adult (female) figures, Bene represents an inherent evil – akin to that which lurks ominously on the other side of the front gate. In Angela's eyes, Bene is a supernatural creature who may or may not be linked with diabolical forces but who, regardless, has an intimate connection with the phantasmagoric realm. Angela's brother, Santiago, seems to share her vision of Bene, as he relates on one occasion a dream in which Bene's appearance frightened him, because she was wearing a long dress that 'moved in the wind in a strange way, because she had no feet' (p. 68). Thompson interprets this dream through psychoanalysis, alleging that the lack of feet under Bene's dress is a sign of Santiago's foot fetish.[25] However, within the Gothic context – and given Santiago's predisposition to supernatural signs – we can read this dream sequence as yet another indication of Bene's phantasmagoric aura: the long, flowing dress and her manner of gliding along with the wind are among the classic images of the ghost in Gothic fiction. If we combine this image with the later scenes of Bene's phantom lover, we can infer that this dream foreshadows Bene's later conversion into a ghostly presence that will haunt Santiago and his sister, ultimately impelling both of them to accept death and to join her in the supernatural realm.

Angela's aunt and tutor successfully project the monster image onto Bene in a very explicit manner, always referring to her diabolical nature. Elisa, for example, remains 'convinced of her wickedness' (p. 69) and Rosaura warns that '[t]he evil Bene is caught up with is not of this world' (p. 71). It is these adult women who create and project the monstrous, diabolical image onto the teenager, exacerbating Angela's own fears and superstitions, making her believe wholeheartedly that the terrible things they describe must really be true. The descriptions of Bene, therefore, alternate between monster and devil, always casting a negative light on her and consistently maintaining around the girl a certain rhetorical wall that the other characters do not want to cross. The women's use of literal and figurative boundaries is part of their strategy to remove themselves from any and all contact with the unknown, thereby highlighting Kristeva's twin dichotomies of Inside/Outside – seen in the restrictive nature of the house – and I/Other, seen in the women's treatment of Bene as a monster.

Both Elisa and Rosaura draw upon Bene's sexuality as a key aspect of her diabolical nature; in this sense we can consider the girl to be an example of what Mario Praz and others have called the *belle dame sans merci*. Praz comments on the 'diabolical beauty'[26] of these so-called Fatal Women, whose seductive charms are a deadly weapon used to entice and entrap their male prey. Angela's aunt and tutor both take their turns gossiping about Bene's past, almost always with the implied notion of Bene's sexual promiscuity. On one occasion, Angela overhears a conversation between her aunt and tutor in which the women refer to certain rumours that have been circulating about Bene, clearly convinced that the teenager is trying to seduce Angela's father. Rosaura immediately warns Elisa about Bene's evil nature and the danger she poses to the rest of the family, even admonishing Elisa for not taking her seriously, claiming that her 'disbelief could be the open door through which this wickedness is allowed to enter the house', to which Elisa responds 'We all know what Bene has been and is' (p. 71). In this first serious conversation about the teenager's inherent evil, Rosaura renews the image of the family's boundaries by using the metaphor of the open door; in this case, as she implicitly argues, the family should seek to maintain their separation and entrapment within the house (effectively, to close themselves to external influences), because an open door allows diabolical forces to enter at free will. Later in the novella, Catalina (a maid in Angela's home) echoes a similar sentiment when she implies that Santiago might be in trouble because of Bene, warning Angela to never leave her brother alone (p. 90). As the narrator reflects back on these scenes, she eventually realises that Santiago's 'love for Bene was like possession by something superhuman, and seemed to come from death itself' (p. 103). Bene's supernatural power over Santiago, as well as her threatening gestures toward Enrique, make her the Fatal Woman in the eyes of the adult female figures of the house (and even, eventually, in Angela's perspective as well).

Sedgwick famously described the Gothic as having an 'aesthetic of pleasurable fear'.[27] Sexuality has long been connected to Gothic otherness and frequently combines with race to inspire fear and longing; in fact, Judith Halberstam has asserted that '[t]he sexual outsider in Gothic . . . is always also a racial pariah, a national outcast, a class outlaw'.[28] In the beginning of the novella, Angela mentions Bene's Roma father as the person who has separated her from Juana in order to put her to work. Although Angela herself does not seem to understand the implicit meaning of Bene's work, we can interpret this passage as a sign that the teenager has been forced into prostitution in order to support her family financially. When talking about Bene's boyfriend, Juana admits: 'He was very good-looking, and also very wicked.' When Angela asks if he hit Bene, Juana responds: 'No. He did worse things than that' (p. 84). Though it is never quite clear exactly what Bene's job was, nor what her boyfriend did to her that was so unspeakable, we are again led to believe that she has worked as a prostitute when Juana tells Angela about Bene's unique traits:

> At night . . . Bene's eyes turn into something else. I've seen them and it looks as though they are made of glass. But it's glass from a different world. With them she can see everything, even things that are invisible . . . She also told me that sometimes she sees things which can't be talked about . . . She only lets men see her like that, and me, because I'm her sister. (p. 86)

Thus, to the adult women in the household, and inadvertently to Juana, Bene's monstrosity exists in direct correlation with her sexuality. Juana, knowing that these forced sexual acts are wrong and demeaning to her sister, refuses to speak openly and clearly about Bene's past, effectively creating a barrier between Angela and the truth that she so desperately seeks. For the adult women, Bene's sexuality is a threat to the stability of their household, thereby forcing them to close the metaphorical door to the evil and monstrosity that she represents within their already secluded environment.

Bene as monster is a multi-faceted image that García Morales develops more intensely as the story progresses. Angela repeatedly uses the first episode in the tower as her point of reference for

Bene's dark character, noting: 'The shadowy figure silhouetted in the black of night, into which she was transfigured during that split second, up there in the tower, became for me the proof that the terror attributed to her really existed' (p. 74). As the novella continues, Angela employs this type of pathetic fallacy even more frequently in her descriptions of Bene, almost always noting the dark atmosphere, the ominous shadows or the strange way in which the (moon)light reflects off Bene's face. One of the most unsettling descriptions of Bene occurs when Angela, again reflecting on the incident in the tower, tries to decipher the reason for her own sense of unease:

> Once again there was the expression of death which didn't seem to belong to her, as though it were a frightening mask put on from the outside . . . At those moments her icy look had the power to summon from our surroundings a different dimension, terribly empty and threatening. (pp. 75–6)

Bene's transformation into what seems to be a phantasmagoric presence – a member of the living dead – ignites in Angela feelings of disgust and anguish. In this passage we see clearly that Bene has a kind of supernatural power that disturbs and even threatens the young girl. Moreover, the forces emanating from Bene can also change the nature of the atmosphere around her: her gaze converts the space into one that is threatening, empty and different. Because she is Roma, Bene's inevitable role as other within Angela's wealthy Spanish home is translated into the role of monster in the Gothic space of García Morales's novella, thus portraying the historically-based fear of difference in this post-war Spanish society.

Despite her terrified reaction to Bene's monstrosity, Angela's almost obsessive need to interact with Bene and to seek the teenager's approval remains unchanged. Angela Curran notes that 'the monster can evoke a dual response in which viewers admire the monster's wielding of power even as they are repulsed by the evil the monster represents'.[29] This appears to be the case with Angela: she does not approve of Bene's diabolical nature (and is certainly frightened by her as well), but at the same time she cannot help but admire her and want to win her affection. On one occasion she even admits: 'I felt the need to look at Bene, as if her image were a mirror in which all the obscurity surrounding her would be reflected' (p. 82). This passage is an explicit statement of García Morales's Gothic motive: by studying the monster's image, we can better understand the darkness and anxiety that accompany our present reality. Angela's relationship with Bene, then, is an odd sort of (anti)hero-worship, with Bene wielding an incredibly influential power over Angela that attracts at the same time as it disgusts her.

García Morales combines these notions of the abject and the sublime to emphasise Bene's monstrosity as well as to connect all other phantasmagoric apparitions to her. One night, after clearing away the condensation from a small section of her bedroom window, Angela witnesses the first apparition of Bene's boyfriend in the garden below, and he appears to return her gaze. Angela's reaction is one of simultaneous fear and intrigue, and she explains:

> I knew at the same time that this was not exactly a man but something else, something unthinkable, for which I hadn't any words . . . I could not tear my eyes away from the gypsy and the space around him, transformed by his presence into a sombre ghostly scene from which, I was sure, Bene had just emerged. (pp. 80–1)

The reactions of both characters in this scene are quite telling, as is the space that García Morales has delineated for this first contact with the phantom. Angela maintains her ability to observe the ghost through a small clearing in the window (notably a kind of barrier that allows one to see but not to interact with the outside world). She is unable to move and establish contact with the ghost because of her fright at this sublime vision, and yet she is also prohibited from doing so because of the actual physical barrier between them. The phantom, likewise, appears to be looking into the house, but remains motionless just on the other side of the gate. Angela's immediate recognition of this ghost as Bene's boyfriend – as well as her insistence on believing that Bene has also been a member of this supernatural scene – again calls attention to the notion of monstrous other that Bene embodies for all of the members of the household. From this point onward, all fantastic apparitions are understood to be inherently and unequivocally connected to Bene.

In one particularly dramatic scene during an afternoon picnic, Bene's monstrous conversion is accompanied by a spectral apparition that Angela describes as 'a transparent shadow with a human form' (p. 92). Due to Bene's reaction to this ghostly figure, Angela immediately intuits that this is the teenager's gypsy boyfriend and, although the phantom vanishes within seconds, the young narrator is terrified by the thought that he might return. Unable to cope with Bene's powerful monstrosity, Angela lets out a savage howl that denotes her terrified response to the sublime vision. This moment marks the beginning of Angela's final quest for the truth about Bene's past – a task that will prove impossible to accomplish. The phantom gypsy's powerful influence on Angela herself marks the beginning of the tragic downward spiral of Bene, Santiago and the young narrator, as she admits:

> I felt pushed right to the edge of a sinister land. It was the place where the gypsy lived. The signs announcing his arrival multiplied all around, making faces at me from every corner . . . My panic was the only thing that was certain, beyond doubt. And yet, in spite of this, there was something exciting about the idea that this monster was coming looking for me and not Bene . . . I felt I was being pushed toward an inevitable transformation. (pp. 105–6)

Angela is too absorbed in the sublime to be able to pull herself away from its destructive forces, even though she is aware that her inevitable spiritual death will occur as a result. This moment is crucial in foreshadowing the phantasmagoric metamorphosis that Santiago and Angela will undergo by the end of the novella as they succumb to the supernatural forces around them.

On the same evening that the above incident takes place, Santiago locks himself in the tower for the first time. As an indirect result of his self-imposed isolation, and directly related to the fact that Bene is the principal cause for Santiago's retreat to the tower (since she is supposedly there with him), Angela is forcefully locked into her own bedroom, but the young girl realises for the first time that closed doors are no longer seen as barriers to the evil forces weighing in upon the household. Knowing this, she feels not comfort in her entrapment, but absolute fear, and she explains:

'I didn't even need to look at the gate, because I had the distinct sensation the gypsy's face was floating in the air all around me, watching me. I was swathed in a malignant atmosphere, born of his invisible presence' (p. 108). The prohibitive space that García Morales described initially is now completely open and accessible, susceptible to the forces that at one time lay beyond the garden gate. Though the older women seem to believe that they have finally solved the problem by getting rid of Bene (after believing that her hands burned when she held a missal – to them, a classic sign of diabolical possession), they do not seem aware of Angela's continued terror within the still haunted environment. After running away with Bene and then being forced to return home by the Civil Guards, Santiago locks himself in the tower once more. Díaz notes the sombre significance of this second and final seclusion, describing the tower as 'un lugar de encierro y muerte' ['a place of confinement and death'] at the end of the novella (p. 232). Here, physical space transforms in direct proportion to the psychological deterioration of the characters: once marked as a site of self-imposed sequestration in which the children encouraged the supernatural to merge with the natural world around them, the tower is, by the end of the novella, a location of pure Gothic entrapment, signalling decline, destruction and, ultimately, death.

The loss of her brother is what leads Angela to succumb to the overwhelming power of the phantom, ending with a scene that many interpret as the girl's metaphorical death. In the final passage of *Bene*, Angela envelops herself in the sublime vision of the phantasmagoric forces around her and describes them in mysterious terms:

> He was looking at me intensely from a distance. I could see nothing but him, as if, at that moment, his was the only image in the night. He was at the gate, only this time not behind, but in front of it, and was moving almost imperceptibly, advancing slowly towards me. (pp. 114–15)

By this final paragraph of the novella, any notion of boundaries and barriers is now completely erased and, instead, replaced with an uninhibited interaction between the Inside (I) and the Outside

(Other). Now Angela can see nothing but the ghost of Bene's lover, and she willingly submits to him because of her inability to resist the sublime force: 'It was horror itself, appearing in this world through a human face. I felt I could not bear the vision of such terror . . . I willingly surrendered to that mode of death' (p. 115). The terror of the unknown and the pleasure that results from her interactions with it is what motivates Angela's final submission to the ghost. In this manner, she is also able to experience the phantasmagoric realm now inhabited by Bene and Santiago, thus opening the doors of her own mortal world to the supernatural forces that she had, for so long, only been able to imagine from the other side of the gate.

As we have seen, the notion of monstrosity is a vital aspect of García Morales's first publication, and the author depicts the complex relationships between the dichotomised I/Other and Inside/Outside in terms of race, class, sexuality and the boundaries established in an attempt to contain and expel alterity. In *Bene*, García Morales takes a close look at the transition from disturbing difference into threatening force in her portrayal of a teenage girl who is marked by an overwhelming sense of otherness within a highly charged Gothic environment. Bene's function as monster is due to her familial relation to the impoverished Roma people as well as to rumours about her sexual promiscuity. Moreover, her monstrous image is multi-faceted, allowing for different interpretations (Fatal Woman, devil, phantasmagoric threat) that all culminate in the eventual physical deaths of Bene and Santiago and the metaphorical death of Angela. Bene's mysterious past acts as a sublime force, simultaneously attracting and repelling Angela and ultimately opening the once obsessively secure home to the diabolical, phantasmagoric powers of the teenager and her phantom lover.

Throughout the narrative, entrapment is a tool that belongs entirely to the adult women in the house: Elisa and Rosaura close and lock doors, gates and windows as a way to create boundaries between their home and the outside world. In both scenarios, the women's practice of segregation and confinement attempts to separate the Inside (self) from the Outside (other). As is the case in most Gothic stories, Bene fails to reintegrate herself into the world around her. Her status as monster marginalises her from the surrounding environment, leading to her eventual self-destruction.

García Morales's text, like many Gothic works, positions the monster as the character who does not conform to prevailing societal standards and expectations. Bene, then, performs a vital role in reflecting real-life fears and anxieties from within the author's own Spanish community. These fears often deal primarily with the question of alterity, since the classic Gothic monster image is rooted in signs of difference. Bene's Roma heritage and social class mark her as always already different within a post-war Spanish society that forcibly repressed otherness in an attempt to forge a monocultural national identity. By not conforming to the prevailing standard of 'Spanishness', Bene was destined to become the monster in this upper-class Spanish home.

In *Bene*, therefore, García Morales presents us with her own version of the haunted house motif in which alterity itself becomes a ghostly, monstrous presence that threatens to destabilise the boundaries of the household by breaking down the relationships between those living inside and those just beyond the gate. As reflections of the self, monsters provide clues to our own fears and anxieties, pinpointing individual and collective acts of transgression by alienating them from the rest of the community; however, as Fred Botting remarks, in the end 'one must love one's monster/vampire/self'.[30] García Morales attempts to reconcile these notions of I/Other and Inside/Outside by allowing her young narrator to ultimately accept the monstrosity around her, admitting the phantasmagoric presence into her house and body and, in doing so, problematising the restrictive notion of 'Spanishness' in the post-Franco era.

3

A (Haunted) Room of One's Own: The Evolution of Gender Roles and Female Sexuality in Adelaida García Morales's Aunt Águeda *and* Elisa's Secret

After Adelaida García Morales (1945–2014) achieved literary fame in 1985 with the publication of both *The South and Bene* and *The Silence of the Sirens*, she continued her work as a novelist throughout the following decade. Developing her own unique narrative voice, García Morales focused her texts primarily on the evolving role of Spanish women during and after the dictatorship of Francisco Franco. Her novels employ the Gothic as a way to highlight women's entrapment in a patriarchal system that relied heavily on the imposition of religion – Franco's National Catholicism – to maintain order and tradition. Women's voices carry the plots of García Morales's novels, perhaps in conjunction with the author's own need to process her personal experience of growing up as a young girl under the dictatorship. It is noteworthy that her writing – like that of many twentieth-century Spanish women authors – coincided with the Transition era, in which the beginning of democracy granted women more personal liberties and a chance to make their voices heard after years of oppression.

The present chapter, divided into two parts, studies the change from dictatorship to democracy in Spain through an examination of traditional gender roles with a focus on women's lived experiences as portrayed in García Morales's novels *La tía Águeda* [translated here as *Aunt Águeda*] (1995) and *El secreto de Elisa* [*Elisa's Secret*] (1999). Both novels develop these themes by employing the haunted house motif as a way to accentuate women's anxiety and entrapment in the domestic space. Haunting and terror combine with alternating images of sexual promiscuity and purity to challenge the standard Francoist discourse about ideal womanhood. The first part of the chapter considers haunting in *Aunt Águeda* as largely related to gendered anxieties produced by an adherence to the traditional lifestyle mandated by Franco. The national obsession with women as chaste and morally-driven servants of the regime, augmented by the Women's Section of the Spanish fascist party, directly results in Águeda's eventual psychosis and death. The second part of this chapter will focus on *Elisa's Secret*, in which we will note the need for protagonist Elisa to cast off these traditional binds through the newly-acquired right to divorce (a result of the transition to democracy), liberating herself from her ex-husband and two teenage sons who constantly doubt her ability to live without them. When she fulfils her lifelong dream of buying a house in a small country village, Elisa discovers that the house is haunted by the spirits of a mother and son who died there in a murder-suicide years ago. Over the course of the novel, Elisa's infatuation with the ghost of the son turns into an exploration of sexuality and the achievement of personal liberation from societal expectations and state-imposed traditions. Studied together, these two novels provide a detailed portrait of women's life during and after the dictatorship, giving particular insight into the influence of National Catholicism on women's sexual and economic freedom.

Aunt Águeda *(1995)*

When 10-year-old Marta's mother dies, her father sends her to live with her older aunt Águeda in a large country house in the outskirts of Seville. Águeda, a severe and domineering woman, expects

Marta to obey her very traditional rules, and the girl soon becomes desperate to leave the house and return to her father. Águeda's husband, Martín (whom she married later in life), is much gentler with Marta, but he is an alcoholic who brings other women to the house, scandalising Águeda and leading others to believe that he only married the woman for her money and large estate. When Martín complains of chest pains one evening, Águeda refuses to let the maid call for the doctor, and Martín dies. After his death, Águeda suddenly starts noticing her deceased husband's possessions appearing in random places throughout the house, and she becomes convinced that his spirit is haunting her as punishment for letting him die. During this time, Martín's son Pedro comes to live with Águeda and Marta, and the two children become quite close. Although Águeda does not like Marta to spend time with Pedro for fear that he will corrupt her innocence, her increasing frailty makes her less able to monitor them, and Marta takes advantage of her aunt's illness to regain a certain amount of freedom. Águeda gradually succumbs to madness due to the nightly hauntings, and when she complains of chest pains one evening, the maid – in payback for what Águeda did to Martín – refuses to call the doctor. When Águeda dies, Marta's father comes to bring her back to Seville and Marta never again returns to the house.

Aunt Águeda has received little scholarly attention, due in part to the lack of an English translation of the novel. Among those who have written about the text, Janet Pérez only briefly mentions it in her article on Spanish women's neo-gothic fiction, noting Águeda's madness as 'characteristic gothic form'.[1] Abigail Lee Six devotes a chapter of her book on García Morales's fiction to this novel, comparing its development of fear within the house to that of Horace Walpole's *The Castle of Otranto*, highlighting 'the sense of claustrophobia, of being trapped inside a building . . . and the ingenious establishment of an almost seamless relationship between the hostile architecture and the unwelcome and unlawful authority of its owner'.[2] Carlos Vadillo Buenfil approaches the novel as a dialogue between *Bildungsroman* and confessional, stating:

> La tía Águeda es un *Bildungsroman* y una ficción confesional que reviste sus propias señas de identidad, pues el dolor que estimula

a la confidencia no es la desaparición física de la progenitora de la heroína . . . sino la vivencia dolorosa que supuso para la neófita el trato con el ser que encarnaba todos los atributos contrarios a la benevolente imagen recordada de la madre.

[*Aunt Águeda* is a *Bildungsroman* and a confessional fiction that takes on its own signs of identity, since the pain that motivates this confession is not the physical disappearance of the heroine's mother . . . but rather the painful experience entailed in the child's interactions with the being who embodied all the attributes that were contrary to her memory of the benevolent image of her mother.][3]

For Vadillo Buenfil, the confessional form that the novel takes on is key to understanding Marta's dramatic transition from young girl to pre-teen, spurred on by loss (her mother, uncle and, eventually, her aunt) and her initiation into sexual exploration.

All of the critics who have commented on *Aunt Águeda* have noted the atmosphere of terror and entrapment within Águeda's rural house, a characteristic that is key to my own reading of the text as a haunted house narrative. Here, I would like to propose a Gothic, feminist reading of this novel in which haunting is a manifestation of the inability (or, perhaps, refusal) to maintain a feminine domestic space. As we will see, Águeda's obsession with image and gender roles contrasts with her own lack of traditional femininity and her long-held status as unmarried (older) woman and landowner. Although she upholds the National Catholic standards for young Marta's upbringing, Águeda herself does not comply with the 'Angel in the House' ideal, and it is precisely her noncompliance that leads to the terrifying nightly hauntings and her eventual death.

When José Antonio Primo de Rivera founded the Falange (the Spanish fascist party) in 1934, his sister Pilar Primo de Rivera soon rose to power as the leader of the 'Sección Femenina' [Women's Section], which espoused the traditional values set forth by the fascist organisation and defined clear gender-based roles for Spanish citizens. Once Franco's Nationalist troops had won the war and his regime was officially installed, the Women's Section played a vital role in the dissemination of propaganda directed toward women, who were seen as an integral part of the fascist strategy. As child-bearers, women were the mothers of future generations of the regime, and the first and most important teachers of National Catholicism in the home. As contemporary author Dulce Chacón notes, the new regime used the Catholic Church and the Women's Section to '"reeducar" a la mujer para reducirla al ámbito doméstico y limitar sus aspiraciones' ['"reeducate" the woman to reduce her to the domestic sphere and limit her aspirations'].[4] Emilio Silva explains the new standard of womanhood as defined by National Catholicism:

> Durante la Guerra y a lo largo de los años cuarenta, a través de la Iglesia y de la Sección Femenina se propagó una imagen de las mujeres de la *España Nacional* como vírgenes o buenas madres, inmaculadas, pasivas; unas guardianas del orden moral sumisas y pías. En contrapartida, las mujeres *rojas* fueron presentadas – con cierta incongruencia – como prostitutas y al mismo tiempo como *no-mujeres*.
>
> [During the war and throughout the 1940s, the Church and the Women's Section propagated an image of the women of *National Spain* as virgins or good mothers, immaculate, passive; submissive and pious guardians of the moral order. In contrast, *red* women were presented – with certain inconsistency – as prostitutes and at the same time as *non-women*.][5]

The very definition of womanhood relied on a form of purity culture that required women to be simultaneously alluring to men (to attract a husband) and virginal. Those who did not comply with this image were acting against the regime itself and were therefore viewed as dangerous 'non-women' who put in jeopardy the entire propaganda machine revolving around domesticity and maternity.

Motherhood was a woman's ultimate goal under National Catholicism. Eider de Dios Fernández states that the 'capacidad de generar nuevos y disciplinados individuos se convertía en su única aportación a la sociedad y el único fin de su existencia' ['capacity to generate new and disciplined individuals turned into her only contribution to society and the sole purpose of her existence'].[6] Franco gave the Spanish Catholic Church complete control over the national school curriculum, resulting in separate curricula for girls and boys as part of the Primary Education Law of 1945. Beginning in primary school, young girls were trained in the tasks and spiritual ideology necessary to turn them into successful wives and mothers as adults. According to Dios Fernández, these lessons were extended to high school girls, who were taught that a woman should be a 'cocinera, doncella, costurera, bordadora, zurcidora, planchadora, recadera, enfermera, contable, economista, maestra e higienista' ['cook, maid, seamstress, embroiderer, darner, ironer, messenger, nurse, accountant, economist, teacher and hygienist'].[7] In one of Pilar Primo de Rivera's 1943 newsletters for the Women's Section, she summarises this curriculum and entire ideology when she writes: 'El niño mirará al mundo, la niña mirará al hogar' ['The boy will look toward the world, the girl will look toward the home'].[8]

In *Aunt Águeda*, García Morales positions her narrative within the National Catholic tradition of rural southern Spain in 1957. Águeda, a 42-year-old woman, is a landowner and was married for the first time only three years prior. In fact, the first real knowledge that we have of Águeda's background is that the family believes that Martín only married her out of economic interest: 'Al parecer tenía la intención de ocuparse de las tierras de la tía Águeda . . . No podían concebir que un hombre pudiera enamorarse de la tía Águeda' ['It seemed that he had the intention to take on aunt Águeda's lands . . . They couldn't conceive that a man could fall in love with aunt Águeda'].[9] The fact that she was single for so many years seems to make her the object of suspicion in town; perhaps unsurprisingly, a regime that emphasised marriage and motherhood as women's primary objective was highly critical of older, unmarried women. As Alejandro Camino Rodríguez explains:

> [D]urante los años cuarenta el discurso oficial del régimen . . . fue muy crítico con la soltería, ya que se percibió como un fracaso de la maternidad y/o una forma de rebelarse ante su subordinación frente a los hombres. En consecuencia, las solteras fueron consideradas como un cuerpo social extraño que va a ser sujeto de burlas y humillaciones.
>
> [During the 1940s the regime's official discourse . . . was very critical of spinsterhood, since it was perceived as a failure of maternity and/or a form of rebelling against their subordination to men. As a

consequence, single women were considered a strange social group that was going to be the subject of taunts and humiliations.]¹⁰

Our perspective of Águeda is, from the beginning of the novel, defined by her 'flawed' womanhood: she was single until the age of thirty-nine, never had children and possesses her own land and house. The townspeople think she is 'rara' ['strange'] (p. 32), Pedro (Martín's son) describes her as 'muy seria . . . a veces es hasta antipática' ['very serious . . . at times even mean'] (p. 67), and Marta sees her as 'malvada y cruel' ['evil and cruel'] (p. 74). Instead of fulfilling the ideal feminine image propagated by the Women's Section of the Falange, Águeda is its severe counterpart.

As Marta relates her memories of her time living in Águeda's home, she continually emphasises the environment of the house itself in terms of Gothic terror. Fear is the primary emotion through which Marta experiences the home and everything that occurs inside. The young girl directly attributes her general unease in the house to Águeda, describing 'la atmósfera desagradable e inquietante que la tía Águeda, con su carácter agrio y rígido, creaba a mi alrededor' ['the unpleasant and disturbing atmosphere that aunt Águeda, with her bitter and rigid character, created around me'] (p. 32). The home – a warm, inviting domestic space when curated by the 'ideal' woman – is, under Águeda's care, a threatening environment that according to Marta is like 'una prisión' ['a prison'] (p. 82).

Within the prisonlike walls of her house, Águeda's attempts at child rearing are equally severe. A devout Catholic who attends mass weekly, Águeda upholds the traditional standards denoted for young girls in Franco's Spain, establishing strict rules for Marta that limit the young girl's freedom and keep her shut inside the house for the majority of her non-school hours. On Marta's first morning in the house, Águeda presents her with an antique doll that was once hers as a little girl. The doll, dressed in a white lace gown, immediately terrifies Marta: 'Sus ojos negros brillaban como si estuvieran vivos y me miraban amenazadoramente desde un mundo . . . que se me antojó siniestro y casi de ultratumba' ['Its black eyes shone as if they were alive and they looked at me threateningly from a world . . . that seemed sinister and beyond the grave'] (pp. 12–13). This doll, a symbol of Águeda's attempt to pass on tradition to her niece, becomes a point of contention between them: Águeda wants Marta to practice her domestic skills by taking care of the doll and sewing it a new dress, but the doll repulses Marta and she has no interest in playing with it or displaying it in her room, as her aunt demands. After Martín's death, Marta – associating the doll with Águeda – rushes to her room and purposefully breaks the doll, smashing it into the floor while imagining that it is Águeda herself.

Águeda's insistence on maintaining tradition in her rearing of Marta extends itself not just to domestic training, but also to religion: the woman requires her niece to attend mass with her, pray the rosary daily and visit her relatives' graves in the local cemetery. Águeda explains to Marta one afternoon: 'Tal vez no te guste mi carácter, pero yo trato de educarte en una disciplina que siempre es necesaria en la vida' ['You may not like my character, but I'm trying to educate you in a discipline that is always necessary in life'] (p. 48). Thus, Marta's new life consists almost entirely of school (with a National Catholic curriculum for little girls) and domestic tasks in the home. This discipline, however, is not enforced on Pedro, who is allowed to come and go as he pleases once he moves into Águeda's house. Marta notices the obvious separate standard, and she admits: 'Le envidié por la libertad que él mismo imponía. ¿Por qué no podía hacer yo lo mismo? Estaba cansada de recibir siempre órdenes de la tía Águeda y de vivir pendiente de sus permisos' ['I envied him for the freedom that he himself imposed. Why couldn't I do the same? I was tired of always receiving orders from aunt Águeda and of waiting for her permissions'] (p. 108). Although she allows Pedro to do anything and go anywhere he chooses, Águeda constantly deems his influence on Marta as damaging to the young girl's innocence. When Marta refuses to pray the rosary one evening, Águeda immediately screams at her: '¿Tienes el demonio dentro del cuerpo?' ['Do you have the devil in your body?'] (p. 128). Marta explains that since Pedro does not have to pray, she will not do so, either, to which Águeda replies: '¡Otra vez Pedro! ¿Ésa es la influencia que está ejerciendo sobre ti?' ['Pedro again! Is that the influence he is exercising over you?'] (p. 128). In every instance in which Águeda discovers Pedro's influence on

Marta, it is the latter who is punished for failing to perform her expected role as a submissive, pious young girl.

Águeda's separate expectations for Marta and Pedro align entirely with the ideology of the Franco regime, including in matters of sexuality. The young girl's innocence is a recurring topic throughout the novel, as Águeda insists on maintaining rigid standards for Marta in accordance with the expectations of the era. When Marta refuses to put her hair in braids (Águeda's required hairstyle for her niece) one Sunday, Águeda shouts at her: '¡Me vas a matar a disgustos, Marta! Si sigues así, no podré seguir teniéndote en esta casa' ['You're going to be the death of me, Marta! If you continue like this, I won't be able to keep having you in this house'] (p. 129). Marta's refusal to maintain the childish hairstyle is a direct result of her newfound sexual curiosity and her feelings for Pedro, with whom she has already had an initial, brief sexual encounter. When Águeda gives up the fight and Marta is able to keep her hair down, the young girl notes that 'finalmente había salido triunfante ante los ojos de Pedro' ['I had finally emerged triumphant in the eyes of Pedro'] (p. 130), demonstrating that although Águeda's reactions are extreme, her belief that Marta is disobeying her because of Pedro's influence is, perhaps, not entirely inaccurate.

Throughout the narrative, it is clear that Águeda views men as a perversion of her personal space. Aside from her view of Pedro as a corrupting influence on her niece, Águeda's relationship with her husband is tense and unbalanced, and their primary methods of communication – as Marta observes – are either shouting or absolute silence. On one such occasion, Martín reacts to Águeda's criticisms by telling her: '¡Ni eres mi mujer ni eres nada para mí!' ['You are neither my wife nor anything to me!'], and then he shows Marta a photo of his deceased former wife, telling the girl: 'Ésta es a la que amo. Mírala bien, fíjate qué guapa y bondadosa es' ['This is the one I love. Look closely at her, see how beautiful and good-natured she is'] (p. 20). From the beginning of the novel, García Morales repeatedly demonstrates that Águeda, the complete opposite of Martín's former wife, will never be able to fulfil the role required of her in 1950s Spain. Far from the 'beautiful and good-natured' ideal, Águeda refuses to submit to her husband and, instead, ridicules and openly despises him. She reminds him of his own financial reliance on her – at one point telling him 'Es muy fácil hacer regalos con el dinero de otro' ['It is very easy to give presents with someone else's money'] (p. 31) – and rebukes him when he returns home drunk or with female friends, whom she calls prostitutes. He takes advantage of her money and estate, and she clearly has internalised that this is the reason he married her, as her friends and family have always suspected. In southern Spain, as David Gilmore has noted, the very notion of masculinity is highly dependent on men's rule in and outside of the home: 'For these men to maintain their honor they must rule themselves, be their own master; hence they are manly. To be "ruled," by which is meant to be controlled by or dependent upon others, is to be dominated, with almost a ring of emasculation about it.'[11] Martín's impotence is accentuated by Águeda's dominance, and their respective failure to follow the separate gender roles that society under Franco mandated indirectly leads to Martín's death and the terrifying haunting that follows it.

When Martín complains of chest pains one evening, Águeda's complete lack of sympathy leads her to ignore his distress and order the maid, Catalina, not to call the doctor. She goes to her own room and falls asleep, while Marta listens to her uncle's agonising cries. When the noise suddenly stops, creating a 'silencio amenazador que se extendió por toda la casa' ['threatening silence that extended throughout the whole house'] (p. 71), Marta realises that Martín has died. Águeda, showing little emotion immediately upon this discovery, finally tells Catalina to call for the doctor to confirm Martín's death. After this point, the terrible silences that Marta so frequently noted throughout the first part of the narrative become even more accentuated and the house more prisonlike and nightmarish for the little girl, who admits that she begins to 'sentir miedo en pleno día, miedo de todo' ['feel fear in the middle of the day, fear of everything'] (p. 80).

Águeda's physical and mental transformation begins immediately after Martín's burial. She becomes more rigid and bad-tempered, often stares absently into space, and locks herself in her room, only leaving for meals or Sunday mass. It is at this point that Águeda begins to receive nightly hauntings from a sinister spirit that she claims is Martín. Marta frequently observes the woman shouting into the air, screaming for him to go back to hell. Águeda soon discovers some of Martín's possessions in random places in the house, and she believes that Martín's ghost has moved them there to manipulate her fear and to drive her mad. (Marta suspects that Catalina is the one who has moved the objects, but the maid insists it is not her.) The young girl tells us that her aunt 'parecía no poder distinguir lo real de lo irreal' ['seemed unable to distinguish the real from the unreal'] (p. 84). As terror invades the house, Águeda's mental state has a profound impact on Marta, who becomes nearly paralysed with fear and unable to process the thought that the dead can intermingle with the living. In fact, as Marta explains, Martín's presence in the house is more noticeable after his death than while he was alive: 'un aliento de muerte invadía la casa. Él estaba más presente que nunca. Su fantasma se paseaba por el dormitorio de la tía Águeda casi cada noche y sus objetos se le aparecían a mi tía con mucha frecuencia' ['a breath of death invaded the house. He was more present than ever. His ghost passed through aunt Águeda's room almost every night and his objects appeared to my aunt with great frequency'] (p. 89). As she sits awake, trembling in the dark each night, Marta begins to perceive 'una presencia maligna e invisible que invadía la casa . . . y siempre acudía a la habitación de la tía Águeda, a atormentarla' ['a malignant and invisible presence that invaded the house . . . and always went to aunt Águeda's room, to torment her'] (p. 117). These nightly visits convince Águeda that Martín 'viene desde el infierno' ['comes from hell'] and 'tiene ahora la forma de un diablo' ['now has the form of a devil'] (p. 101). This blend of the supernatural and the Catholic teachings regarding sin and the afterlife serves to heighten Águeda's madness and Marta's terror; the young girl, believing wholeheartedly in what her aunt has taught her, tells us that it seems that 'el infierno mismo se había instalado en la oscuridad de la casa' ['hell itself had moved into the darkness of the house'] (p. 105). Águeda's house, never a domestic haven, is finally converted into a site tinged with the supernatural terror of the afterlife and, as a symbolic hellscape, it exudes the twin notions of penance and sacrifice.

Águeda is unable to withstand the physical and mental impact of the hauntings, and she eventually succumbs to the illness the ghost has brought upon her. Catalina, unforgiving after Águeda let Martín die, now returns the favour, refusing to call the doctor when Águeda begins to complain of chest pain. As the woman lies dying in bed, Marta admits that 'no sentía nada hacia ella, solo miedo' ['I didn't feel anything for her, just fear'] (p. 145). The terror the young girl feels toward her aunt after death denotes Águeda's lack of benevolence in life; even in death, she is always already the embodiment of the 'non-woman': one who does not follow the traditional role assigned to her, one who lacks the alluring beauty, kindness, grace and maternal instincts that were the constant subject of the Women's Section reviews at the time.

It is noteworthy that Martín's ghost seems to focus almost entirely on Águeda's bedroom, thus invoking the intense feeling of violation that hastens her decline. Diana Wallace has noted a correlation between haunting and marriage, stating: 'Some of the most powerful of women's ghost stories deal with the physical and psychic violence enacted on women within marriage, figured through the haunted house and the abjected (or out-of-place) body or corpse.'[12] Wallace then later suggests that the ghost itself often comes to symbolise 'women's feeling that their identity, both past and present, has been repeatedly, and often violently, denied and repressed'.[13] Haunting in García Morales's novel is the result of Águeda's refusal to abide by the gender norms of her time; while on the one hand she does, in fact, uphold the traditional standards in her upbringing of Marta (focusing on domestic tasks and religious education), she herself does not fit the ideal image of wife and mother. Her severe countenance and lack of maternal benevolence make her somehow less-than-woman in the eyes of those around her. Even Catalina, the maid, abhors Águeda's lack of subordinance and goodwill toward her husband, and for this reason she allows Águeda to die in the same manner that Águeda allowed Martín to die.

The invasion of Águeda's space begins with her marriage to Martín and continues to escalate after her husband's death. What once represented a frustrating lack of control for Águeda becomes a terrifying and total loss of agency as it is no longer just her physical space but also her emotional and mental wellbeing that are constantly subjected to supernatural threats. In this novel, therefore, the house – a symbol of domesticity and ideal womanhood – becomes a battleground for control: the masculine presence within the house both in human and ghostly form serves as a constant reminder of Águeda's refusal to abide by the social norms of her era, accentuating her dominant persona as a monstrous form of non-woman and non-mother. The house is haunted by the unfulfilled need to maintain an idealised domestic space in which the feminine is subordinate to the masculine. Águeda's choice to maintain control over herself and her house (seen here as an extension of her body) leads to the eventual violation of that space, resulting in her descent into madness and, finally, death.

García Morales employs the haunted house motif in this novel in order to highlight the impact of the rigid gender roles first established by the Women's Section of the Falange in the 1930s. Women who did not abide by the standards of National Catholicism and its insistence on their primary role as wives and mothers were seen as rebellious, strange and even non-women. The image of a dominant, independent woman contrasted sharply with the feminine ideal, which was a fundamental aspect of the regime's plan to produce generations of children raised under the watchful, benevolent eye of mothers dedicated to the nationalist cause. By creating a protagonist who is the opposite of that ideal, García Morales portrays rather vividly the dangers the regime posed for those who were different, and the terror provoked by the loss of individual agency for countless women living under Franco.

Elisa's Secret *(1999)*

In her 1999 novel *Elisa's Secret*, García Morales once again takes on the haunted house motif in connection with her female protagonist's attempt at personal freedom. Unlike *Aunt Águeda*, this novel takes place after the Franco regime, during the final years of the Transition era in the early 1990s. Elisa, fifty-two, separates from her husband after discovering his affair with a younger woman. She moves from their house in Madrid to a small, isolated town in the outskirts of the capital, where she rents and eventually buys an old house from elderly neighbour Eulalia. The woman's sister, Encarna, and nephew, Daniel, lived in that house until just over twenty years ago, when Encarna murdered him and killed herself in a violent rage provoked by Daniel's abandonment of her with his move to Madrid. Their rooms at the back of the house are haunted every night by the sounds of their anguished cries and tortured last breaths. Elisa finds a collection of letters, photos and other personal objects belonging to Daniel, and she becomes obsessed with him, eventually finding herself falling in love with the ghost of a man she has never met. She tries to communicate with him through seances, and this method finally works when Daniel tells her to find a woman in Tejuela named Gloria, who performs a ritual to rid the spirits of their eternal pain. Although Encarna fades away, Daniel admits that he has fallen in love with Elisa and vows to stay with her forever; Elisa, however, cannot stand the thought of his gaze always following her throughout her home, and the idea of her complete lack of privacy begins to drive her mad. Daniel finally leaves, and Elisa decides to write about his future life in the spiritual world as a form of closure.

As in the case of *Aunt Águeda*, few scholars have specifically studied *Elisa's Secret*, again due primarily to a lack of English translation. Among those who have mentioned it, Lourdes Albuixech briefly considers the text alongside García Morales's other novels, which she sees as sharing important autobiographical elements such as 'isolation, North versus South or countryside versus city, strict social norm or convention versus marginal anti-norm, or freedom versus repression'.[14] Albuixech also notes that 'the phantasmagorical atmospheres, the supernatural or fantastic dimensions . . . the mystery of death, the theme of secrets, the predominance of interior spaces . . . all seem to point to the existence of an unattainable, invisible (un)reality'[15] in García Morales's literary works. We will certainly note the presence of all these elements in *Elisa's Secret*, a novel which shares striking similarities to the narrative pattern established in *Aunt Águeda* and *Bene*. Beatriz Trigo studies *Elisa's Secret* as a *Bildungsroman* within the fantastic tradition, comparing it to Olivia Howard Dunbar's 1914 tale 'The Long Chamber'. According to Trigo,

> En *El secreto de Elisa*, el elemento fantástico está entonces vinculado a lo que yo denomino la esfera íntima de la mujer, estableciendo desde un principio una correlación entre el elemento fantástico y el género,

que en este caso funciona como una herramienta que posibilita en la protagonista un viaje de autodescubrimiento.

[In *Elisa's Secret*, the fantastic element is therefore linked to what I call the woman's intimate sphere, establishing from the beginning a correlation between the fantastic element and gender, which in this case functions as a tool that makes possible the journey of self-discovery in the protagonist.][16]

Trigo also emphasises the fact that Elisa is surrounded by women in the small town, marking her removal from a masculine-centred urban space (her home in Madrid) to a feminine-centred natural space (her home in the countryside), concluding: 'Se podría decir que en este sentido, la depresión de Elisa desaparece gracias a este universo femenino que la acoge' ['One could say that in this sense, Elisa's depression disappears thanks to this feminine universe that takes her in'].[17] In her dissertation on neo-Gothic elements in García Morales's literature, Laura Ponce Romo differs from Trigo's fantastic reading of the novel by cataloguing and commenting on the various characteristics that make *Elisa's Secret* a Gothic text, noting the remote location,[18] the forbidden room,[19] the overwhelming silence,[20] the presence of phantoms,[21] and the love between Encarna and her son, which she considers to be an example of Gothic incest.[22] (On this last point I would disagree: if we understand this novel to be a representation of women's lived experiences, Encarna's obsession with Daniel relates more to anxiety stemming from motherhood as her sole role in life; thus, a failure of her child to amount to anything is a failure of the worst kind for a woman in a traditional town under the Franco regime, because her entire sacrifice is fruitless.)

In my reading of *Elisa's Secret*, I will consider the Gothic motifs and gender roles noted above as interrelated elements that, like in *Aunt Águeda*, serve to highlight García Morales's socio-political consciousness. Whereas Águeda was confined to a domestic space that became haunted in relation to her departure from the traditional norms established during the early Franco era, Elisa leaves the modern urban capital and purposefully installs herself in a remote rural house to reclaim her independence as a newly single woman. If Martín's spectral visits to Águeda's room are a consistent reminder of her lack of femininity and desirable sexuality (and, as such, a violation of her personal space – read as a violation of her body), Elisa's supernatural encounters with Daniel's ghost are highly eroticised and, until the very end of the novel, intensely sought by Elisa herself. Using Marianne Hirsch's notion of postmemory, I will examine Elisa's interactions with the objects and photographs in the house as an important part of her reconstruction of Daniel's memories, which converge with her own life until the boundaries between the real and the unreal, the physical and the supernatural, are entirely blurred. What both novels share in common is the portrayal of the masculine presence inside the house as an invasion of the women's personal liberty and, ultimately, a reminder of the difficulty women faced even in the post-Franco era in attaining true independence.

Marriage and motherhood are, from the beginning of the novel, a continuous baseline against which women's happiness and success are measured. The very first sentence already positions domestic partnership as a focal point of the narrative: 'Después de veintiocho años de matrimonio, Elisa empezó a sospechar, por vez primera, que su marido le ocultaba la existencia de una amante' ['After twenty-eight years of marriage, Elisa began to suspect, for the first time, that her husband was hiding the existence of a lover'].[23] As she reflects on her married life, Elisa recalls the sacrifices she made to raise their two sons: before they were born, she had finished a degree in history and was teaching in a private school, but Gabriel, her husband, was a psychiatrist and they relied on his income to sustain the family once they had children, so she quit her job to become a stay-at-home mother. A recurring theme throughout the novel is maternal guilt and unhappiness; after twelve years at home, Elisa feels 'frustrada por su inactividad y decepcionada de su matrimonio' ['frustrated by her inactivity and deceived by her marriage'], leading her to 'un estado de angustia que no sabía cómo superar' ['a state of anguish that she did not know how to overcome'] (p. 6). Gabriel prescribes her antidepressants, but to no effect. Like the protagonist in Charlotte Perkins Gilman's classic tale 'The Yellow Wallpaper', Elisa feels trapped in a domestic environment that is smothering her freedom and happiness. Juliann Fleenor has noted that in the female Gothic, such as Perkins Gilman's story, 'women are punished for having babies because doing so imprisons them in the social structure symbolized by the house. The house is again employed as a major symbol; it is haunted . . . by female vulnerability and the sin of maternity.'[24] The house – always already a symbol of domesticity – once again becomes a space of haunting in García Morales's narrative; unlike *Aunt Águeda*, however, in *Elisa's Secret* we have two distinct forms of haunted houses: the modern house in Madrid that haunts Elisa with thoughts of her continual self-sacrifice, and the country house, with its restless, agonising ghosts.

The discovery of her husband's affair is what leads Elisa to decide to upend her life in Madrid and move to an isolated village on the outskirts of the capital. Here we must recall that prior to 1975, the Spanish civil code had strict rules regarding women's conduct within marriage. Divorce was illegal and, as John Hooper notes, *permiso marital* [marital permission] gave men nearly complete power over their wives:

> Without her husband's agreement, a wife could not embark on any sort of activity outside the home. She could not take a job, start a business or open a bank account. She could not initiate legal proceedings, enter into contracts, or buy and sell goods. She could not even undertake a journey of any length without her husband's approval.[25]

As such, in the early 1990s when this novel takes place, divorce and women's freedom of movement and legal agency were relatively new concepts for Spaniards. Even then, unmarried older women were still viewed with certain suspicion, and Elisa only has one friend – Raquel – who has chosen this path for herself. Perhaps unsurprisingly, Raquel becomes a model for Elisa's newfound independence when she realises that her unmarried, childless friend 'se encontraba satisfecha con su vida' ['was satisfied with her life'] and that 'la vitalidad, el optimismo y la ternura de Raquel se le contagiaban' ['Raquel's vitality, optimism and tenderness rubbed off on her'] (p. 8). Desperately seeking this positive outlook for herself, Elisa decides to abandon the city – which for her has become synonymous with anxiety and depression – and move to the countryside, leaving her children in the care of her husband and his mistress.

Although Elisa's move to the country represents, on the one hand, a break from tradition and from her marriage, it nevertheless serves as a constant reminder of her financial dependence on Gabriel. She believes that she will never be able to become fully independent because of the sacrifices she has made until this point: 'se sentía impotente para mantenerse a sí misma, una independencia económica era imposible para ella. Se veía marginada por completo del mercado laboral' ['she felt helpless to support herself, economic independence was impossible for her. She was completely marginalised from the labour market'] (p. 72). It is Gabriel who finances her move and provides money for the rental and eventual purchase of the house and for everything else that Elisa needs; therefore, even her own house in the country represents, to a certain degree, an actual lack of freedom. As Darcie Rives notes, 'For women writers of gothic fiction in particular, the home represents more generally how women have historically been cut off from the outside world, denied participation in public affairs, and prevented from controlling their own finances and lives.'[26] Although Elisa has left her primary home in the city – a space that came to symbolise domestic-induced claustrophobia – she has entered yet another home that still, inevitably, forces her dependence on her now ex-husband.

The isolated village to which she moves immediately evokes images of death and the afterlife. Upon seeing it for the first time, Elisa is drawn to its remote, almost other-worldliness. To her, it appears to be a 'lugar fantasmal, extraño' ['ghostly, strange place'] (p. 17) where empty roads pass by ruinous, silent houses through the centre of town to the church and cemetery, creating an atmosphere in which the inhabitants 'aparentaban no pertenecer ni al pasado, ni al presente, ni al futuro, sino a un tiempo distinto' ['seemed to pertain neither to the past, nor the present, nor the future, but rather to a distinct time'] (p. 26). The dilapidated, deserted houses and overwhelming silence of the town contrast sharply with the urban city from which the protagonist has come, and she frequently describes her experience living there as if she were in another realm – a sort of alternate reality that blends the physical with the spiritual.

When Elisa first enters the house that she has decided to rent, it is as if she has entered a time capsule: all of the former inhabitants' possessions are still in every room of the house, left in their original places for more than twenty years. Elisa quickly perceives 'una extraña quietud que impregnaba todo cuanto contenía, incluso sus propias paredes . . . como si algo de los dos difuntos se hubiera quedado en aquella sala' ['a strange stillness that impregnated everything within it, including its own walls . . . as if something from the two deceased owners had remained in that room'] (p. 21). This first entrance into her new home has a profound effect on Elisa: 'se sentía agobiada y oprimida por la atmósfera cargada' ['she felt overwhelmed and oppressed by the charged atmosphere'] (p. 23), and she feels 'sumergida en aquel pasado que . . . habitaba entre las paredes . . . un pasado que amenazaba con aprisionarla en una sutil e invisible pero inquebrantable tela de araña, penetrando en ella con su extraño aliento de vida' ['submerged in that past that . . . lived within the walls . . . a past that threatened to imprison her in a subtle and invisible but unbreakable spider web, penetrating her with its strange breath of life'] (p. 25). This sense of claustrophobia that Elisa experiences inside the house is, according to Rives, 'an essential element for the creation of terror in gothic fiction'[27] and is particularly noteworthy in the female Gothic. Nevertheless, despite the intense fear that Elisa immediately feels within the house, she is determined to make it her own, and she begins to plan new furnishings in each of the rooms.

Throughout the novel, García Morales continually points to the objects within the home as a gateway to the supernatural forces that reside there. These objects play an integral role in Elisa's ability to communicate with the two spirits trapped in her house, and Daniel's letters and photographs are what allow her to feel a special kinship with him by recreating his memories as part of her own lived experience. Marianne Hirsch has coined the term 'postmemory' to describe the process by which memory can be formed by and extracted from sources that bridge the divide between the first generation who directly experienced trauma and the subsequent generations who rely on such sources to recreate the memory for themselves. She explains the particular importance of photography to postmemory:

> Photographs in their enduring "umbilical" connection to life are precisely the medium connecting first- and second-generation

remembrance, memory and postmemory. They are the leftovers, the fragmentary sources and building blocks, shot through with holes, of the work of postmemory. They affirm the past's existence and, in their flat two-dimensionality, they signal its unbridgeable distance.[28]

Hirsch references Barthes and his consideration of photographs as 'a physical, material emanation of a past reality'.[29] As such, photographs are inherently connected to notions of materiality and, therefore, haunting. Indeed, Hirsch further explains that the subject of a photograph 'is both present (implied in the photograph) and absent (it has been there but is not here now). The referent haunts the picture like a ghost: it is a revenant, a return of the lost and dead other.'[30] Moreover, she notes: 'Photographs, ghostly revenants, are very particular instruments of remembrance, since they are perched at the edge between memory and forgetting.'[31] Likewise, Patricia Keller asserts that 'photographs are nothing if not ghosts – the texture of time and light transformed into meaning, the invisible visualized. Walter Benjamin, who perceived photography's radical and indeed revolutionary potential, understood well its underlying spectral quality.'[32]

When Elisa finds a box of photographs of Daniel, she is instantly able to recreate his life in images: first as a young boy, then gradually growing older until reaching maturity in his last photo, dated 1971. Through the pictures, Daniel's intense gaze seems to stare back at Elisa, 'descubriéndola y observándola' ['discovering and observing her'] (p. 31). In this moment, Daniel suddenly becomes an active part of Elisa's life; the touch of her hands on the photos and letters in the boxes in his room combines with the young man's eyes staring back at her, lifelike, through the paper to create a palpable sense of his presence next to her. Elisa is immediately drawn to Daniel, sensing that he is 'muy atractivo, de una gran belleza y virilidad' ['very attractive, of great beauty and virility'] (p. 31). Her desire to know more about the mysterious death of this man and his mother – the circumstances of which she has not yet discovered – is enhanced by her sudden physical attraction to Daniel. Elisa thus becomes determined to recreate Daniel's memories, and she will end up combining them with her own present reality until the lines between the past and present are entirely blurred.

The former owners' objects throughout the house seem to Elisa to be part of a kind of 'memoria impersonal, una memoria que pertenecía a la casa, como si ésta poseyera algo de humano' ['impersonal memory, a memory that belonged to the house, as if it had a human quality'] (pp. 33–4), later explaining that she herself is a participant in this impersonal memory, in which 'los objetos que tocaban sus manos se le habían aparecido como figuras imaginarias que se materializaban, prodigiosamente, con su contacto' ['the objects that her hands touched appeared to her like imaginary figures that materialised, prodigiously, with her contact'] (p. 42). Aside from the photographs (the last of which Elisa even takes with her on a trip to Madrid), Daniel's letters to his mother are the most important objects in the home because they give a voice to the spirit who is trapped inside the house, helping Elisa to reconstruct the last years of his life and to better understand the reasons for his haunting presence. She is convinced that 'Daniel existía en forma de recuerdos' ['Daniel existed in the form of memories'] (p. 48) both in his former possessions as well as in the memories of the townspeople who knew him. The 'impersonal memory' that she associates with the back rooms where these objects are located also corresponds to the distinct atmosphere of that part of the house – a space delineated in terms of claustrophobia and cyclical moments of terror.

As she spends time in Daniel's room looking through his photographs and reading his letters to his mother, the house repeatedly induces a feeling of severe claustrophobia in her, forcing her to 'respirar de manera agitada, tratando de que penetrara más oxígeno en sus pulmones' ['breathe in an agitated manner, trying to get more oxygen to penetrate her lungs'] (p. 32). Her physical response to the room is accompanied by an inescapable feeling of terror that Elisa realises she must try to overcome if she is going to be able to make contact with the spirits. This is more difficult than expected, however, because every night at two o'clock she awakens to the horrific sounds of agonised breaths and cries coming from Daniel's room. Realising that there is no rational, earthly explanation for these sounds, Elisa succumbs to sheer terror and panic on an almost nightly basis as she listens to the ghostly wails emanating from the back room.

García Morales repeatedly emphasises throughout the novel the overwhelming fear that Elisa experiences within her new home, almost always in connection with her protagonist's intense sexual attraction to Daniel. This sublime mixture of terror and desire begins during Elisa's first night in her new home, when she hears the ghosts' tortured breaths for the first time. Wanting to know what secrets the back rooms contain, she admits that 'su ansiedad por correr de inmediato hacia ellas era tan intensa como el terror que agitaba su cuerpo' ['her anxiety to run immediately toward them was as intense as the terror that shook her body'] (pp. 40–1). The result of these terrifying experiences is 'una euforia que le producía el constante recuerdo de su reciente e inexplicable experiencia' ['a euphoria that produced in her the constant reminder of her recent and inexplicable experience'], which – by daylight – becomes 'una emoción intensa y placentera' ['an intense and pleasurable emotion'] (p. 47). The back rooms quickly become, for Elisa, a sublime space that provokes intense emotional and physical responses that she has not felt during her monotonous years in the city. Given that these feelings are due to her newfound connection with Daniel, it becomes impossible for Elisa to separate the departed man's spirit from her present lived reality, and she finds herself falling in love with him.

Elisa's attraction to Daniel is further accentuated by the fact that the nightly hauntings occur in his bedroom. Emma Liggins has studied the occurrence of haunted bedrooms in May Sinclair's ghost stories, and she considers 'the bedroom as a room of death/mourning and of an often disturbing sexual intimacy . . . The haunted bedroom with its "nightmare-haunted" beds becomes a space of conflict and terror.'[33] As Elisa eventually learns, Daniel's bedroom was the site of his violent death: his mother, fuelled by angst at the thought of losing her son to the city that was slowly destroying him, killed him while he was lying in bed asleep, and then slit her own throat next to him. This grisly scene happened shortly after Daniel slept with Rosaura, a young woman who had been in love with him since early adolescence and whom he had repeatedly ignored until that night. The bedroom therefore becomes a space marked by sexual intimacy and violent death, and this sublime attraction/repulsion permeates the very walls of the room that Elisa comes to know so well.

S. L. Varnado notes that in texts that feature a character who has fallen in love with a ghost, 'the romance generally has been doomed to failure'.[34] The initial problem for Elisa – aside from the terror she cannot help but feel while in Daniel's room – is the lack of physical intimacy that she craves. Gazing constantly at his photograph, Elisa has incorporated Daniel into her own memory and life, and 'su emoción amorosa se despertaba de nuevo en su interior, creándole esperanzas imposibles y deseos irrealizables' ['her romantic feeling awakened once more inside her, creating for her impossible hopes and unrealisable desires'] (p. 134). As a newly liberated woman living in the post-Franco era, Elisa seems to abide by the modern concept that Mary Nash explains as 'la expresión de la sexualidad femenina, sin vínculo con la procreación y la maternidad' ['the expression of feminine sexuality, without a link to procreation and maternity'].[35] Hooper also makes note of the correlation between women's liberation in Spain and 'sexual permissiveness'.[36] Unlike aunt Águeda, who lived under the oppressive doctrine of National Catholicism that essentially prohibited overt sexuality in women, Elisa has agency over her body and can act on her desires, which is what prompts her to attempt to make contact with Daniel's ghost. Over the course of many nightly sessions in Daniel's bedroom, during which Elisa gradually learns to control her terror to open herself to communication with the spirits, the protagonist finally achieves contact with Daniel when she briefly feels the touch of his hand on her own. This momentary success compels her to try even harder to communicate with him, and she eventually speaks with Encarna and, later, Daniel, who tells her to find a woman named Gloria who will be able to help them pass on to the next realm. One evening, after hearing the agitated breathing from the room, Elisa sits next to the bed and sees that the pillow is slightly depressed in the centre, as if a head were lying on it. She reaches out and feels Daniel's face, recognising his features from the photograph she had committed to memory, then discovers, horrified, that she has blood on the palm of her hand, which disappears when she attempts to wipe it on her pants. This moment is the definitive proof that Elisa needs to believe that her world and that of Daniel are intimately connected, 'que lo inexplicable también podía ser real' ['that the inexplicable could also be real'] (p. 230).

Although Elisa is initially elated at the thought that she might, in fact, be able to have a relationship with Daniel in some form, her excitement rapidly dissipates after Gloria performs a ritual in the room to relieve the spirits of their agony and to free them from the house. Once the ritual is complete, Daniel speaks through Gloria, thanking her for freeing his mother and telling Elisa: 'permaneceré en este espacio terrenal, en esta misma casa, junto a Elisa. En todo momento estaré a su lado, de manera constante, sin ninguna interrupción' ['I will remain in this earthly space, in this very house, next to Elisa. At every moment I will be by her side, constantly, without interruption'] (p. 238). After this moment, Daniel gradually begins to appear in physical form to Elisa, first showing just his hand and then his entire body, for only a few seconds at a time. This sight provokes in Elisa a confusing 'estremecimiento, mezcla de euforia y de miedo' ['shudder, mixture of euphoria and of fear'] (p. 243). Although the ability to see and touch Daniel is what Elisa has wanted since she first saw his photograph, she suddenly reverts to a state of anxiety and terror as she realises that he will always be there, perhaps unseen but present, constantly watching her.

The male gaze as a source of Gothic terror is a well-established motif especially among women writers of the genre. Judith Halberstam considers it in relation to Gothic paranoia, which she explains as 'a fear of being watched that produces both fear and desire in the female body and provokes a male sexual response'.[37] Susanne Becker asserts that authors have used the Gothic mode 'to expose the imprisonment through the male gaze'.[38] Rives has even described the Gothic as 'a genre centered on the lack of privacy, freedom, and safety for women in an isolated, gloomy mansion that harbors malevolent violence'.[39] Elisa is terrified at the sudden lack of privacy that Daniel's ghostly presence implies; even in the complete darkness of her own room, she perceives 'la mirada de Daniel con un peso que inmovilizaba su cuerpo y le creaba una ansiedad que le impidió conciliar el sueño' ['Daniel's gaze with a weight that immobilised her body and created an anxiety in her that made it impossible for her to fall asleep'] (p. 244). In the days that follow, she constantly feels his eyes watching her and 'le horrorizaba el saberse observada de una manera constante, quizá incluso pudiera conocer todo cuanto pensase' ['it horrified her to know that she was constantly being observed, that maybe he could even know everything she was thinking'] (p. 252). This paranoid response to Daniel's vigilance is further intensified by Elisa's perception of the house as belonging to another realm in which the supernatural and the real exist simultaneously; thus, the notion that Daniel could even read her mind follows the logic of the house itself, and serves to amplify Elisa's terror. She is no longer a free agent in her own home, but rather a prisoner trapped inside it by the seductive, relentless gaze of the ghost. In fact, García Morales employs prison imagery in her description of Elisa's physical and emotional response to Daniel's gaze, which

> se le presentaba como una suerte de cárcel que la paralizaba con una angustia nueva que nunca, anteriormente, había conocido. Elisa sentía sobre ella la mirada de Daniel, sus ojos tan bellos, tan amorosos y a veces tan tristes, poseyéndola por completo, adentrándose en su propio interior.
>
> [presented itself like a type of prison that paralysed her with a new anguish that she had never known before. Elisa felt Daniel's gaze upon her, his beautiful eyes, so loving and at times so sad, possessing her completely, penetrating her own interior.] (p. 254)

Just like Águeda, whose house is violated by the presence of the masculine phantom that haunts her nightly, Elisa's personal space also becomes a site of violation through haunting. What had once provoked a sublime response to the simultaneous feelings of seduction and fear becomes, in the end, an inescapable source of terror and entrapment.

For reasons that García Morales never explains, Daniel eventually decides to leave Elisa and continue to the next realm, where he says they will one day see each other again. Given that his departure is the only way in which Elisa could ever regain her freedom, she is, by the end of the novel, happy once more. Having attained complete control of her own space at last, she decides to start writing the story of Daniel's life as she imagines it must be now in the spiritual realm. Through her writing, Elisa continues to create new (post)memories that blur the lines between reality and fantasy but also allow her to have certain freedom and authorship over the narrative and her own role in it.

Conclusion

In *Aunt Águeda* and *Elisa's Secret*, Adelaida García Morales traces the evolution of women's role in the domestic sphere from the first decades of the Franco dictatorship to the late Transition era, providing a critical portrayal of the restrictive gender norms to which Spanish women were subjected throughout the twentieth century. In *Aunt Águeda*, the moral tradition of National Catholicism is the baseline against which Águeda's lack of submissiveness and benevolence is measured; as an older woman without children of her own, she attempts to rear her niece in the nationalist tradition while simultaneously refusing to abide by the standard of ideal wife imposed upon her by 1950s Spanish society and the propagandistic Women's Section. Here, haunting is a result of perceived moral failure and rejection of her prescribed role as subordinate wife; Martín's presence is a perversion of her home both during his life and after, and his demonic ghost haunts her in nightly violations of her personal space until she finally succumbs to madness and death.

In *Elisa's Secret*, our protagonist leaves her stifling domestic life behind in the modern city and journeys to the remote countryside in search of personal freedom and happiness. Her need for adventure and romance makes her an especially willing participant in the nightly haunting episodes involving the two deceased former inhabitants of her new home. The objects and photographs within the home allow her to recreate Daniel's past and construct new memories (postmemories) for herself, positioning herself as an intimate witness to Daniel's life. Once she has established contact with him and he vows to never leave her side, however, the sublime thrill that she first felt cedes to absolute terror at the imposing masculine gaze, which she perceives as a ghostly presence at all times in the house. This violation of her privacy leaves her in a state of constant anxiety and claustrophobia, and we can assume that she might have suffered a similar fate to Águeda if Daniel had not finally decided to leave the house.

Both novels employ Gothic haunting to demonstrate women's forced dependence on the men in their lives, and both illustrate the deleterious effects of submission to the traditional domestic roles of wife and mother. Through the trajectory of these novels, García

Morales makes clear that women who rejected the standard under Franco were seen as non-women who posed a threat to the regime's success, and that those who did assume the expected roles were not necessarily rewarded with happiness. The persistent haunting in both these texts symbolises the female protagonists' loss of control and entrapment in a patriarchal society that – even at the end of the Transition – continued to siphon women's agency within and outside of the home. García Morales provides some hope at the end of *Elisa's Secret*, however, in the form of female authorship, which allows for the blending of the supernatural and the real in a space defined and controlled exclusively by the protagonist herself, thus embarking on the final creation of a new (written) room of her own.

4

War at Home: The Haunted House as Battlefield in Ana María Matute's Family Demons

❧

Ana María Matute (1925–2014), considered one of twentieth-century Spain's most important authors, is known for her narratives portraying silence, absence and the loss of childhood innocence. Born in Barcelona in 1925, Matute spent most of her childhood summers with her family in Mansilla de la Sierra, a small town in the northern community of La Rioja where her mother was born. Her time in the countryside was highly influential to her writing, and childhood memories are a frequent focal point of her literary works. She credited her summers in Mansilla with the awakening of her social consciousness, explaining in an interview: 'Allí fui tomando conciencia, casi sin saberlo, de esos terribles "nosotros" y "los otros", y esas diferencias siempre han estado presentes en mi obra' ['That is where I began to become conscious, almost without realising it, of those terrible "us" and "the others", and those differences have always been present in my works'].[1] Matute's experience living through the civil war as a young girl permeates her writing, and as an author in the post-war era she was frequently the target of literary censorship for her portrayal of the effects of the war and the Franco regime on Spanish society. Nevertheless, she received numerous literary awards throughout her career (including the acclaimed Cervantes Prize, which she was awarded in 2010) and was inducted into the Spanish Royal Academy. Although Matute achieved wide recognition and literary fame in Spain, the majority of her works have not been translated – a fact that has severely limited both international readership and scholarship on her works in English-language academic circles.

Matute's last novel, *Demonios familiares* (hereafter translated as [*Family Demons*]), was left unfinished at the time of her death in 2014 and was published posthumously in its original form that same year. In this novel our protagonist is Eva, a 16-year-old student who is sent home from her convent school as the civil war breaks out in Madrid. Her overbearing father, a retired, wheelchair-bound Colonel who fought in Morocco, supports Franco's Nationalist troops as they advance through the centre of the country. The Colonel is helped by Yago (his secret son from a previous relationship) and maid, Magdalena, who has acted as mother to Eva since her own mother died during childbirth. The house in which they live is a large estate in the countryside and it is haunted by the ghosts of Fermín (the Colonel's brother who died in childhood) and Mother, the Colonel's imposing, severe mother, whose portrait (now removed to the attic) looms over the family and whose presence after death seems even more overpowering than when she was alive. As the war rages in the background, Eva escapes to her beloved forest one day only to discover an injured Republican soldier who has crashed his plane in the woods outside her house. Yago and Eva conspire to help the man – Berni, a childhood friend of Yago – by hiding him in their attic, where Magdalena and the Colonel will not be able to find him. As Eva provides him with medicine and food every night, she begins to feel a powerful attraction to this man and experiences love for the first time in her life. Mother, however, appears to her each time, admonishing her for her contact with Berni. The novel ends here, leaving us wondering what might have happened to this illicit relationship and to the many ghosts that populate the large, silent house.

The decision to publish this book in its unfinished state is a testament to Matute's literary legacy and to the timeless power of her narratives. María Paz Ortuño, in her notes at the end of the novel, explains that Matute was writing this book at a time when her health was failing her: 'El parto de *Demonios familiares* fue una auténtica lucha, un entregarse en cada una de las frases, de las palabras, de las ideas' ['The birth of *Family Demons* was an authentic struggle, a surrender to each one of the sentences, the words, the ideas'].[2] Parallel to the novel she was writing, Matute herself was engaged in a battle for health and time. She suffered from unending pain and from such terrible vertigo that, as Paz Ortuño explains, 'llegó a pensar que en realidad eran sus propios demonios, y barajó llamar a la novela *Vértigo*, como ese malestar obsesivo que la acompañaba constantemente' ['she came to believe that in reality they were her own demons, and she considered naming the novel *Vertigo*, like that obsessive malaise that constantly accompanied her'].[3]

Although Matute has been a frequent focus of scholarship among literary Hispanists, this novel has received little critical attention, perhaps in part due to its unfinished state (and, like many of the other novels studied here, its lack of an English translation). Natalie Noyaret has examined the role of what she calls the 'poétique du silence' ['poetics of silence'][4] in *Family Demons*, comparing it to Gaston Bachelard's notion of the poetics of space. Notably, Noyaret considers the village in which the novel takes place as a 'microcosme de l'Espagne d'alors' ['microcosm of the Spain of that time'],[5] facilitating commentary on the role of silence within both the fictional house and the historical period of the Spanish civil war. Concepción Torres Begines also applies Bachelard's poetics of space to this novel, studying the use of physical space within and outside the home in Matute's *Family Demons* and *Paraíso inhabitado* [*Uninhabited Paradise*] (2008) as a method of highlighting various social dichotomies present in both texts. Her study of these spaces reveals that 'hay una constante dialéctica entre el mundo de los adultos y el de los niños' ['there is a constant dialectic between the world of adults and that of children'][6] in Matute's works. Silvia Bermúdez argues that *Family Demons* should be read alongside Matute's 1959 novel *Primera memoria* (translated in English as *School of the Sun*) as a history lesson about the civil war era, asserting: 'Matute comes full-circle with her inner demons but also, it appears, with those of Spain as is evident in the recent debates about historical memory and narrating the past'.[7] Pere Gimferrer, in his prologue to Matute's novel, points to the similarities it shares with her previous novel

Uninhabited Paradise, noting that it features 'la misma guerra civil vista por los ojos de quien viaja a la adolescencia desde el crepúsculo vespertino de la infancia sellada en la incógnita clandestinidad del "castillo interior"' ['the same civil war seen through the eyes of one who travels to adolescence from the evening twilight of childhood sealed in the clandestine unknown of the "interior castle"'].[8] Paz Ortuño describes the main themes of the text in relation to the title *Family Demons*:

> Los personajes de esta novela viven en una casa poblada por demonios: el odio, las órdenes, los silencios, los llantos y el poco cariño que ha albergado a lo largo de los años. Todos ellos viven entre las viejas paredes. Pero en esta casa surge también el amor, aunque sea un amor prohibido e imposible.
>
> [The characters of this novel live in a house populated with demons: hatred, orders, silences, crying and the little affection that it has harboured over the years. All of them live within the old walls. But in this house love also emerges, although it is a prohibited and impossible love.][9]

It is worth noting that none of the scholars who have commented on *Family Demons* have considered it from a Gothic perspective, despite all the trappings of the genre that Matute has purposefully included in her novel. In the present chapter, I will examine the Colonel's house as an example of the classic Gothic haunted house motif that Matute employs in *Family Demons* in conjunction with the symbolic and persistent representations of war and memory throughout the text. The many forms of haunting that plague the Colonel's estate are engaged in simultaneous warfare against those living within its walls. Mother, in particular, permeates the house, infiltrating every corner and waging war on those within it, converting the house into a symbolic female body and locus of terror that posits female spectral monstrosity against the militant corporeal masculinity of the Colonel and his undying nostalgia for the war in Morocco. The fact that the novel is unfinished and was published posthumously lends it an even greater phantasmagoric quality; given the themes of the text at hand, it seems quite appropriate that an author who lived in an illusionary world of silences and ghostly apparitions would, in the end, become one of those spectral presences in her own, final novel.

Matute's haunted house embodies Fred Botting's characterisation of the traditional Gothic motif when he writes: 'as both building and family line, it became the site where fears and anxieties returned in the present. These anxieties varied according to diverse changes: political revolution, industrialisation, urbanisation, shifts in sexual and domestic organisation, and scientific discovery.'[10] The country manor on the outskirts of Madrid is perfectly poised both as the classic haunted house (a remote estate passed down through generations) and as a natural witness to the unfolding war, given that the battle begins in the capital city. In this manner, the Colonel's house is already primed for two distinct forms of haunting in accordance with Botting's observation: haunting resulting from political anxiety and from generational changes in domestic life, catalysed primarily by Mother's death.

As we have seen in previous chapters, the haunted house is a frequent motif in the female Gothic because of its inherent ability to subvert traditional domestic discourse through a focus on entrapment and claustrophobia and its incitement of terror. The Colonel's house is, from the beginning of the novel, a site of ghostly apparitions, fear and generalised dread. The townspeople varyingly refer to the house as the 'Palace' and the 'House of Ghosts', immediately calling attention to the dichotomy between the estate and the town surrounding it: it is at once a house many times larger than the average home in town (thus demonstrating ostentatious wealth to the people of much lesser means living nearby) and a space where the living and the dead converge in a perceptibly supernatural way. Eva describes the atmosphere of the house as a mixture of 'una demoledora y persistente melancolía que cubría la casa de un polvo invisible y ecos de voces desaparecidas' ['a devastating and persistent melancholy that covered the house in an invisible dust and echoes of disappeared voices'].[11] This is a house in which 'nadie tenía buenos sueños' ['no one had good dreams'] (p. 33), whose walls are 'hechas de silencio, hasta de aliento contenido' ['made from silence, even from held breaths'] (p. 89), and whose creaking floors contrast with eerie silences to provoke a near-constant fear in the teenage protagonist. Eva admits that she has been afraid her entire life in that house, although 'lo peor era que la mayoría de las veces se trataba de un miedo misterioso, que no podía definir' ['the worst was that the majority of the time it was a mysterious fear, that I couldn't define'] (p. 162). Matute thus provides a transgressive domestic atmosphere as the setting for her novel, emphasising from the very beginning the important role of fear and the supernatural forces within the home.

Part of the distinct other-worldly feeling of the house is due to the proliferation of mirrors hanging in various rooms. The largest of these hangs at an angle in the front room – Mother's preferred way of installing them – so that the reflected images are slightly unbalanced, giving them a surreal quality. The Colonel spends much of his time gazing into this mirror, at times hearing the ghostly voice of his mother. It is also through the mirror that he was able to see the first signs of the fire at the convent where Eva was studying, thus hastening the teenager's return home. Torres Begines notes the role of the mirrors in establishing a sense of space in the novel:

> Para Eva, el elemento desestabilizador será el espejo, símbolo de la dualidad entre el espacio habitado por el Coronel y el fantasma de Madre y su espacio hasta entonces: el convento. Frente al espejo inclinado del salón en el que el padre se mira, la hija se da cuenta de la ausencia de espejos en el convento justo en el momento en el que las monjas la evacúan.
>
> [For Eva, the destabilising element will be the mirror, symbol of the duality between the space inhabited by the Colonel and Mother's ghost and her space until then: the convent. In front of the inclined mirror in the front room in which her father looks at himself, the daughter becomes aware of the absence of mirrors in the convent at the exact moment that the nuns evacuate her.][12]

The lack of mirrors in the convent contrasts sharply with the prevalence of them in Eva's large home, which – upon her return – appears even more saturated with supernatural energy. The mirrors themselves provide a glimpse of not just the characters' own reflections, but also of the past: the Colonel frequently sees Mother looking back at him through the glass, and Eva states that 'todo se convertía en la mirada de Madre' ['everything turned into Mother's gaze'] through the inclined mirror (p. 55). Mirrors, then, are not only a reflection of the present state of the living, but also an inescapable reminder of the memory of the dead, converting the home into a space in which the past and present converge seamlessly and the spirits of the departed coexist with – and even exert certain control over – the living.

This troubled sharing of the domestic space with the supernatural is a primary source of tension for Eva and her father, as both are victims of endless psychological torment caused by the ghostly apparitions. In his essay on ghost stories, Nick Freeman explains that the haunted house

> supplies continuity in that it exists in the present as both a historical artefact and a contemporary residence, aging and changing as the years pass. Its spectral inhabitants, by contrast, lack this ability to develop and adapt . . . Their historical fixedness is one reason why they cause such horror and distress: their intrusion upon the present is too abrupt, unmediated by the events of intervening years.[13]

It is not surprising, then, that Matute begins her novel by telling us: 'Algunas noches el Coronel oía llorar a un niño en la oscuridad' ['Some nights the Colonel heard a boy crying in the darkness'] (p. 17). This ghostly apparition – the spectral presence of the Colonel's brother, Fermín, who died of illness in early childhood – sets the tone for the narrative and becomes a repetitive presence in the text. For the Colonel, the ghostly cries are a constant reminder of his own unhappiness: he was never good enough for Mother, who preferred Fermín to the Colonel and remembered him as the perfect child, the one who did not grow up. The Colonel, therefore, is trapped in a continuous cycle in which the past returns to the present, extending the trauma of his childhood by eliminating the barriers between memory and current experience.

In much the same manner, history itself becomes a spectral presence in the novel because of the Colonel's inability to distinguish between the present and the past. As Matute tells us in the first paragraph of the novel, in addition to the recurring ghosts of his brother and Mother, the Colonel also experiences 'los tenebrosos fantasmas de la campana de África' ['the sinister ghosts of the African campaign'] (p. 17). The war in Morocco (known as the Rif War, which took place between 1921–6), was a frequent source of nationalistic propaganda during the civil war era, and the road to political power for Miguel Primo de Rivera (who would become dictator of Spain from 1923–30) and his then-general, Francisco Franco. Moreover, as Bermúdez notes, a common reading of twentieth-century Spanish history is the 'argument that the Spanish Civil War partially originated from the unresolved issues' of the Moroccan war.[14] The historical acknowledgement of the relationship between these two wars supports Matute's portrayal of the civil war as an inherent invocation of the Moroccan conflict. The lingering spectral presence of the African campaign will come to dominate the Colonel's life as the civil war begins just outside his property line; as we will see, this new war will resurrect old phantoms and create new ones for both the Colonel and his daughter.

Despite the hyper-masculine character of the Colonel, bolstered by his war memories, the house is entirely dominated by the singular spectral presence of Mother. In her book on the female Gothic, Juliann Fleenor focuses on maternal images and the role of the mother in female-authored texts, noting: 'the Female Gothic expresses a real and frightening contraposition in the center of the female identity – the conflict with the mother'.[15] Likewise, Diana Wallace and Andrew Smith describe this principal Gothic motif as 'the conflict with the archaic all-powerful mother, often figured as a spectral presence and/or as the Gothic house itself'.[16] In *Family Demons*, both the Colonel and his daughter are haunted by Mother. For the former, the elderly woman's presence is an emasculating one; her preference for her 'perfect' deceased son contrasts sharply with her feelings for her surviving child, and in life she was quick to point out that the Colonel, 'que lloraba de noche porque tenía miedo de la oscuridad, se fue a matar gente por ahí, y se hizo con la fama de hombre valiente' ['who cried at night because he was afraid of the dark, went off to kill people, and gained the reputation of a brave man'] (p. 40). Within his mother's house, the Colonel remains the little boy who was afraid of the dark; Mother's memory (and his memory of Mother) is an insurmountable force even for the war hero. Although he attributes the night-time crying to his ghostly brother, we can perhaps intuit that this is yet another manifestation of the blending of the past and present: he is haunted by the terrified cries of a young boy in the darkness – a young boy who could very well have been (or may well be currently) the Colonel himself.

Eva's experience with Mother's ghost is far more intrusive and fear-inducing than that of her father. It is important to note that Mother (always capitalised throughout the text) is actually the girl's grandmother, but Eva never knew her own mother (who died in childbirth), and so she grew up calling the elderly woman 'Mother', as did her father and all other members of the household. For the teenage protagonist, her grandmother's ghost is both a tangible presence and a reminder of maternal absence: the pain of losing a potentially benevolent biological mother is augmented under the critical spectral glare of this ever-present (M)other. Mother's ghostly apparitions are always a source of terror for Eva, who frequently senses her presence throughout the house and especially in response to actions or decisions of which Eva believes the woman would not have approved. On one such occasion, Eva tells us: 'La siento, sube detrás de mí, oigo el roce de sus zapatillas junto al crujido de la madera. Está asombrada por lo que he hecho' ['I feel her, she rises up behind me, I hear the brush of her slippers along with the creaking of the wood. She is shocked by what I have done'] (p. 53). On one evening as Eva sneaks out to the forest, she hears 'las zapatillas de fieltro, silenciosas pero terriblemente presentes de Madre. A la espalda. Siempre a la espalda, no sabía si protegiendo o amenazando algo. Pensándolo, temblaba' ['Mother's felt slippers, silent but terribly present. At my back. Always at my back. I didn't know if she was protecting or threatening something. Thinking about it, I trembled'] (p. 95).

Eva's deep fear of her grandmother is inevitably associated with the house – Mother's ancestral home – both because of the legacy it carries and because of the deceased woman's numerous possessions and portraits that still fill its rooms. Eva remembers vividly the fear she felt at the portrait of the woman that once hung in the hallway near her bedroom: 'Temblaba. Más que temor, era pavor lo que me invadía al mirar sus ojos, negros y brillantes, que parecían vivos' ['I trembled. More than fear, it was terror that invaded me upon seeing her eyes, black and shining, which seemed lifelike'] (p. 38). Interestingly, although most of the elderly woman's possessions and furniture have remained in their original places in the house after her death, the Colonel has had the portrait removed to the attic. Nevertheless, even in its absence the portrait continues to be a reminder of Mother's intimidating gaze, as it has left a slightly pale area on the wall where it once hung (p. 118). Emma Liggins has asserted that 'for women writers the cryptic space is not always the nostalgically conceived childhood home but the darkly mysterious house of the female ancestors, embodied in the phantom or lost rooms as much as in the dusty portrait galleries which recur in tales of the supernatural'.[17] Mother's presence permeates the house through all her possessions, photographs and the memories they invoke, and even the attic – once Eva's intimate space where she was free from the fear-inducing world downstairs – is now no longer safe because the Colonel has had Mother's portrait stored there. When Eva discovers it, she is immediately terrified, and the image stirs up resentment at her memories of the past: 'Ella fue la culpable de que yo fuese una niña prisionera . . . Y tampoco sé lo que es querer a alguien' ['She was the one who was responsible for making me a child prisoner . . . And I don't even know what it is like to love someone'] (p. 39).

Mother's association with entrapment and a complete lack of love and affection makes her a kind of anti-mother for Eva: she represents the opposite of what the girl has always imagined maternal warmth to be. Instead of benevolent, Mother is unforgiving and critical; instead of feminine, she is rigid and domineering. Paz Ortuño, in reference to the novel's title, characterises the elderly woman as '[e]l demonio más grande que hay en esa casa' ['the biggest demon in that house'].[18] Like the title character in Adelaida García Morales's *Aunt Águeda*, Mother is the dominant figure in Matute's narrative who evolves to be the true masculine presence in the house. Guadalupe Cabedo Timmons has noted that motherless children tend to be a common theme in Matute's literary works and that the author frequently provides a less-than-ideal female substitute for the orphaned children: 'Las madres muertas son muchas veces sustituidas por otras figuras maternas, símbolos de una sociedad patriarcal, autoritaria y machista, a las que las protagonistas rechazan abiertamente' ['Dead mothers are many times substituted by other maternal figures, symbols of a patriarchal, authoritarian and chauvinistic society, which the female protagonists openly reject'].[19] Mother, a symbol and product of patriarchal tradition, is the authoritarian figure that Eva will reject as she increasingly defies the rules and breaks the bonds of her imprisonment in the house.

Interestingly, the beginning of the war provides Eva with an opportunity to reclaim much of her freedom. As the Colonel starts to spend his days in front of the large mirror in the living room, absorbed in memories of the past and the spectres that continue to join him in the present, he pays less attention to Eva's whereabouts. The girl who had become accustomed to an oppressive, solitary life inside the house begins to spend more of her time outside in settings that have been typically off limits to her. Matute employs these dichotomised spaces of outside and inside to further develop the relationship between history and haunting: inside, the atmosphere is charged with the ghostly apparitions of the dead, who insist on maintaining control in the present by imposing order through tradition; outside, the town and forest are visibly marked with signs of war and death, triggering memories of the previous war and its aftermath. Whereas the Colonel customarily forbade his daughter to spend time in the outside world (for fear of her moral corruption), his present emasculated state allows Eva more bodily autonomy than she has ever had. As she explains:

> los acontecimientos que cambiaron el ritmo de nuestras vidas (en la casa, en el pueblo y en el país entero) fueron suavizando la actitud e incluso las costumbres y pensamientos de mi padre. De un hombre impedido pero tiránico, acostumbrado a ser siempre obedecido sin rechistar, se convirtió en un padre indiferente, distante, casi patético en su reconcentrado autoaislamiento.
>
> [the events that changed the rhythm of our lives (in the house, in town and in the entire country) softened my father's attitude and even his habits and thoughts. From a crippled but tyrannical man, accustomed to always being obeyed without complaint, he became an indifferent father, distant, almost pathetic in his intensified self-isolation.] (p. 55)

Eva understands her newfound freedom as developing parallel to the socio-political changes around her; the outside world and the family's estate are, in many ways, mirror images of each other. Therefore, the fact that the Colonel first sees the war through Mother's mirror becomes yet another metaphor for the home as a reflection of the nation and, as such, Eva's rebellion against her father's rules can be understood as symbolic of the political upheaval taking place just beyond their property line.

Outside the home, the dangers commonly associated with the forest are accentuated by new fears of violence in town and beyond; in the village, however, the threat of bodily harm is seemingly outweighed by the perceived moral dangers of illicit sexual relationships and pregnancy outside of marriage (and, ultimately, the consideration of abortion, as Jovita becomes pregnant with Berni's child). This perceived connection between the outside world and the loss of innocence is reflected in the treatment of women throughout Spanish history; as Abigail Lee Six explains:

> One of the age-old Spanish responses to the perceived need to control female sexuality – predating the Gothic by centuries and a cornerstone of Golden Age drama – is to keep women enclosed in the home. While the issue of female enclosure is a transnational staple of the Gothic, it thus has especial resonance in the Spanish cultural context, with its long-standing link between women's virtue and their staying indoors.[20]

In *Family Demons*, this is particularly notable in the Colonel's order for Eva to 'Permanece en casa' ['Stay inside'] (p. 60). Until the beginning of the civil war, Eva had spent most of her life shut inside the silent, eerie house or locked in a convent – yet another way to control the adolescent's budding sexuality by denying it altogether.

It is no coincidence that Matute's references to war become more frequent in the text as Eva seeks more independence (and, consequently, experiences Mother's hauntings in an increasingly vivid, intrusive manner). Due to their proximity to the front lines of battle, the family hears almost constant gunfire and explosions that shake the walls of their house and shatter the customary silence within. Eva explains: 'Estábamos tan cerca del frente que a veces parecía que las descargas de la artillería se producían en la misma sala. O que del mismo techo caían los truenos de una invisible tormenta, capaz de hacer temblar los muros de la casa' ['We were so close to the front that at times it seemed like the artillery discharges were produced in the very living room. Or that from our very roof fell the thunderclaps of an invisible storm, capable of making the walls of the house tremble'] (p. 87). Here, the house and the battleground seem almost indistinguishable, blurring the boundaries between the outside and the inside, as if the house itself were host to the war. In fact, the Colonel indicates just that when he states: 'Resulta inquietante ese avanzar y retroceder de las líneas enemigas [. . .] en horas, en tu propia tierra [. . .], en tu propia casa, se podría decir' ['That advancing and receding of the enemy lines is rather disturbing [. . .] within hours, on your own land [. . .] , in your own home, you might say'] (p. 88). At this turning point in the narrative, Matute makes it clear that the war cannot – and will not – be contained to the area beyond the property line, highlighting instead the house as the scene of a new ongoing battle when, by the end of this chapter, Eva and Yago find Berni lying injured in the forest after he has crashed his plane. This discovery results in the sudden dismantling of the barrier between inside and outside, intruding on Eva's personal space while also offering her the opportunity to finally transition to adulthood. Knowing that Berni will be killed as a traitor if their father or his friends discover him, the siblings decide to hide him in the attic, which neither the Colonel nor Magdalena are able to access. Although Eva is not thrilled at the thought of having to share her intimate space with this man whom she barely knows, she cannot help but feel like this is going to change her in an unexpectedly desirable way, and she remarks: 'Aún no me había dicho a mí misma que a menudo cuando un deseo se cumple, todo un mundo muere' ['I had not yet told myself that often when a wish is fulfilled, a whole world dies'] (p. 100). With this premonition, Eva recognises the relationship between the fulfilment of desires and punishment and, almost immediately, Mother appears: 'frente a mí, no tras de mí como acostumbraba. Tenía los brazos abiertos, pero no prefiguraban un abrazo, más bien eran una barrera, una prohibición' ['in front of me, not behind me as she tended to do. She had her arms open, but not in anticipation of a hug, but rather as a barrier, a prohibition'] (p. 101). From the moment Berni enters the attic,

Mother appears more frequently to Eva, seeming to demand subordination in response to the failure of the girl's father, who has abandoned his vigilance altogether.

As Eva begins to spend more time in the attic with Berni and in town with Jovita, the boundaries between outside and inside further erode, and she sees that her obedience under her father's once tyrannical rule has prolonged her childhood naiveté and prevented her from experiencing love and desire. Jovita further opens Eva's eyes to the outside world when she remarks: '¿Pero no te has dado cuenta de la diferencia de vida que llevan las mujeres con respecto a los hombres [. . .]?' ['But haven't you realised the difference in life that women have compared to men [. . .]?'] (p. 164). Eva, who had already begun to take account of this in her own life, suddenly realises that this is why, 'por primera vez, era capaz de desobedecer al Coronel. Incluso el hecho de haber escondido en el desván a Berni tenía su origen en aquellas reveladoras palabras: "la diferencia de vida"' ['for the first time, I was able to disobey the Colonel. Even the fact that I had hidden Berni in the attic had its origin in those revealing words: "the difference in life"'] (p. 164). Her newfound freedom and rebellious nature grow as she spends more time with Berni in the attic, fostering a relationship that hastens her loss of childhood innocence by introducing her to sexual desire.

Eva's rejection of her father's rules leads to more frequent apparitions of Mother, now always materialising in front of the girl instead of behind her. When Eva rests her cheek on Berni's chest, for instance, Mother suddenly appears: 'Desde los cojines esparcidos en el suelo, seguía atravesándome la mirada negra, brillante, de Madre. "No estás portándote bien [. . .]", decía, y yo la oía. "Oía" aquella mirada' ['From the cushions scattered on the floor, Mother's black, shining stare continued to pierce me. "You're not behaving well [. . .]", she said, and I heard her. I "heard" that stare'] (p. 145). Mother continues to treat Eva like a little girl, admonishing her for not behaving well during shared moments of intimacy in the attic. On yet another occasion, Berni playfully teases Eva for being inexperienced with alcohol as they drink whisky together. When Eva tells him that she has, in fact, tried whisky and cognac and that she has decided to give up the convent, Mother again appears in front of her: 'Estaba sentada en el taburete, y sus ojos negros parecían dos botones de azabache. La voz aterciopelada y susurrante decía: "Vete, ya es hora [. . .]". Pero había un punto de burla, tanto en su mirada como en su voz' ['She was seated on the stool, and her dark eyes looked like jet-black buttons. Her velvety and whispering voice said: "Go, it's time [. . .]". But there was a bit of mockery, both in her stare and her voice'] (p. 155). In both instances, Mother's appearance coincides with Eva's own mutterings of self-doubt; first, about her own desires and actions in the attic – which she says confuse her and remind her of her friend Jovita (who, as we recall, is pregnant with Berni's child) – and, later, about her need to learn how to lie and drink alcohol. Thus, for Eva, Mother's hauntings are an inevitable reminder of her stifling upbringing in a very traditional home, and the spectral appearances may even be understood as a manifestation of Eva's own internalisation of the patriarchal world in which she has been raised. According to Cabedo Timmons, this is a key part of Matute's literary project:

> Eliminando en sus obras a las madres de sus protagonistas y sustituyéndolas por otras mujeres que estas niñas no querían, Matute rechaza esa educación machista y patriarcal de la "madre patria" impuesta a las niñas y adolescentes. Haciéndolas rebelarse contra esas madres suplentes (abuelas, tías), como la Madre del coronel, en *Demonios Familiares* . . . define que las madres reales de sus protagonistas no podían ser así; ellas no podían ser como el régimen franquista quería, autoritarias, duras y poco afectivas.
>
> [Eliminating in her works the protagonists' mothers and substituting them with other women that these girls did not love, Matute rejects that chauvinistic and patriarchal education of the "motherland" imposed upon girls and adolescents. Making them rebel against these substitute mothers (grandmothers, aunts), like the Colonel's Mother in *Family Demons* . . . establishes that the protagonists' real mothers could not be like that; they could not be how the Franco regime wanted them, authoritarian, rigid and lacking emotion.][21]

In life and in death, Mother symbolises for Eva the need to abide by the strict rules of her father's authoritarian home. Even though her father himself has become weak and has seemingly given up his control over the teenager, Mother is always present as a reminder of the patriarchal, nationalistic society in which they live, and which the Colonel and his friends strive to maintain in this new war.

Because Matute left the novel unfinished at the time of her death, there is no resolution to these interwoven conflicts and their hauntings. Nevertheless, *Family Demons* remains a masterful example of the author's literary conventions and her frequent themes of love, absence and loss. Matute portrays both war and desire in this novel in terms of present absences: through Eva's first experience with love – which is only possible because of the war – the teenager realises that her life has been defined by a complete lack of affection (an absence that began with the death of her mother in childbirth). Likewise, the war itself is a constant symbol of loss, but also of returns: a return of desire and love, a return of friendship and – for the Colonel and his fellow veterans – a return of the glory and ghosts of the past. In his *Specters of Marx*, Jacques Derrida discusses spectrality as a constant returning presence: 'A question of repetition: a specter is always a *revenant*. One cannot control its comings and goings because it *begins by coming back.*'[22] In this manner, we can come to understand war itself in Matute's text as a Derridean revenant: always already a spectral return of the past and an inevitable glimpse of the imminent future.

Matute, then, establishes her haunted house as the site of convergence of all the revenant forms in this novel: within its old walls, the tomblike silence is punctured by the sounds of war; the Colonel sits absorbed in his chair, staring into the mirror for a fleeting glance of the past; and Eva cautiously steals away to the attic for a chance of affection, only to be terrified by the intimidating gaze of Mother. In her book on women's ghost stories, Liggins reminds us that '[w]omen's troubled inhabiting of the home in the ghost story is revealing of cultural anxieties about tradition and modernity, about the old and the new; the spaces of the past leave traces in the present which clash and terrify'.[23] In Matute's novel, these clashes provide a compelling commentary on the nation's own fight over the right to define itself either in the cloak of tradition or the path toward modernity and progress. As an author who experienced this era during childhood and who subsequently battled against the regime-imposed censorship of her texts, Ana María Matute recognised this fight as central to her writing, telling Gazarian

Gautier: 'Decían que yo destruía los valores sociales, que destruía a la familia, que destruía la religion . . . Yo quería cambiarlo todo. Era el grito de libertad de una muchacha contra un mundo que le parecía falso, hipócrita, explotador y mentiroso' ['They said I was destroying social values, that I was destroying the family, that I was destroying religion . . . I wanted to change it all. It was the shout of independence of a girl against a world that seemed to her to be false, hypocritical, exploitative and lying'].[24] Thus, in Matute's very last novel, that young girl – a version of Matute herself – again is the protagonist seeking freedom from the oppressive environment in which she has always lived, just as the world outside the confines of her home attempts to do the same. Through the unwritten pages of her narrative, Matute becomes a present absence in her own text, guiding us through a personal and collective history that reflects the anxieties and fears of her generation while allowing us to imagine a potential (but perhaps unnecessary) resolution.

Part II
Silent Spaces

Introduction

Silence, like a ghost, is the presence of absence. It can be felt and experienced; it can be 'deafening' despite producing no audible sound; it can be 'unspeakable' and instil a very real terror. By being aware of silence we are also aware of what is not, or what was but is no longer. One could infer, then, that silence is a form of spectrality, and – like an always returning phantom – silence can haunt us. This is especially true in texts that rely heavily on trauma as a driving factor in the plot; for many contemporary Spanish authors, the natural silences of the rural countryside have become a focal point for an elaboration of a memory landscape that recognises the recent past as an ongoing source of collective trauma and fear.

Silence and haunting have always been key interrelated features of Gothic fiction, in which secrets abound and terror manifests itself as fear beyond words. Eve Kosofsky Sedgwick has famously highlighted the notion of the unspeakable as a central Gothic motif, noting that in many of the original Gothic texts the words 'unspeakable' or 'unutterable' appear frequently when describing reactions of fear. More than just the use of this vocabulary, Sedgwick explains that 'the novels deal with things that are naturalistically difficult to talk about, like guilt; but they describe the difficulty, not in terms of resistances that may or may not be overcome, but in terms of an absolute, often institutional prohibition or imperative'.[1] David Punter has described the ghost story as 'the emblematic version of cryptonymy, that process of the psyche which continually cries out for explanation while it is equally continually silenced because what it would have to say is, strictly speaking (as it were) unutterable'.[2] Nicholas Abraham and Maria Torok have theorised the role of secrets as a 'transgenerational phantom' in the subconscious, asserting that 'what haunts are not the dead, but the gaps left within us by the secret'.[3] For Abraham and Torok, the phantom is symbolic of shame, guilt and trauma (the 'secret') that is passed through generations of a family and, due to its inherent potential for harm, is therefore unspeakable. Drawing out the phantom requires speaking the secret – giving a voice to the trauma of the past – in order to stop the inherited cycle of haunting.

Due to its long history of mandated silence beginning in the Franco dictatorship and continuing in the Transition era with the 1977 Amnesty Law and Pact of Forgetting, Spain has been a frequent focus of the debate regarding the role of silence in historical memory and its continuing impact on contemporary politics. Joan Ramon Resina, referencing the 1977 law, points to the implied relationship between amnesty and amnesia: 'Amnesty is institutionalized oblivion, the deliberate erasure of a part of the civic past that otherwise would cling to the present.'[4] Enrique Gavilán explains that '[e]l silencio forzado, esa segunda forma de represión, en cierta medida más insidiosa, ha agravado la herida. Se nos ha dicho que vivíamos en una sociedad sana y nos lo hemos creído, poco o nada conscientes del trauma que albergamos en el centro de nuestra historia' ['forced silence, that second form of repression, to some extent more insidious, has aggravated the wound. We have been told that we lived in a healthy society and we've believed it, little or not at all conscious of the trauma that we harbour in the centre of our history'].[5] Journalist Juan Luis Cebrián has likewise noted the continuing pervasive presence of silence in post-Franco Spain: 'Hay una cosa que me llama mucho la atención, y es el silencio, al principio de la transición, sobre el propio franquismo, silencio que todavía se sigue produciendo' ['There is one thing that really calls my attention, and that is the silence, at the beginning of the transition, about Francoism itself, silence that is still being produced'].[6] The ongoing silence about the dictatorship and its victims indicates that this trauma has been inherited and, indeed, Carmen Moreno-Nuño suggests this when she states: 'There is no doubt that many children of the war's survivors grew up surrounded by a silence that could never be broken and by a pervasive fear, because anything could bring about a terrible fate.'[7] Abraham and Torok's transgenerational phantom continues to return in contemporary Spain as a sign of unresolved trauma in the form of silence.

For some Spanish authors, silence is not just a device that denotes fear, but it is also a trope used to represent the rural traditions of small towns and the way in which their inhabitants – like the physical towns themselves – are haunted by the spectral presence of the dying past. As more and more people leave rural communities throughout Spain in favour of larger metropolitan areas, those left behind continue their customary way of life while knowing that it is slowly becoming extinct. This mass exodus has been the subject of several recent critically acclaimed texts, including Sergio del Molino's *La España vacía* [*Empty Spain*], in which he presents the vast, empty landscape of rural Spain as a result of what he calls the 'Great Trauma': the abandonment of small villages (and, thus, cultural traditions) as Franco's focus on modernising urban centres dramatically reduced economic opportunities in the outlying countryside throughout the twentieth century.[8] Emilio Gancedo has recently described his experiences in rural Spain in the form of a travel essay called *Palabras mayores* [*Strong Words*], in which he sees the past as a constant presence outside the urban centres in provinces where ancient regional dialects continue to be spoken, giving these small towns the sense that time has stood still.[9] Internationally-renowned author Javier Cercas has also recorded rural Spanish life in his 2017 book *El monarca de las sombras* (officially translated as *Lord of All the Dead*), which depicts his search for information about his great-uncle, Manuel Mena, who fought for Franco in the civil war. By the end of the text, as Cercas visits the houses and other buildings in the village that was once his ancestral home, he reflects on his experience and the ghosts that still populate the countryside around him, declaring 'Nadie se ha ido. Nadie se va' ['No one has left. No one leaves'].[10] For these authors, the Spanish rural experience is inevitably an experience of and in the past – a space where the concept of time is not linear but rather cyclical.

Part II of *Spectral Spain* examines the haunting presence of silence and its relationship to memory and mourning in the Spanish rural landscape through close readings of Julio Llamazares's *Wolf Moon* (1985) and *The Yellow Rain* (1988), and Cristina Fernández Cubas's *El columpio* [*The Swing*] (1995). The tension between the urban and the rural that is often central to Spain's realist fiction is also a driving force behind much of its Gothic fiction, in which authors imbue the rural landscape with threatening features that act as a catalyst of fear, madness and death. In their portrayal of isolated Spanish towns, these authors frequently imply an inherent connection between the land and the past, invoking spectres as a representation of memory that continues to haunt the abandoned countryside. Therefore, where Raymond Williams has shown the country to traditionally denote 'the idea of a natural way of life: peace, innocence, and simple virtue',[11] we will instead see it here as a space that Spanish Gothic authors employ to comment on the impossibility of avoiding the cyclical returns of memory in spectral form. The ghostly landscapes of rural Spain thus become a natural site of mourning, which, as Dominick LaCapra notes, 'brings the possibility of engaging trauma and achieving a reinvestment in, or recathexis of, life which allows one to begin again'.[12] In these Spanish novels, that possibility is problematised by ongoing trauma that does not necessarily allow a clear resolution, reflecting the authors' perspective on the state of memory in the Transition era and beyond.

5

The Ghost Howls at Night: Silence, Death and the Politics of Fear in Julio Llamazares's Wolf Moon

~

Julio Llamazares (1955–present) is one of contemporary Spain's most lauded authors, a recipient of numerous literary awards and twice a finalist for the prestigious National Prize for Literature for his novels *Wolf Moon* (1985) and *The Yellow Rain* (1988). Llamazares was born in 1955 in Vegamián, a small town in the León province that quite literally disappeared during the author's childhood when a dam was constructed on the Porma River, permanently flooding several villages in the region. His experience in the rural Leonese countryside had a profound impact on his view of the Spanish landscape and his understanding of the socio-political culture of twentieth-century Spain, both frequent themes in his literary works. During childhood summers spent in his grandparents' small town, he listened to the mythologised tales of the 'resistance fighters' – the fugitive men who lived in the northern mountains, continuing the fight against the Franco regime into the mid-1940s. These stories fuelled Llamazares's imagination and became the basis for his first novel, *Wolf Moon*.

In this text, narrator Ángel and his three friends (Juan, Gildo and Ramiro) are members of the Republican forces fighting against Franco's Nationalist troops during the civil war. As the troops descend into the northern regions of Asturias and Cantabria in 1937 at the beginning of the novel, the four friends are forced to flee into the mountains, where they hide out in caves, barns and occasionally the houses of friends and family, only coming out at night and always hoping that their time as fugitives will come to an end once Franco is defeated. Over the course of nine violent and traumatic years, Juan, Gildo and Ramiro are all killed by the Civil Guard and only Ángel survives. His time in hiding has turned him into a ghostly creature of the night, and his association with the remaining members of his family only continues to endanger them. At the end of the novel, his sister begs him to leave them forever, and he boards a train and heads out, unsure of how – or how long – he will survive. In the afterword to *Wolf Moon*, Llamazares explains that he based the narrative on the true story of Casimiro Fernández Arias, who was the last surviving member of the resistance fighters in the León province and who, as Llamazares tells us, 'unwittingly played the leading role in the stories of my childhood dreams and who, in the fullness of time, would inspire the novel in which I tried to recount those stories'.[1]

Wolf Moon is, as Jo Labanyi asserts, one of the 'first novels to engage with the forcibly silenced memory of Republican victimization in and after the war'.[2] As a product of the Transition era, Llamazares's novel underscores the need to acknowledge the traumatic past. Its emphasis on memory and remembrance are frequently the subject of academic study; López de Abiada and López Bernasocchi, for instance, consider 'la expandida presencia de la memoria histórica y a los múltiples motivos inherentes a la transición' ['the expanded presence of historical memory and the multiple motives inherent to the transition'][3] at the root of this text. Labanyi sees Llamazares's authorial mission as 'an exercise in historical witnessing',[4] which she compares to Marianne Hirsch's concept of postmemory; in this case, authorship itself becomes the tool through which the authors (and, by extension, the readers) come to understand the generational trauma they have not personally witnessed, but rather inherited. Due to his vivid portrayal of the northern landscape and rural traditions, some scholars have considered Llamazares among the contemporary writers of Spanish 'regional literature'; Dorothée Riele, however, disagrees with this categorisation and argues that much of Llamazares's descriptions of the Spanish countryside and small towns could be equally representative of any remote region in the rural north.[5] These natural settings and isolated towns thus become a wider commentary on the rural Spanish collective memory and experience in the post-war era. In a study of this natural setting based on Bachelard's poetics of space, Li-Jung Tseng emphasises the important dialectic between the mountains (representative of freedom but also of the unforgiving cruelty of the land, which turns the men into animals) and the valleys (associated both with the warmth of home and family as well as the dangers posed by the Civil Guard who lie in wait).[6] Susan Martin-Márquez also comments on Llamazares's use of space in her study of the novel as an example of Jeremy Bentham's Panopticon, invoking the Foucauldian notion of the European penal system to show that the narrative 'is structured by a visual regime which could be characterized as panoptic, and that in this way it reflects the significance of this pattern of surveillance within the larger cultural context'.[7] Not only do the guards keep a constant vigil of the mountain, but the land itself appears to be imbued with monstrous features that John Margenot considers emblematic of demonic archetypes and spaces of fear in accordance with Bachelard and Frye.[8]

Using the above-mentioned works as a point of departure, in this chapter I propose to analyse the representation of Llamazares's resistance fighters as spectral, Gothic monsters who rely on silence and the darkness of night to survive in the mountainous countryside of northern Spain. In *Wolf Moon*, the intersection of mourning and the (un)dead provides a fascinating commentary on the role of the recent historical past in the collective memory of the rural north. Within Llamazares's memory landscape, the atmosphere of censorship and violent oppression turns the four young men into phantom-like werewolves that only emerge at night for fear of being hunted during the day. Mourning is an inherent characteristic of this rural space, where the Gothic motifs of silence, darkness and death combine to portray the impossibility of hope and the inevitability of loss.

Until the publication of *Wolf Moon* in 1985, much of what was known about the Spanish resistance was shared through oral tradition.[9] The severe repression and censorship throughout the dictatorship and the 1977 Pact of Forgetting silenced the stories of these Republican *maquis*, many of whom continued their fight against the Franco regime until the 1960s. Cristina Ruiz Serrano explains that aside from the strategic use of violence and terror, the regime also purposefully covered up information related to the resistance fighters due to their 'carácter político' ['political character'], noting 'la manipulación franquista de la historia y la falta de un apoyo institucional decisivo a la restauración de la memoria histórica en la ya España democrática' ['the Francoist manipulation of history and the lack of decisive institutional support for the restoration of historical memory in the already democratic Spain'] as the primary reason for the delayed acknowledgement of the group's activities.[10] León, Llamazares's home province, was an early battleground for these fighters because of its immediate status as Nationalist territory at the beginning of the war; as López de Abiada and López Bernasocchi explain:

> A partir de entonces comenzó la represión contra los ex combatientes republicanos o de ideología izquierdista que intentaban regresar a sus casas; muchos de ellos terminaron en los campos de concentración de la zona y sus familiares sufrieron frecuentes represalias. De ahí que algunos de los ex combatientes que veían amenazadas sus vidas decidieran ocultarse en los montes sin planificación previa; la mayoría de ellos eran mineros y campesinos, pero también había maestros y de otras profesiones.
>
> [From then on began the repression against the former Republican fighters or those of left-wing ideology who attempted to return to their houses; many of them ended up in concentration camps in the zone and their family members suffered frequent reprisals. Hence, some of the ex-fighters who saw their lives endangered decided to hide themselves in the mountains without previous planning; the majority of them were miners and farmers, but there were also teachers and people of other professions.][11]

According to Julián Casanova, maintaining an atmosphere of fear was a key tactic in the newly-minted regime: 'This state of terror, a continuation of the state of the war, transformed Spanish society through the destruction of entire families and by inundating daily life in Spain with the constant threat of punishment and through numerous instances of carrying out that threat.'[12] As Casanova clearly states, the war did not end in 1939 for the victims of the regime; the fear of retaliation was profound and devastating.

Carmen Moreno Nuño has used the term 'politics of silence' to refer to Franco's forced repression of collective trauma in the post-war era, which she considers to be a primary motif in contemporary Spanish literature. For Moreno Nuño, the widespread silence about the war and its aftermath is like 'a ghost which obsessively reappears to a second generation who seeks its identity in connections with a past that has resisted oblivion'.[13] In *Wolf Moon*, the atmosphere is charged with ghostly silences that heighten the characters' endless terror and anxiety. From the very beginning of the narrative, Ángel unwittingly foreshadows the impossibility of reclaiming their political voices when he describes the silence of their surroundings as '[d]ense and profound. Indestructible' (p. 20). This silence is portrayed as an inviolable part of the landscape itself when Ángel later says that 'thick silence holds up the sky's dome, like an arch of black water curving gently over the valley' (p. 28). In fact, nature appears to obey the rule of silence when it is 'so tense that even the rain has gone quiet in anticipation of the dénouement' (p. 49). Throughout the text, Llamazares continually returns to metaphors in which silence and nature appear inextricably linked; thus, in the cold, damp mountains, Ángel asserts that '[g]radually everything becomes buried under the profound weightlessness of silence' (p. 80).

The terror implied in the extended silence of Llamazares's landscape is multiplied through the pervasive presence of darkness in the narrative. Because of their status as fugitives, the four men spend daylight hours hidden and only come out in the cover of night. Ángel describes the first night in the novel like 'a cold black stain on the outline of the beech groves, which climb up the mountain and into the fog like ghostly armies of ice' (p. 18). The distorted reality of darkness is, from the beginning, fertile ground for the invocation of fear and for the men's conversion into spectral monsters. The interplay between death and darkness is made obvious within the first few pages of the novel, when Ángel remarks that '[d]aylight is not good for dead men' (p. 21). Already signalling their identity as living dead, Ángel's understanding of their fugitive status takes on a decidedly Gothic tone. Existing in perpetual darkness and often hiding themselves under piles of hay or rubble during the day (repeatedly acting out their own burials), the four friends only experience life through death. For them, 'it is always night-time. There is no sun, no clouds, no wind, no horizons . . . You lose your memory and your consciousness in an endless round of hours and days' (p. 38). When the sun does appear in the text, it is always blood-red (a reminder of the certain dangers of the daytime) and blinds the men, whose eyes have grown accustomed to the darkness.

Despite the conditional safety of the night-time hours when the men are better able to hide from the Civil Guard, it is also a time of unique dangers in the inhospitable mountains. The landscape, which Ángel describes as 'grey, futile, desolate' and 'abandoned to the remorseless voraciousness of time and oblivion' (p. 44), is even named in accordance with the symbolism of darkness and death. Margenot lists several of these names as an indication of the diabolical in Llamazares's novel: 'Peña Negra, Peña Malera, el lago Negro, el río Negro, la Sierra de la Sangre, el bosque de las Loberas, el prado de la Llamas, el valle de los Osos, fuente Amarga y el puente del Ahorcado' ['Black Rock, Evil Rock, Black Lake, Black River, Blood Mountain, Wolf Den Forest, field of Flames, Valley of the Bears, Bitter Fountain and the Bridge of the Hanged'].[14] That the human inhabitants of this isolated region have given such names to their physical surroundings is evidence of the unforgiving nature of the environment around them and accentuates the Gothic tone of the text. Within this cruel landscape marked by darkness and silence, the men's fate seems to be predetermined. Riele notes that despite the clear indications of danger presented to them through and in their natural surroundings, 'the attachment of the characters to their region makes it hard for them to leave, even though they sense that staying will result in death'.[15] Thus, for personal and political reasons, the men are determined to continue their fight to survive in their homeland, even amid the continuous threats of hostility and violence from both the landscape and – acting as its extension – the Civil Guard.

Silence and darkness are equal catalysts for fear in Llamazares's novel, making it the principal emotion of the narrative. Indeed, every village inhabitant in the text is at one point or another a victim of terror, often at the hands of the Civil Guard though also occasionally due to the four protagonists, who at times use threats of violence to get food, shelter and other favours from the mountain dwellers. Llamazares's characters continually act and react through cyclical terror propagated by the circumstances of their socio-political environment. We see victims 'gripped by terror and the cold' (p. 22), 'completely unhinged' (p. 57), 'dead still' (p. 59), 'eyes popping out of their sockets' (p. 75), 'paler beyond the limits of fear' (p. 76), 'on the verge of screaming in panic' (p. 91), 'collapsing in a faint on the table like a rag doll' (p. 97) and 'like a statue seized by panic' (p. 125). By part three of the novel, Ángel remarks: 'It's been like this for six years now, living in silence, terrified, torn between pity, which moves them to help us, and the ever-increasing fear of reprisals' (p. 116). As a reflection of its historical context, the narrative repeatedly stresses the ongoing trauma in the Spanish countryside as an individual and collective experience rooted in fear and violence.

In response to this dark and terror-filled environment, the people living within it become increasingly dehumanised. We can therefore read the title *Wolf Moon* as an allusion to all the nocturnal creatures that populate Llamazares's menacing landscape, including the four *maquis*. The narrator frequently mentions the wolves that prowl the rugged mountainside in search of prey; these animals become a central symbol in the text, often reflected in the natural surroundings (where the wind and snow howl and the fog roars) and in the men themselves, who gradually take on the form of nocturnal beasts resembling wolves (or, in Gothic terms, werewolves). It is no coincidence that Ángel first describes Ramiro 'like the profile of an animal that is motionless, perhaps dead' (p. 17). The narrator views himself and his friends through the constant dual imagery of animalisation and death, which responds to and reflects the harsh conditions in which they live. The more time they spend in the darkness, the less human and more monstrous they become. Thus, the opening scenes in which Ramiro 'sniffs the night like an injured wolf' (p. 18) and Ángel crawls 'through the heather like a mangy dog' (p. 28) inevitably result in the narrator telling us, by part four, that he has 'turned into a real predator . . . A predator whose presence shocks both man and beasts' (p. 149). Margenot explains that the animalisation of both the *maquis* and the Civil Guard emphasises their brutality and that 'la cacería del hombre como si fuese un animal deshumaniza tanto a los republicanos como al bando nacionalista cuyo fanatismo no tiene límites' ['the hunting of man as if he were an animal dehumanises both the Republicans and the Nationalists, whose intolerance has no limits'].[16] López de Abiada and López Bernasocchi similarly consider the main theme of the novel to be 'el acoso constante y progresivo del hombre por el hombre, el inhumano acorralamiento, la despiadada persecución y el exterminio del hombre por el hombre' ['the constant and progressive pursuit of man by man, the inhumane cornering, the ruthless persecution and extermination of man by man'],[17] and Inge Beisel considers that the constant threats from the Civil Guard and the terror of their environment lead the men to 'aislamiento, a la adaptación al nivel de las fieras y a la reducción de lo humano al simple instinto de supervivencia' ['isolation, adaptation to the level of beasts and to the reduction of the human being to the simple instinct of survival'].[18] When the *maquis* kidnap the mine owner in hopes of getting money to cross the border into France, Ángel, in a moment of introspection, tells the man: 'Take any domesticated animal, the best-behaved dog . . . lock it in a room and beat it. You'll see how he turns and bites you. You'll see that he'd kill you if he could' (p. 99). Here, the narrator attributes his own animalisation to the inhumane treatment he has received during his many years in hiding. He importantly acknowledges wrongdoing, but also recognises the circumstances around him as the catalyst for his monstrous conversion.

Four years after the kidnapping of the mine owner (which results in the death of Gildo), Ángel and Ramiro display their animalistic transformation when they hunt down the local priest, Don Manuel, under the light of the moon in what the narrator describes as 'the dull throb of revenge' (p. 110). Acting with animal-like rage, they terrorise the clergyman in the hope of hearing his confession: that he was the one who – with 'unusual and feverish enthusiasm' (p. 110) – denounced Juan and many of the other Republicans in town who have been killed by the Civil Guard. By including this scene in his novel, Llamazares points to the complicity of the Catholic Church in the creation of the hostile landscape that he portrays; aside from the Civil Guard who hunt their enemies and instil terror in their victims, the clergy also wield profound control over the village dwellers and assist the hunters by leading them directly to their prey. Julián Casanova, in his book *La iglesia de Franco*, explains that the Catholic clergy played an important role in Franco's politics of terror: 'La complicidad del clero con ese terror militar y fascista fue . . . absoluta y no necesitó del anticlericalismo para manifestarse . . . La actitud más frecuente fue el silencio, voluntario o impuesto por los superiores, cuando no la acusación o la delación' ['The complicity of the clergy with that military and fascist terror was . . . absolute and did not require anticlericalism in order to manifest itself . . . The most frequent attitude was silence, voluntary or imposed by superiors, when not accusation or denunciation'].[19] In this scene, what is perhaps most telling is that Ramiro and Ángel do not end up killing the priest, despite their plan to do so. In an exchange of roles, the two young men – at first acting as vicious beasts after their prey – regain part of their humanity by letting the priest go; Don Manuel, however, does not appear to admit or repent for his sins and, upon release, immediately runs to the Civil Guard to tell them where the men are. With this act, Llamazares casts the priest as the true monster in this chapter: he willingly sacrifices the children of his church to the wolves who lie in wait under the cover of night.

As Llamazares's references to animalisation increase throughout the text, so too do the comparisons of the men to ghosts, living dead and shadows. Interestingly, Labanyi considers werewolves, vampires and Frankenstein's monster within the category of 'ghosts' – an assertion that highlights their common feature of marginalisation in darkness.[20] Likewise, Andrew Smith notes that 'early folktales included a diverse range of forms that were associated with haunting, such as werewolves and vampires, which were not ghosts'.[21] The conflation of (were)wolf and ghost in *Wolf Moon* therefore emphasises the marginalised state of the four young men, who find themselves losing touch with their humanity as the community increasingly builds a wall of silence around them. Forced to be creatures of the night, the narrator and his friends experience life through the lens of death. When Ángel states in chapter two that 'our lives are now totally dependent upon how successful we are at not being seen' (p. 27), he directly relates survival to ghostlike invisibility; in this manner, the men become phantasmagoric presences haunting the countryside. Death permeates everything around them, seeping into the landscape itself, and yet despite the endless trauma they suffer in the mountains, their connection to the land binds them to it, much like ghosts fated to the futility of endless returns. Ángel explains that their resistance to leave is due to 'our attachment to this lifeless land – lifeless and hopeless – which weighs down on us like a tombstone' (p. 94). The men's familial and cultural bonds keep them locked in a cycle of violence and death, and ultimately necessitate their spectrality, which the narrator admits early in the novel when he proclaims: 'It's like we're dead. As if there's nothing apart from this' (p. 36). Simultaneous to their portrayal as werewolves, Llamazares also describes the friends as 'three shadows walking silently into the wind' (p. 74) and as 'ghosts emerging every now and then from the shadows' (p. 107). Because of the Panopticon-like vigilance around them, invisibility is key to their survival, and they begin to insist that their victims and family members do not recognise their materiality – a demand evidenced in Ramiro's threat to the foreman: 'Us? We're not here. No one's seen anyone' (p. 81). This present absence that the young men come to embody recalls what Avery Gordon has said regarding the spectral nature of the disappeared in Luisa Valenzuela's works: 'a disappearance is real only when it is apparitional'.[22] Here, the opposite is equally true: in order to know the men exist as living beings, the townspeople must first (and then only ever) see them as ghosts. In this sense, the four friends truly experience life as revenants, always returning and yet never fully arriving, dematerialising into shadowlike projections of their former selves that actively resist being seen while also desperately yearning for the chance to recover their humanity.

Inherently connected to notions of silence, darkness and spectrality that Llamazares purposefully interweaves in his text, death is the inevitable result of the traumatic landscape of the post-war era. Through death – which, for Ángel, is likened to being slowly 'buried alive' (p. 179) – our narrator, the last surviving member of the group of four friends, comes to understand the futility of his situation in the mountains. When his sister Juana begs him to leave, Ángel finally realises, after nine long years, that she is right, stating: 'I have to escape from this cursed land and put kilometers of silence and oblivion between me and the memory of me, between me and this tomb where the heat and desperation fuse together into one putrefied substance that is starting to spread through my body' (p. 179). Here, the physical and mental degeneration that Ángel experiences in hiding is explicitly linked to memory; if life as a fugitive is actually a slow death, then memory – the experience that binds him to the land and the nostalgic past – is an agent of decay. Ángel therefore considers his only option for survival to be the simultaneous extermination of memory and physical separation from his homeland.

Llamazares problematises this process, however, in Ángel's evolving attitude toward silence and memory. Whereas in the beginning of the novel, silence was an integral part of the threatening, hostile landscape, by the end – when Ángel is the sole survivor – it suddenly seems like a welcome presence that the narrator describes as 'the only friend I had left', explaining: 'Now the silence is my strongest ally in this long struggle against death, and it comes out to greet me at the entrance of the cave, like a dog, when I return' (p. 151). If silence was, initially, a community-wide response to the fear of torture and death at the hands of the Civil Guard, it is now the only tool that Ángel has to survive the mental and emotional anguish of complete solitude. This new acceptance of silence is, then, a form of self-censorship in which Ángel blocks out his memories of recent trauma in order to preserve his mental state – a process that mimics the pervasive role of silence in post-Franco Spain. Salvador Sánchez Terán, former Minister of Labour under Adolfo Suárez (Spain's first democratically-elected Prime Minister after Franco's death, serving from 1976–81), noted in an interview with Montse Armengou and Ricard Belis: 'Había ya, como en toda la transición, un interés en no revolver el pasado. Uno de los pilares de nuestra transición es el no hablar de nuestros muertos, ni de nuestro pasado, ni de la guerra civil, ni de lo anterior ni de lo posterior a la guerra civil' ['There was already, as in the entire transition, an interest in not stirring up the past. One of the pillars of our transition is that we do not speak about our dead, nor about our past, nor about the civil war, nor about the era prior to or after the civil war'].[23] As Sánchez Terán notes, silence was the defining feature of the Transition, primarily because of the widespread belief that remembering would mean extended political strife. Paloma Fernández Aguilar has explained the perceived political and societal advantages of silence during the Transition, stating: 'Los silencios expresan de forma latente una autocensura colectiva, la existencia de cicatrices políticas abiertas, de problemas vivos subyacentes en la vida del país. Sin embargo, el olvido puede llegar a ser tan importante como la memoria para cimentar la convivencia pacífica de una nación' ['Silences express in latent form a collective self-censorship, the existence of open political scars, of intense underlying problems in the life of the country. However, oblivion can come to be as important as memory for founding the peaceful cohabitation of a nation'].[24] This representation of the relationship between silence, memory and nation building as vital for democracy is one that continues to persist in Spanish politics even in the twenty-first century. Cristina Moreiras Menor elaborates on the use of silence in the transition and notes its potential for damage:

> Esta escena de la vida democrática española es ejemplar de los procesos de silenciamiento que dirigen la transición a la democracia, y aún la democracia misma, en la medida en que confirma una práctica que, desde la misma muerte del dictador, se instaura en el país en torno a la historia reciente de España: la borradura de un pasado que se empeña en perderse en una lógica de la desmemoria y que, desde la oficialidad institucional, se instala en el colectivo nacional bajo la premisa de una imperativa necesidad de abrirse a una nueva realidad que nada tiene que ver con su anterior.
>
> [This scene of Spanish democratic life is exemplary of the processes of silencing that direct the transition to democracy, and even democracy itself, in that it confirms a practice that, since the very death of the dictator, has established itself in the country around the recent history of Spain: the erasure of a past that insists on losing itself in a logic of amnesia and that, from institutional officiality, is installed in the national collective under the premise of an imperative need

to open itself to a new reality that has nothing to do with its previous one.]25

Much like the silence of the post-war era and, later, the Transition, which was an attempt to split the present from the recent past, silence is, for Ángel, a method of avoidance. When his total isolation becomes compounded by grief at the news of his father's imminent death, Ángel portrays memory itself as an instrument of torture: 'the memory of my father explodes in my brain, shattering into a thousand pieces, into a painful avalanche of shrapnel or shards of broken glass, which can only just reach into my hidden pain before continuing into the bottomless mire of oblivion' (p. 158). If the pain of remembering is too unbearable, Ángel will not be able to maintain the concentration needed for his survival in the wilderness; therefore, silencing memory appeals to him as an immediate solution.

After he accepts silence as part of his reality, however, he begins to realise that he is no longer just hiding from the Civil Guard, but also from his past – a truth that he acknowledges when he describes one day as '[a]nother day spent running away from myself with no rest and no hope' (p. 171). Although he has initially resigned himself to accepting silence as an ally, Ángel knows that he cannot last much longer in isolation, and he decides to accept Juana's request and take a train across the border into France. This final scene is a metaphorical exhumation and resurrection, as Ángel emerges from the tomblike hole in the floor of the goat pen where he has been hiding and enters the land of the living and of the sunlight, which initially blinds him. His journey, which he describes as a path toward 'death or oblivion' (p. 180), is open-ended, as Llamazares provides no resolution to the story – reflecting, perhaps, the widespread silence that still defined Spain at the time of his writing.

When read as a Gothic text, *Wolf Moon* becomes a record of silence and death brought to life through the act of mourning, highlighting in particular the collective memory of the rural north that Llamazares recalls as part of the foundational mythology of his own childhood. Timothy Baker, in his study on mourning in the Scottish Gothic, explains that mourning is 'the process that provides the appearance of death. It is, in a manner of speaking, the way the self relates to death, and through which an image of death is formed.'[26] In this sense, Ángel's narrative is part of his own process of reconstructing identity through loss; despite having identified himself as a dead man throughout much of the text, it is only through the act of mourning his friends and his former life that he is able to finally separate himself from death and, by extension, his hometown. Despite his assertion at the end of the narrative that he is potentially journeying into death or oblivion, the mere retelling of his story simultaneously avoids both of those conclusions: through his tale, he and his friends will continue to exist as a record of the past that has become part of the memory carried by readers in the present.

In this manner, the text itself is a testimonial that memorialises the resistance fighters, whose very existence was erased from Spanish collective memory through the oppressive politics of silence that defined Franco's regime. The act of writing – in this case, the act of recalling the past – is therefore doubly important in this narrative: through telling his story, Ángel begins a new life in exile, free from oppression and able to remember his loved ones without fear of reprisal; and, in writing this novel, Julio Llamazares restores memory and voice to his real-life hero whose story had yet to be told. As Labanyi notes: 'Their story is threatened with extinction by the last surviving resistance fighter's expulsion from his family's memory at the end of the novel – but, in relaying his first-person narrative to contemporary readers, the novelist is keeping him (and his already dead comrades) alive.'[27] In fact, Llamazares himself has recognised his authorial project as a personal mission to salvage memory, admitting in interviews that 'he writes from memories of a world which is disappearing and which he wants to prevent from sinking into oblivion'.[28] As a Transition-era author whose own hometown was lost below the floodwaters of a river during his childhood, Llamazares knows well the indelible impression that landscape and silence make on memory. In *Wolf Moon*, their combined presence invokes the spectral past in recognition of trauma and of the need to recover the voices that have been erased from official histories.

6

Life in a Ghost Town: Gothic Landscapes, Rural Memory and the Silence of Loss in Julio Llamazares's The Yellow Rain

∽

Julio Llamazares's second novel, *The Yellow Rain*, achieved instant critical acclaim upon its publication in 1988, ultimately becoming a finalist for the National Prize for Literature in 1989, just three years after his first nomination for his novel *Wolf Moon* (1985). In many ways, *The Yellow Rain* is a profound reflection of the author's own experience growing up in the isolated rural landscape of León. The narrator-protagonist, Andrés de Casa Sosas, lives in a small village called Ainielle in the Pyrenees of Aragon, where he is the sole inhabitant left in the town after all the others have either died or moved away in the years since the Spanish civil war. Narrating the story from his deathbed, Andrés describes in flashbacks the death of his 4-year-old daughter years earlier, the loss of his son Camilo (who went missing in the war and is presumed dead in a mass grave), the absence of his middle son who moved away to Germany to escape the village, and, eventually, the more recent suicide of his wife during a harsh winter of isolation. With just his dog for companionship, Andrés is terribly lonely and becomes increasingly terrified of going mad because of the overwhelming solitude. He starts to see 'shadows' (ghosts) of his mother and other deceased members of his family and village, many of whom come to visit his kitchen in the evenings. In his final years, nature seems to completely take over the town, turning its houses into crumbling ruins and giving the village itself the appearance of a cemetery. Living among these ghosts, Andrés spends his final hours consumed by his memories of the past and waiting for death to finally release him.

Scholarship on *The Yellow Rain* frequently focuses on the narrator's connection to nature and physical space, in which the rural landscape becomes yet another protagonist in the text. For this reason, Ellen Mayock groups Llamazares with other contemporary Spanish authors like Camilo José Cela, Miguel Delibes, Rosa Montero and Carmen Gómez Ojea for their similar literary themes such as:

> el crecimiento de los espacios urbanos y el abandono de la vida del campo, la dureza del medio ambiente, la crisis de la fe frente al poder del medio ambiente, el enfrentamiento entre el determinismo y el libre albedrio, la creciente importancia de las ciencias y, sobre todo, de la herencia genética.
>
> [the growth of urban spaces and the abandonment of life in the countryside, the harshness of the environment, the crisis of faith against the power of the environment, the confrontation between determinism and free will, the growing importance of sciences and, above all, of genetic inheritance.][1]

Mayock centres her study on the role of determinism and free will in *The Yellow Rain* through the relationship between death and the environment that Llamazares portrays in his text. Rosa María Díez Cobo also sees the depiction of nature as key to Llamazares's narrative, which she considers to be an example of the growing genre of neo-rural literature in contemporary Spain. As such, she relates it to earlier forms of rural literature by William Faulkner, Juan Rulfo and Gabriel García Márquez, noting the shared 'sentido de lo fatídico, de lo violento y del aislamiento geográfico y humano' ['sense of the ominous, of the violent and of the geographic and human isolation'] in these newer texts which links them 'con otra tendencia de narrativas rurales precedentes: la propensión a construir cartografías y cosmogonías míticas; nuevos Yoknapatawphas, eternas Comalas, inesperados Macondos' ['with another tendency of the previous rural narratives: the propensity to construct mythical cartographies and cosmogonies; new Yoknapatawphas, eternal Comalas, unexpected Macondos'].[2] For Jo Labanyi, who mentions Llamazares alongside the cinema of Victor Erice, the author's 'sense of place . . . is extraordinarily strong – but in all cases these are spaces where the possibility of collectivity and communication is denied or at best curtailed'.[3] Indeed, the severe isolation the narrator experiences in Ainielle serves to create what José Antonio Llera calls the 'universo claustrofóbico' ['claustrophobic universe'] of *The Yellow Rain*,[4] in which 'se ha borrado la distancia entre lo vivo y lo muerto' ['the distance between the living and the dead has been erased'].[5] Both Llera and Robert Baah see interactions between memory and individual identity as an important tool that Llamazares employs to address Spanish history, and Baah considers the author's use of emotions and self-reflexion 'a stylistics of compassion, which Llamazares develops in response to the theater of human desperation played out in Spain's rural communities after the civil war'.[6] Similarly, Li-Jung Tseng, in a study of the value of space in three of Llamazares's novels, asserts that *The Yellow Rain* is, in essence, 'una poesía de soledad, silencio, locura y muerte' ['a poetry of solitude, silence, insanity and death'].[7]

Despite the frequent focus on the portrayal of space in *The Yellow Rain*, none of the scholars who have studied this novel have considered it from a Gothic perspective, which would further illuminate the interactions between the narrator and the threatening landscape of the rural north. What I propose in the present chapter is a new reading of *The Yellow Rain* as a Gothic narrative that employs overwhelming silence and fear as the primary motifs through which Llamazares provides a glimpse of life in one of the many ghost towns of Spain's contemporary countryside. The landscape itself serves as a catalyst for the narrator's obsessive fear of going mad, which only intensifies when he begins to see the ghosts of his mother and others from the town who have died. The spectral presences throughout the text are a constant reminder of the physical decay of not just the human body and the country town, but also of the traditional way of life associated with the era prior to the civil war, which Llamazares portrays in its final death throes in this novel. In this manner, the concept of 'ghost town' is imbued with particularly poignant symbolic meaning: the town itself, envisioned as a cemetery, is a marker of memory in which Andrés, as its sole survivor, lives his last days resigned to his impending death. Within this Gothic atmosphere, the act of mourning thus becomes central to Andrés's understanding of death and the persistent, haunting presence of memory.

As numerous scholars have noted, Llamazares's portrayal of the small mountain town of Ainielle is in many ways a depiction of the historical experience of isolation and solitude in Spain's rural countryside. The gradual extinction of the country's rural villages prior to the civil war quickly became a dramatic mass exodus in the years that followed. As Michael Richards explains:

> Before 1936, 29 percent of the Spanish population lived in urban centers of more than 20,000 inhabitants; by 1958 (even before the 'boom' of the 1960s) this proportion had grown to 40 percent . . . The shift was rapid and continued in the 1960s, and took place within the space of little more than a generation. In 1950, one of every four persons active in agriculture was a wage worker. By 1965 the proportion was one of every ten.[8]

For the villages that retained inhabitants, access to basic technology was limited at best. John Hooper notes that Pardamaza, a village in the León province, did not even have electricity until 1996 and remained without street lighting until 2004[9] – a clear example of the lasting impact of rural exodus on the remote Spanish countryside. The glacial pace of modernisation in these villages ultimately drove even greater numbers of migrants to the urban centres (primarily Madrid and Barcelona, which remain the largest metropolitan areas in Spain).

Sergio del Molino, in his seminal 2016 essay *La España vacía* [*Empty Spain*], considers this mass exodus to be the 'Gran Trauma' ['Great Trauma'] of the post-war era.[10] Although this shift in migratory patterns is not unique to Spain, Molino explains that the circumstances around it – tied inherently to the mass trauma of the civil war – and the extent of the damage are very much part of contemporary Spanish cultural identity. He notes: 'El paisaje que ha pintado ese Gran Trauma define el país y ha dejado una huella enorme en sus habitantes. Hay una España vacía en la que vive un puñado de españoles, pero hay otra España vacía que vive en la mente y la memoria de millones de españoles' ['The landscape that the Great Trauma has painted defines the country and has left an enormous mark on its inhabitants. There is an empty Spain in which a handful of Spaniards live, but there is another empty Spain that lives in the mind and memory of millions of Spaniards'].[11] For Molino, empty rural Spain is, in many ways, a palimpsest in the country's collective memory: the traces of what were once vibrant centres of shared traditions now weigh on the Spanish subconscious as a present absence – a loss that is part of Spain's generational inheritance. As Molino notes, this Great Trauma has inspired an entire literary genre focused on the rural Spanish landscape (exemplified in Llamazares's *The Yellow Rain*), but most importantly is what Molino highlights as 'una forma de mirar y de mirarse a sí mismos que es difícil de comprender en otros contextos geográficos. Un odio. Un *autoodio*' ['a form of looking and looking at themselves that is difficult to understand in other geographical contexts. A hatred. A *self-hatred*'].[12] Beyond the large metropolitan centres, Spain's autonomous communities are filled with absences: abandoned towns dot the landscape with their vacant houses and overwhelming silences. Travelling through these isolated regions, Molino asserts, is 'una experiencia inigualable' ['an incomparable experience'] unlike anything one might expect to find elsewhere in Europe: 'Paisajes extremos y desnudos, desiertos, montañas áridas, pueblos imposibles y la pregunta constante: quién vive aquí y por qué. Cómo han soportado, siglo tras siglo, el aislamiento, el sol, el polvo, la desidia, las sequías e incluso el hambre' ['Extreme and naked landscapes, deserts, arid mountains, impossible towns and the constant question: who lives here and why. How have they tolerated, century after century, the isolation, the sun, the dust, the apathy, the droughts and even the hunger'].[13] These questions are all central to Llamazares's novel, in which his narrator's entire life is marked by the constant battle against an inhospitable landscape and the devastating effects of the loss of community hastened by this Great Trauma.

Llamazares opens *The Yellow Rain* with a note that Ainielle, the town portrayed in the text, actually exists, thus emphasising from the beginning a certain realism to his work; however, this assertion of reality serves to heighten the irreality with which the author describes the town, as hostile natural forces and fear-inducing spectres quickly distort the reader's (and the narrator's) perception of time and place. The first paragraph of the text begins:

> By the time they reach the top of Sobrepuerto, it will probably be growing dark. Thick shadows will advance like waves across the mountains, and the fierce, turbid, bloody sun will humble itself before them, clinging, feebly now, to the gorse and the heap of ruins and rubble that (before fire overwhelmed it while all the family and the animals were sleeping) was once the solitary house at Sobrepuerto.[14]

With these opening lines, Llamazares immediately establishes this northern region as a *locus terribilis*: in the rugged Pyrenees of Aragon, nature is cruel and vengeful, claiming victims among humans and animals alike and leaving only the skeletal remains of a burned-down house as evidence of its destruction. From this vantage point atop the mountain, Ainielle appears like 'an avalanche of crazed tombstones . . . amid the utter stillness, the silence, and the shadows' (p. 2). Llamazares repeats these images throughout his text, frequently calling attention to the cemetery-like atmosphere of the town which, like a 'sad, unburied corpse' is cloaked in 'sepulchral silence' (p. 4). His persistent depiction of Ainielle's abandoned houses as corpses or tombstones combines with the dark, threatening landscape to create from the outset a Gothic tone to the narrative.

Indeed, nature itself is an unforgiving, seemingly malicious force throughout the entire novel. Llamazares frequently mentions nettles and their invasive and 'terrible power', which he envisions as beginning to 'invade and profane the hearts and memories of the houses' (p. 3). Houses, here again seen as living beings, are also markers of memory in this inhospitable space, inevitably associated with the families who once lived in them and constant reminders of the sense of community that defined the town in years past. Now these buildings and the memories they carry are in a process of slow, persistent decay aided by the brute forces of nature around

Life in a Ghost Town

them. Thus, in true Gothic form, the wind howls 'like a rabid dog' (p. 10), the winter snow is an 'ancient white curse' (p. 13) of death that threatens the man's survival, the apple tree is 'possessed by the blood of Sabina' (p. 129), and the narrator himself imagines the group of men finding his body 'devoured by the moss and by the birds' (p. 8).

Within this environment, as Julio Ángel Olivares Merino notes, Llamazares places special symbolic significance on color: 'Se trata de la multiplicación y saturación de elementales invasivos, generalmente asociados a una sustanciación densa del cromatismo blanco – ausencia – , amarillo – como óxido o herrumbre – o negro – epítome de lo siniestro' ['It has to do with the multiplication and saturation of invasive elements, generally associated with a dense substantiation of the use of the colour white – absence – , yellow – like oxide or rust – or black – epitome of the sinister'].[15] The novel's title image, yellow rain, is given particular importance in the text as a prime symbolic device that connects nature with the notions of decay, death and loss (of loved ones and of memory). Llera considers the yellow rain to be a bisemic symbol representing 'las hojas desprendidas de los árboles, que inundan el valle en otoño, y también el paso del tiempo, el dolor, la tristeza, la muerte' ['the leaves fallen from the trees, which inundate the valley in fall, and also the passing of time, pain, sadness, death'].[16] Mayock interprets the colour yellow as a sepia-tone photograph of memory that depicts 'un retrato en vivo del pasado – de la memoria y de la nostalgia – y del presente – de los preparativos para la muerte' ['a living portrait of the past – of memory and of nostalgia – and of the present – of the preparations for death'].[17] Given the Gothic's preoccupation with death and decay, it is no coincidence that the titular image is an almost obsessive presence in the text. Llamazares often associates yellow rain, as a product and force of nature, with fear and destruction; notably, Andrés first feels fear in his eyes, where 'the yellow rain is gradually erasing all memory from them' (p. 9). The autumn countryside soon becomes a 'landscape of death . . . inhabited by bloodless men and trees and by the yellow rain of oblivion' (p. 31). Later, Llamazares repeats this imagery when his narrator tells us that 'this yellow rust became my sole memory, the sole landscape of my life' (p. 71). As death approaches, yellow appears as a stain that covers everything in Andrés's line of sight, even permeating the memories he has of the town and countryside. When he decides to chop down Sabina's diseased apple tree, he quickly realises that the act would be futile because '[t]he sap of death had already filled the whole village, it was gnawing at the wood and the air of the houses, impregnating my bones like a yellow creeping damp. Everything around me was dead, and I was no exception, even though my heart was still beating' (p. 111). The drumbeat-like repetition of these phrases throughout the narrative makes the vocabulary itself a spectral presence in Llamazares's novel; the yellow landscape, yellow stain and yellow shadows all represent already returning presences – ghostly words – in the text. Like memory, these images are an inevitable connection to previous experiences that become even more vivid as death draws nearer.

In this Gothic atmosphere, isolation, abandonment and mourning all manifest themselves as and through silence. In her study of *The Story of Lucy Gault,* Joanne Watkiss talks of 'an unnecessary fear that fuels a silence of loss'.[18] This notion of a 'silence of loss' perfectly describes the state in which our narrator exists in Ainielle; silence, which he says fills his house 'like black slime' (p. 6), permeates every physical and mental space in *The Yellow Rain*, seeping through cracks in Andrés's subconscious as a catalyst to rot. In fact, he tells us that at times 'the howling silence was so loud, so deep, that I would leave the kitchen, unable to stand it any longer' (p. 16). This silence threatens the narrator's very existence by making his home – a normally welcoming space – nearly uninhabitable. In this manner, silence itself becomes a spectral presence in the text, constantly invading the protagonist's personal space and innermost thoughts. By the end of the novel, silence even takes on the role of gravedigger as Andrés insists that 'Like sand, the silence will bury my eyes' and 'Like sand, the silence will bury the houses' (p. 114).

Seen as a simultaneous force of nature and an ominous spectral sign of memory, silence is thus a powerful metaphor for the Great Trauma described by Molino, rendering it a mechanism through which Llamazares invites discussion of the devastating effects of the civil war and its aftermath in rural Spain. Baah notes that in *The Yellow Rain*, 'the mimetic base rests on collective and communal histories, the history of Spain before, during, and after the civil war, and that of rural communities torn apart by the conflict and later abandoned by their inhabitants'.[19] For Baah, the dichotomised before and after of the text therefore imply that 'the present experiences of loneliness, silence, madness, and hunger contrast dramatically with those of community, companionship, and saneness that marked the protagonist's life prior to the civil war'.[20] Llera also calls attention to the historical basis of the novel, noting that 'estamos frente a una novela política, que no oculta las causas del abandono que padecen el protagonista y su entorno' ['we are in the presence of a political novel, which does not hide the causes of abandonment that the protagonist and his surroundings suffer'][21] and, likewise, Olivares Merino asserts that 'Llamazares se enfrenta a los fantasmas de la Guerra Civil y la Dictadura españolas' ['Llamazares confronts the ghosts of the Spanish civil war and dictatorship'].[22] These ghosts of the past, appearing as memories in sepia tone, inevitably return as markers of individual and collective trauma for which the only cure, according to Andrés, seems to be oblivion.

Although the socio-political situation of twentieth-century Spain is rarely mentioned explicitly in the novel, Llamazares gives us enough clues with which to draw our attention to the continuing role of silence in the post-war Spanish community. In various flashbacks, Andrés explains that everyone left the town when the civil war began; for the narrator, the most difficult of these departures is that of his son, Camilo, who left to fight in the war and never returned. Andrés and Sabina never receive an official death notice, so their son is considered missing. As Andrés tells us: 'Only his shadow returned to the house and melted in among the other shadows in the rooms, while his body rotted in a mass grave in some village in Spain and in the frozen memory of the troop train that left one morning from Huesca station never to return' (p. 45). This absence is traumatic for Andrés, who explains that unlike the finality of death, '[d]isappearance, however, has no limits; it is the contrary of a fixed state' (p. 44). The uncertainty surrounding Camilo's disappearance and presumed death is made more painful precisely because of the regime-mandated silence that sweeps through the countryside in the aftermath of the war.

Silence is often a natural expression of fear derived from one's surroundings; in Llamazares's novel, the landscape is an extension of the atmosphere of post-war Spain. As Franco's troops made their way through the rural villages removing outspoken and rumoured enemies of the regime from their homes (often in the cover of darkness), silence became the civilians' mechanism to combat the terror of being discovered and potentially tortured or killed. Pere Ysàs explains: 'Además de llevar a los cementerios, a las cárceles y al exilio a centenares de miles de españoles, inoculó el miedo a millones, asegurando así el silencio y la pasividad política de buena parte de la sociedad, especialmente durante el primer *ventennio franquista*' ['Aside from taking hundreds of thousands of Spaniards to the cemeteries, jails and exile, they injected fear in millions, thus assuring the silence and the political passivity of a good part of society, especially during the first twenty years of Francoism'].[23] Montse Armengou and Ricard Belis, award-winning journalists and documentary film-makers who have chronicled the process of exhuming mass graves in contemporary Spain, note that silence and fear continue to be an undercurrent among older, rural citizens in particular: 'Sin embargo, el miedo hace que en la zona todavía haya un silencio que a menudo es impenetrable; los pocos que hablan lo hacen en voz baja y volviendo la cabeza para ver quién escucha' ['However, fear has made it so that in the zone there is still a silence that is often impenetrable; the few who speak do so in a quiet voice and turning their head to see who is listening'].[24] Likewise, Francisco Ferrándiz has explained that '[t]he screen of silence, fear and self-censorship has been particularly strong in local, rural contexts'.[25] Andrés, a literary representation of these rural village dwellers, has quite clearly internalised this silence. Within Llamazares's Gothic atmosphere of fear and anxiety, the narrator understands silence as being necessary to his survival but also, paradoxically, as a terror-inducing catalyst of madness. Richards explains that in post-war Spain, the 'Civil War could only be integrated into the normal narrative of memory under the pressure of profoundly changing circumstances, extreme exploitation, provisionality and fear, invented identities and a dictatorial political system. Inevitably, in effect, this meant "forgetting".'[26] Thus, for Andrés, the 'yellow rain of oblivion' takes on new meaning as a coping mechanism to remove himself from the cyclical trauma of memory.

The narrator's desire to forget the past, however, is made impossible by the saturation of death around him. Living in a metaphorical cemetery, Andrés is continually and inevitably confronted with the ghosts of the departed, which unearth his own long-buried memories and the pain associated with them. After his wife commits suicide, Andrés can no longer look at her photographs because her eyes seem to stare back at him like a phantom. Suddenly perceiving her presence in the house, which feels 'frozen, heavy with menace' (p. 27), he quickly gathers all her possessions and photographs in a trunk that he buries outside. For Andrés, memory is traumatising, and thus silence through forgetting (in this case, through the burial of Sabina's possessions) is preferable. What Andrés does not seem to realise is that burying his wife's mementos is not enough to keep the ghosts at bay. Indeed, as Emma Liggins has asserted in her chapter on Edith Wharton's ghost stories, 'Silence and nostalgic slowness encourage the production of ghosts.'[27] Just like in real post-war Spain, where state-mandated silence developed parallel to the burial of bodies (and memory) in mass graves, in Ainielle silence and memory are also inextricably linked as fertile grounds for the resurrection of the ghosts of the past. These lingering presences are difficult to contain and impossible to ignore; as Andrés admits, 'it is hard to accustom oneself to living with a ghost' (p. 44). Sabina's death is a pivotal moment for the narrator because he is suddenly the sole human inhabitant of his village. As Andrés is left alone among the dead, the accumulating spectres of his departed family members distort his present reality by forcing him to live in the past: Camilo's ghost returns to the family home as an agonising reminder of his eternal absence and Sara, Andrés's daughter who died at age four, is an unexpected ghost whose tortured last breaths are an audible, spectral presence imbued with the pain of loss. When his mother eventually returns as a semi-permanent ghostly figure in the kitchen, Andrés refuses to interact with her, instead deciding to maintain the tomblike quiet of the house: 'I sat in silence . . . After all those years, after all that time separated by death . . . we dared not resume a conversation that had been suddenly interrupted a long time ago. I did not even dare look at her' (p. 76). By acknowledging the ghosts, Andrés will open the door to memory and break the silence that reigns in the house and village. When he is awoken one night by a strange murmuring sound only to discover that all the family's dead have gathered in the kitchen, he immediately runs out of the house, terrified:

> For a few seconds, I stood there, paralyzed. During those seconds – interminable seconds made longer by the wind rattling the windows and doors of the houses – I thought my heart was going to burst . . . I had just left behind me the cold of death, death's gaze, and now, though how I didn't know, I found myself once more face to face with death . . . Terrified, I started running down the middle of the street, with no idea where I was going. (pp. 78–9)

Andrés is suddenly petrified by the thought that every kitchen in the decaying village is host to the dead. Instead of returning to his house, he spends the night outside in the howling wind and stinging nettles. When faced with his own ghosts, Andrés prefers the solitude of the inhospitable landscape around him, which encourages silence and forgetting.

The narrator's fear of facing these spectres is heightened by an increasing fear of madness, which Llamazares mentions throughout the text as his protagonist's principal source of terror and anxiety. The 'endless nightmare' (p. 17) of death and decay in which Andrés lives becomes a catalyst for psychosis; when he first sees Sabina's ghostly eyes gazing at him from her photographs, he worries that the 'fear of madness and of insomnia was beginning to take hold of me' (p. 26). The repeated phrase 'fear of madness' becomes yet another spectral presence in Llamazares's text, punctuating moments of silence with the profound terror of mental degeneration. Thus, Andrés asserts that building 'a thick wall of forgetting around my memories' is the only way he will be able to survive and to avoid going mad (p. 31). Much like the historical 1977 Pact of Forgetting, Andrés's decision to relegate memory to the past through forced silence and lack of acknowledgement of trauma has a deleterious effect: as the ghosts inevitably materialise, the cognitive and emotional dissonance associated with their return forces Andrés to reconcile with his traumatic memories. Thus Andrés, a 'tótem herido de muerte en medio de la ruina y de tejados vencidos' ['hurt totem of death in the middle of ruin and of defeated roofs'],[28] grapples with the ghosts of his family and town just as death itself comes to remove him from his liminal place in Ainielle. According to Olivares Merino, the spectral presences in the text are, for Andrés, 'motor esencial en su pretensión de reconstituir la identidad – a las puertas del deceso – a través del reencuentro con el pasado y la fabulación sobre el futuro' ['an essential driving force in his ambition to reconstruct identity – at the doors of death – through his reencounter with the past and fabulation about the future'].[29] In this sense, spectrality is, itself, a defining feature of Andrés's identity due to his intimate relationship with his town and community, which continue to exist as long as the narrator is alive to remember them.

Fear of remembering thus becomes, by the end of the novel, fear of being forgotten. Memory – a constant source of anxiety for Andrés – is also the sole means through which his town is kept alive. After Sabina dies, the narrator considers memory to be his 'only landscape' (p. 31) and, as memory and time converge, he notes that 'everything else – the house, the village, the sky, the mountains – had ceased to exist, except as a distant memory of itself' (p. 32). This photographic perspective of the ghostly landscape around him is what helps, initially, to distance Andrés from his memories of the past, which he considers to be reflections distorted by nostalgia. However, his growing unease and fear of madness in the face of the ghosts who now visibly populate his town lead him reluctantly through a process of remembering, which Llamazares portrays as mourning. Timothy Baker, in his book *Contemporary Scottish Gothic: Mourning, Authenticity, and Tradition*, examines mourning as a fundamental motif in Gothic fiction, where a chief preoccupation with death and its relationship with identity invites the portrayal of mourning as both an individual and collective experience. As such, Baker asserts: 'In its resistance to narratives of progress, and its insistence on the power of the past to continually haunt and shape present actions, Gothic provides a form, and a forming, that draw readers' attention to the ambiguities and borders of individual and cultural experience.'[30] Andrés's own imminent death is played out in the narrative as a series of out-of-sequence flashbacks that gradually destroy the walls he has constructed around his memory and begin the process of reconciliation through the act of mourning, which

Baker considers death's sole point of access: 'death cannot be known as itself, but is only revealed through mourning. Mourning provides an "image" of death that death itself cannot provide.'[31] Therefore, as Andrés's ghostly encounters increase in number and frequency, forcing him to remember the deceased and to come to terms with his grief and the silence of loss, he simultaneously experiences death in a vivid and much more personal way. As a living representation of memory in corporeal form, Andrés embodies the former life of the town and community in which he was raised; his inextricable connection with the spectral past allows him to come to know death first through fear, and finally through mourning.

As an effective archive of memory for his town, Andrés represents the experience of not just Ainielle, but the entirety of rural Spain in the post-war era. The isolation, loss and absence that Llamazares depicts in his novel are characteristic of much of the twentieth-century Spanish experience outside the urban centres and are invariably rooted in the Great Trauma that was a direct result of the war and Franco's policies during the first two decades of his dictatorship. Baker notes that mourning can also have national implications, especially when in the form of shared rituals that unite a group through the representation of trauma: 'mourning rituals can codify particular aspects of national identity, both uniting the past and present and illustrating the way in which the nation has overcome previous hardships or disasters'.[32] While Andrés's mourning does imply a collective experience greater than just himself or his town, Llamazares also makes it quite clear that this process will not have a typical resolution (if it has any). During his last moments, Andrés repeatedly tells us that he has been forgotten by everyone and that his only wish was 'to be remembered by the one person who can do to me what I did this morning to the dog' (p. 125) – namely, to help him into death to eliminate his suffering. When we realise that Andrés will, in fact, die alone before the group of men can reach him, we must conclude that this wish was unfulfilled. Because Andrés's trauma is ongoing and the only resolution to the narrative is the implied extinction of the town and of memory, mourning – and reconciliation – on a national scale therefore appear impossible; if no one is left to remember the dead, then their very existence becomes part of the sepia-tone landscape of the past. Tseng notes that '[e]l destino del protagonista es un destino compartido por multitud de personas que se ven obligadas a abandonar su tierra, excepto que este protagonista resiste hasta el final de su vida' ['the protagonist's destiny is a destiny shared by a multitude of people who see themselves obliged to abandon their land, except that this protagonist resists until the end of his life'].[33] Andrés's refusal to leave Ainielle is paradoxically both an act of self-preservation and the catalyst for his death. With no one left to remember him – no one to mourn him – silence dominates once more and, as the last line of the novel tells us, '[t]he night returns to its rightful owner' (p. 130).

Llamazares's Gothic 'landscape of memory' is, consequently, a rendering of individual and collective experience in rural twentieth-century Spain. Within the harsh, unforgiving setting of the rural north, Andrés seems resigned to live his last days alone and in fear. The shadows of people and moments from his past – while perhaps in some ways a cathartic experience – remind him of the inevitable silence of loss, which becomes both his burden and his fate. Memory, a ghost he attempts to avoid for his own survival and sanity, permeates the countryside around him, ultimately making its way into his house and his mind. Jeffrey Weinstock has explained that '[t]o be spectral is to be ghostlike, which, in turn, is to be out of place and time'.[34] In *The Yellow Rain*, time and memory are part of the fabric of the rural landscape, which is envisioned as a liminal, spectral space that exists only as long as Andrés is alive to remember it. Llamazares introduces the notion of collective trauma through its manifestation in sepulchral silence; while memory remains buried, silence (and, therefore, trauma) continues to control the rural landscape.

In this manner, Llamazares's novel points to the importance of exhumation, both of physical bodies as well as historical truths. Llera asserts that the text 'puede interpretarse también como una inmersión en las aguas de una memoria silenciada y maldita, la de los vencidos, como la necesidad de revelar todo lo que ha sido sepultado, reprimido o tachado' ['can also be interpreted as an immersion into the waters of a silenced and cursed memory, that of the defeated, as the need to reveal everything that has been buried, repressed or crossed out'].[35] Ainielle thus represents the countless ghost towns across Spain that continue to bear witness to the Great Trauma of the twentieth century. For these towns, the 'silence of loss' implies a loss of lives (in some cases, like that of Camilo, permanently disappeared in mass graves that dot the Spanish countryside) and a loss of voices, rooted in the initial fear of speaking out that became, after Franco's death, a mandated pact to forget. It is important to note that at the time the novel was published in 1988, the mass graves of the civil war remained untouched; it would not be until late 2000 that the first would be exhumed in Llamazares's home province of León. The fear that his Gothic setting provokes in the narrator replicates the Spanish citizens' experience in this historical atmosphere and, ultimately, implies that healing is impossible in an environment in which trauma (here, the forced repression of memory) is ongoing.

7

Unspeakable Truths: Silence, Spectrality and the Artefacts of Memory in Cristina Fernández Cubas's The Swing

෴

Cristina Fernández Cubas, born in Arenys de Mar (Barcelona) in 1945, is one of contemporary Spain's most celebrated authors. Best known for her short stories, which have won numerous literary awards including the National Prize for Narrative in 2016, Fernández Cubas is also a novelist, playwright and essayist. She has named Edgar Allan Poe's stories as highly influential to her work,[1] and Katherine Glenn and Janet Pérez have both commented on the Gothic quality of much of her literature, particularly in the recurrence of doubles, locked spaces and the unspeakable.[2] Fernández Cubas has explained that her early childhood home influenced her love of attics and closed spaces, describing them as 'baúles de recuerdos que me han atraído siempre' ['storehouses of memories that have always attracted me'].[3] She has nonetheless asserted that she has 'deliberately avoided the autobiographical' in her literary works,[4] and she does not consider herself a feminist author. Instead, she has said that she chooses to focus on what she characterises as the 'zona de límites imprecisos' ['zone of imprecise limits'],[5] a quality of liminality that defines her work. Jessica Folkart places Fernández Cubas in the 'generation of '68': the group of Spanish authors born in the immediate post-civil war era for whom the European protests of 1968 were highly influential. She asserts that Fernández Cubas's literary works 'emerge from the context of contemporary Spanish culture and interrogate the issues that inform and define that culture'.[6] For Glenn and Pérez, 'Cristina Fernández Cubas is, without question, one of the most important of the Spanish writers who have begun to publish since the end of the Franco dictatorship'.[7] Despite her critical acclaim in Spain and around the world, very few of Fernández Cubas's works have been translated into English, leaving her relatively unknown to scholars outside of literary Hispanism and almost entirely unknown among international Gothic scholars.

El columpio [hereafter translated as *The Swing*], published in 1995, is Fernández Cubas's second of three novels and embodies what Glenn has called the author's 'often disturbing fictive world which is rich in fantastic and Gothic elements'.[8] Narrator Eloísa, twenty-five, is mourning the loss of her mother (also named Eloísa) who died seven years earlier and whose mythologised tales about her childhood make her daughter long to meet the characters of her mother's former life. The narrator decides to make a visit to the small town where her mother's brothers and cousin still live in their childhood home: a house with a tower overlooking the countryside and village below. The men are very quiet and brooding, and during her week-long stay Eloísa discovers a secret drawer in the armoire of her mother's old bedroom where her uncles have placed all of her mother's letters to them over the years, read and re-sealed as if they had never been read to begin with. After hearing what seems to be the spectral voice of a little girl, Eloísa is increasingly anxious and fearful in the house and, disappointed that her experience has not been what she had expected, she tells her uncles that she will be leaving in two days. The following morning, the men gather all her belongings and take her to the train station without warning, but she tells them she does not have her passport and lets them know that she is aware of the secret drawer. After taking her back to the house, uncle Tomás enters her room and gives her a drink, which he watches her sip and then, after leaving, continues to spy on her through the keyhole of the door. Convinced that it is drugged, Eloísa vomits the liquid into the bathroom sink, then takes her belongings and sneaks outside. She watches her uncles through the dining room window as they seem to enact a kind of theatrical performance at the dinner table, pretending that their sister – as a little girl – is there with them, which convinces Eloísa that the men are insane. She then turns and feels something hit her chest: it is a diabolo, and she sees her mother as a young girl in front of her, like a ghostly apparition. She suddenly feels a cord around her neck – the string of the diabolo – and she begs her mother for help. The girl looks terrified and releases the cord, and Eloísa runs to the inn, where she spends the night. In the morning she discovers that her uncles have dropped off her suitcase and a letter, along with a check for the money that her mother would have inherited from the estate. She rips it all up, then continues her trip on the train back to France, concluding that her mother's childhood seemed more a nightmare than a pleasant dream.

Cristina Fernández Cubas has been a frequent subject of study among literary scholars, who tend to focus on her short stories rather than her longer works. Xavier Aldana Reyes considers her story collections within the panorama of contemporary Spanish Gothic narrative, stating that she 'began to update the Gothic tradition for a modern audience, focusing on warped psychologies and unreliable narrators . . . deconstructive narratives . . . and the double'.[9] Pérez has read *The Swing* as an example of the Spanish female neo-Gothic, describing the narrative as 'an allegory of growing up under Franco – and the insurmountable barriers to realizing oneself as a woman then'.[10] Similarly, Folkart studies the novel as 'a re-interpretation of the Francoist depiction of the historical Spanish subject',[11] noting the swing as a metaphor for the ever-present shifting between past and present in the text. John Margenot interprets the swing as a 'metaphor for the narrator's (in)ability to distinguish between reality and appearances', underscoring the important role of metafiction in the novel,[12] and Catherine Bellver examines what she considers 'overt references' to theatricality in *The Swing*,[13] noting the uncles' behaviours within the home as part of a larger role-playing game in which they act out an elaborate continuation of the past. Silvia Bermúdez and Akiko Tsuchiya both take a psychoanalytic approach to the novel, emphasising the absent mother as a fundamental destabilising factor in the narrator's experience of self.[14] As we have seen with much of Spanish nonmimetic literary criticism, when the supernatural is the subject of study it is almost always from the perspective of the fantastic. Among the scholars who have studied *The Swing*, only Pérez and Glenn have considered it through a Gothic lens, focusing on its primary neo-Gothic characteristics and the use of doubles, respectively.

The present chapter seeks to illuminate the role of Gothic silence in *The Swing* through an examination of its relationship with the artefacts of memory, mourning and haunting in the text. The secluded tower house becomes an archive in which letters, photographs and portraits give the past a living, tangible presence, allowing Eloísa to re-create and adopt her mother's memories as her own in a process similar to Alison Landsberg's theory of prosthetic memory. The Freudian concept of melancholia will inform my reading of the uncles' insistence on avoiding the creation of new memories that acknowledge loss – a forced continuation of the past through denial of the present that leads to ghostly apparitions of the protagonist's mother and fear associated with reliving traumatic loss. Fernández Cubas's Gothic narrative encourages madness, duplicity and irreality, and highlights the tensions between the traditional past and the modern present, bringing to light the problematic silencing of memory that defined the Spanish experience in the immediate post-Franco era.

As with all Gothic narratives, the setting of Fernández Cubas's novel is key to establishing the feelings of anxiety and foreboding that underscore the text. Eloísa has grown up listening to her mother's stories of her childhood in 'un valle perdido al otro lado de los Pirineos' ['a lost valley at the other side of the Pyrenees'].[15] The large house with a tower that overlooks the small town below is the natural focal point of the villagers and also of the reader: Fernández Cubas directs our attention toward the house from the beginning of the novel, when Eloísa tells us that she situates the Tower House 'fuera del tiempo' ['outside of time'] (p. 14), rendering it an already liminal space in the text. Inside, the house is always dark and hazy, making it difficult for the narrator to distinguish details and faces. As her uncles' odd behaviour accentuates the strange atmosphere around her, Eloísa considers the maid's lack of reaction to the activities in the house as a commentary on its otherworldliness, remarking that it is 'como si nada de lo que ocurriera en la casa pudiera sorprenderla' ['as if nothing that occurred in the house could surprise her'] (p. 63). Throughout her time in the Tower House, Eloísa repeatedly notes the darkness as a principal source of her unease, at one point leading her to purchase and install better lightbulbs, which her uncles promptly replace with dim ones. The pervasive darkness combines with locked rooms, secret drawers and eerie silences to create a truly Gothic space that obfuscates reality and heightens anxiety, prompting Eloísa to suddenly feel 'una auténtica urgencia por abandonar la casa' ['a real urgency to leave the house'] (p. 76). As her unease inside the house grows, she begins to spend more time in town, seeking the comfort of what little modernity it has to offer.

The urban-rural divide in *The Swing* is a primary motif that Fernández Cubas employs to emphasise the liminality of the Tower House and the town it inhabits. Folkart sees this divide as evidence of the author's commentary that 'Spain embodies an uneven postmodernity full of contradictions, with the rejected reality of the past still penetrating the hyperreality of the present'.[16] In further demonstration of the rural resistance to modernity, Eloísa's uncles live in the Tower House as landowners of the surrounding countryside, which they rent to the local townspeople in a seeming continuation of the feudal past, 'como si nada hubiera ocurrido, como si el mundo pudiera detenerse con sólo que alguien . . . olvidara la existencia del reloj' ['as if nothing had happened, as if the world could stop if someone just . . . forgot the existence of the clock'] (p. 39). The sensation of shifting between past and present is symbolised in the title, *The Swing*, which also necessarily evokes images of a nostalgic past embodied in a childhood object of play. Moreover, the very notion of an adult narrator from the city reflecting on a childhood (in this case, her mother's) in the country directly parallels the real lived experience of countless Spaniards in the late twentieth century, many of whom moved to urban centres in search of better opportunities after having spent most of their childhood in rural towns (like both Fernández Cubas and Julio Llamazares). One could infer, then, that the rural countryside is an inherently nostalgic space for many contemporary Spaniards and, if time is non-existent in memory, then Fernández Cubas's isolated town does, indeed, exist – as Eloísa tells us – in 'una zona indefinable, fuera del espacio y del tiempo' ['an indefinable zone, outside of space and of time'] (p. 124). The description of the town serves to mark the space as partly inconsistent with this nostalgic past, with its housing developments that are '[e]spantosamente iguales' ['frightfully similar'] (p. 19) and its shop signs that advertise Parisian fashions in what appears to be a desperate attempt to attract and retain tourists and inhabitants alike. A young store clerk confides in Eloísa that the town bores her and that almost everyone there is 'viejos y niños' ['elderly and children'] (p. 82), implying the exodus of young working people to the larger cities outside the remote valley. The modernity of the downtown is thus a façade – a futile attempt to bring the rural space into a present that is incongruent with the memory landscape in which it exists.

Within this rural environment, Eloísa experiences time in a series of repetitive acts bolstered by her uncles' strict daily routines. Their insistence on maintaining a regimented schedule (with Friday as the culmination of the week's events) means that each new week is essentially a copy of the previous one; time, in effect, does stand still in the Tower House, precisely because its inhabitants refuse to let it progress. The text is full of these repetitions, both in actions (the maids' cleaning routine, the dinners with the same aperitif, the conversation topics, Raquel's shout of 'Recuerdos' ['Regards']) and in language, noted especially in Tomás's tic-like 'Bien, bien, bien' ['Good, good, good'] and Eloísa's use of the phrase 'como si' ['as if'], which according to Tsuchiya 'imbues her entire experience with a sense of irreality, of otherworldliness'.[17] The cyclical timeline produced by these repetitions becomes the perfect host to Eloísa's re-creation of her mother's past; therefore, as she first approaches the house, the narrator sees it getting 'cada vez más grande, o quizás era yo quien, intentando revivir otras infancias, iba haciéndome más y más pequeña' ['bigger and bigger, or perhaps it was I who, attempting to relive other childhoods, was becoming smaller and smaller'] (p. 21). Eloísa's entrance into the town marks her simultaneous entrance into her mother's childhood, which she converts into her own series of memories that she experiences in this liminal space between the past and present.

Eloísa's intention to re-create her mother's memories and adopt them as her own is remarkably similar to Alison Landsberg's theory of prosthetic memory, which considers the interaction with various forms of media as a catalyst for the creation of memories that help with the expression and understanding of subjectivity, despite the foundational experiences being remote to the subject itself. Landsberg explains that prosthetic memory

> emerges at the interface between a person and a historical narrative about the past, at an experiential site such as a movie theater or museum. In this moment of contact, an experience occurs through which the person sutures himself or herself into a larger history . . . In the process that I am describing, the person does not simply apprehend a historical narrative but takes on a more personal, deeply felt memory of a past event through which he or she did not live. The resulting prosthetic memory has the ability to shape that person's subjectivity and politics.[18]

For Landsberg, memory 'has always been about negotiating a relationship to the past';[19] this negotiation is crucial to Eloísa's understanding of herself in relation to her mother's childhood, and it is the focal point of Fernández Cubas's text. Although the protagonist does not enter an actual theatre or museum for a multimedia exhibition, Fernández Cubas mimics this sensorial experience in her portrayal of the Tower House as a living museum in which theatricality and collected objects combine to alter Eloísa's perception of time and reality in such a way that she becomes an active participant in the memories of the past.

Eloísa's process of acquiring prosthetic memory begins on her train ride to her uncles' town, when she looks through the 'fotografías antiguas, macilentas' ['ancient, worn photographs'] of her mother playing with the diabolo, and her uncles playing games outside and pushing their sister on the swing (p. 14). Eloísa brings these photos with her on the train as a way to invoke her mother, telling us that with them 'parecía como si mi madre estuviera aún allí, a mi lado, señalando con el dedo, relatando anécdotas' ['it seemed as if my mother were still there, at my side, pointing with her finger, telling anecdotes'] (p. 16). When she first sees the tower on the skyline, the narrator immediately recalls the games her mother and uncles used to play there, remembering one particular episode in which cousin Bebo gave her mother a kiss on the cheek (p. 21).

Later, sitting on her mother's old swing, Eloísa notes that suddenly 'fue como si reviviera una de las fotografías de mi madre' ['it was as if I relived one of my mother's photographs'] (p. 43). When her initial introduction to the Tower House and her uncles is not what she had expected, Eloísa even imagines what her mother might have said to her at one time that could have explained or foreshadowed what she would encounter there, indicating a clear need to base her own subjectivity on the logic of an unlived past experience – a condition that Bermúdez considers emblematic of Eloísa's 'undifferentiated self'.[20] This conjuring of memories is repeated throughout the narrative, always in conjunction with physical spaces and objects in the house that assist in re-creating the sensorial experience of Eloísa senior's childhood.

When Eloísa first enters her mother's bedroom, she recalls the stories about secret drawers in the furniture and she easily discovers one in the desk, where she finds all her mother's letters to her uncles throughout their life in Paris. These letters initially promise to facilitate the acquisition of prosthetic memory, as Eloísa sees them as giving her 'la oportunidad de pasar un rato en su compañía, de escucharla' ['the opportunity to spend a while in her company, to listen to her'] (p. 54). Margenot sees the treatment of letters in the novel as evidence that Eloísa 'not only acknowledges the power of the written word in *El columpio* but also understands that oral discourse can transport characters to other illusory, if not oneiric, worlds',[21] in this case, acting as a point of access to memory. However, when she realises that they have not been opened, her understanding of her uncles – and, more importantly, their treatment of her mother's memory – is ruptured. Until this moment, Eloísa has built her own sense of self with the words of her mother's recollections of the past; story telling – both in written and oral form – is pivotal to the narrator's subjectivity, as she takes on her mother's memories and relives them as her own. The sudden realisation that these newer memories, documented in the letters, have been censored is overwhelming. Eloísa laments the 'indiferencia, el desprecio' ['indifference, scorn'] with which her mother's letters have been treated, noting that it is 'como si no existieran. Como si jamás hubieran sido recibidos. Como si Eloísa, en fin, al abandonar el valle, hubiera arrastrado una condena para el resto de su vida' ['as if they didn't exist. As if they had never been received. As if Eloísa, in short, upon leaving the valley, had born a punishment for the rest of her life'] (p. 55). As the narrator looks at her mother's signature at the bottom of the letters, she notices that her name is written with peculiar swirls that mimic the diabolo's string, and she realises that this is Eloísa senior's way of assuring her brothers that '[n]ada ha cambiado. Para vosotros ni siquiera he crecido. Sigo siendo la de siempre. Eloísa. Vuestra Eloísa' ['nothing has changed. For you I haven't even grown. I am still the same as always. Eloísa. Your Eloísa'] (p. 56). Nonetheless, the discovery of the letters hidden in a secret drawer, out of sight and mind, is a clear indication that the men cannot accept the new memories of an adult Eloísa, despite these reassurances. When the narrator finds that the letters have, in fact, been opened and then resealed (proving that her uncles had indeed read them), she concludes that they have done this as a rejection of the reality of the present in order to continue living in the past, 'como si mi madre no hubiera muerto nunca' ['as if my mother had never died'] (p. 60). As Folkart explains, '[l]etters epitomize the effect that the passage of time and an altered perspective have on the interpretation of a message or an event, by their nature as texts that are written in one moment and then read, at a point later in time, by someone different'.[22] Letters inherently represent the relationship between memory and time, and are an undeniable proof of a linear progression in the past. Given that the men have based their adult lives on cyclical time with its predictable repetitions, the disruption posed by the letters is incongruent with the altered sense of reality in the Tower House and, therefore, the men cast them aside in wilful disregard of their existence.

Due to their treatment as artefacts of memory and, thus, objects to be denied access to the present, these letters, along with other items in the house, become part of a museum-like collection that inevitably invokes the past in spectral form. In addition to the letters, the primary object that connects both Eloísas is a portrait of the mother as a young girl with a diabolo, painted by Bebo and permanently on display in the dining room. It is no coincidence that the men seat their niece directly in front of the painting of her mother at dinner time; Eloísa, the daughter, suddenly becomes the corporeal representation – the double – of Eloísa, the mother, who has until now existed in the house only as a ghostly continuation of the past. As the men toast their guest with the words 'Por nosotros' ['To us'], Eloísa notices that their words do not actually include her, but rather her mother, who 'nos observaba a todos desde su posición inmóvil sobre la consola' ['observed us all from her unmoving position on the side table'] (p. 38). This scene is evidence of the profound psychological disruption that the protagonist's visit causes her uncles: with their sister's child sitting at the table, the image of the young girl they vividly remember (envisioned in the portrait behind their niece) is jarringly out of place. Young Eloísa cannot continue to exist in the same temporal space as her 25-year-old daughter; the narrator is yet another reminder of the linear progression of time that does not exist for the men in the Tower House.

This haunting presence of the past is a repeated notion throughout the text, with the voice of Eloísa senior acting as protagonist for much her daughter's narrative. The peculiar curation of time and memory in the Tower House lends all its inhabitants an eerie, spectral quality from the beginning, when Eloísa first tells us that Bebo looks like 'un espíritu' ['a spirit'] (p. 25). Outside in the garden, when the narrator sits on her mother's swing, Eloísa has her first encounter with a ghost, which manifests itself in the audible presence of an angry little girl's voice, tauntingly yelling that she will marry a French man and never return. This spectral presence, accompanied by the sudden blocking of the sun and a violent wind, does not remind Eloísa of her mother's fairy-tale recollections of her childhood, but rather 'el grito de una niña malcriada, caprichosa, tiránica' ['the shout of an ill-mannered, capricious, tyrannical little girl'] (p. 44). Here, the embodiment of the past in spectral form does not reflect the nostalgia-tinged stories Eloísa has been told and, because of her need to understand herself through her mother's memories, Eloísa interprets this angry voice as a sign of 'oculto resentimiento' ['hidden resentment'] (p. 47) that she must unknowingly harbour against her mother. If her mother's childhood was truly as happy as she always portrayed it, then Eloísa must assume responsibility for its negative re-enactment in the present.

Eloísa hears the little girl's ghostly voice again at the end of the novel, in a pivotal scene that explains her uncles' behaviour and her own experiences in the house as directly related to madness caused by melancholia. After she sneaks outside on Friday evening in an attempt to escape the house, she watches her uncles through the dining room window as they laugh and converse over dinner. The strange effect produced by their voices is unlike anything she has ever heard, and it appears that they are acting as ventriloquists, speaking in each other's voices in a bizarre theatrical (re)production of their daily lives. For Bellver, this scene demonstrates that the men view their life as 'a game, an escape from reality, an enactment of desire' in which the game itself 'is a play – a simulacrum of life, an analogous representation, a mimetic repetition of a single scene'.[23] By reliving the past through these weekly charades, Eloísa's uncles repress their own maturity and extend their childhood in an endless series of repetitions that deny their access to the present. As Eloísa watches the spectacle before her, she suddenly hears a 'voz impostada, falsa, una pretendida voz de niña que jamás podría haber pertenecido a niña alguna en el mundo' ['projected, false voice, a little girl's voice that could never have belonged to any little girl in the world'] (p. 118). Through the windowpane, Eloísa listens to the eerie voice and concludes that her uncles 'estaban rematadamente locos' ['were utterly insane'] (p. 118). Their constant repetitions and repression of the present lead them to believe that young Eloísa is truly there – as if time had not passed at all. Moreover, by including her in their game, they are delightedly continuing their own childhood. What the narrator understands as her mother's spectral presence is, in fact, a corporeal presence for her uncles: 'ellos la creían allí. Ellos la veían. Eloísa, para mis tíos, *estaba* allí. Cada viernes, a las diez de la noche, en el comedor de la Casa de la Torre' ['they believed her to be there. They saw her. Eloísa, for my uncles, *was* there. Every Friday, at ten o'clock at night, in the dining room of the Tower House'] (p. 120).

The men's repression of maturity and denial of the present is best understood through the Freudian concept of melancholia, an extended mourning in which the subject's experience of loss makes them incapable of accepting closure. Melancholia, for Freud, manifests as 'an enduring devotion on the part of the ego to the lost object. A mourning without end, melancholia results from the inability to resolve the grief and ambivalence precipitated by the loss of the loved object, place, or ideal.'[24] Given its intimate connection to the past, Eng and Kazanjian note that melancholia is imbued with spectral potentiality: 'By engaging in "countless separate struggles" with loss, melancholia might be said to constitute, as Benjamin would describe it, an ongoing and open relationship with the past – bringing its ghosts and specters, its flaring and fleeting images, into the present.'[25] For Eloísa's uncles, the acknowledgement of her mother's death would mean the permanent end to their childhood, which they prefer to prolong indefinitely in a purposeful rejection of the traumatic reality of loss. In this case, their devotion to the memory of their love object – their sister, young Eloísa – prevents them from resolving their grief, which began not when they received word of her death (through a letter written by their niece), but much earlier, when 'their' Eloísa left permanently for France upon marrying her husband. This initial loss caused by separation becomes a profound loss through death, and the Tower House is thereby transformed into a spectral museum of memory, dominated by the melancholic psychosis of its inhabitants.

This Gothic spiral into madness culminates at the end of the dinner spectacle, when Eloísa herself finally sees the ghostly apparition of her young mother standing in the garden. Suddenly, she feels 'la sensación de asfixia, de que los ojos se me salían de las órbitas, de que estaba perdiendo el conocimiento' ['the sensation of asphyxiation, of my eyes leaving their sockets, of losing consciousness'], at which point 'todo, al instante, se convirtió en real' ['everything, at once, became real'] (p. 124). She begs for her mother to help her, and the spectre releases the diabolo's cord from Eloísa's neck and stares, aghast, at the image before her: the sight of her own daughter, years in the future, which would later become the foundation of the narrator's own self-concept and the impetus for her trip to the valley. Here again we witness the repetition of the past in the present, as the mother's story becomes reality for the daughter. Tsuchiya relates this moment to the concept of melancholia, explaining:

> The narrator's vision, then, represents a reenactment of her primordial desire to recapture the presence of the Imaginary embodied in the maternal fantasy/phantom. Like the melancholic, whose ego becomes identified with the loved object that has become lost, the narrator has clung, up to this moment, to the phantom of her absent mother.[26]

Although her uncles willingly continue their state of melancholia because of the paradoxical happiness it brings them, Eloísa's experience with her mother's phantom is a horror-inducing break from the cyclical past that has come to define her own subjectivity. Whereas her uncles break the silence of the present with their recreation of the voices of the past (through their ventriloquism that gives young Eloísa a tangible presence in the house), the spectral voice of her mother only produces fear in the narrator, signalling the final rupture of the past from the present and, therefore, the splitting of the mother from the self. Thus, the 'temor inesperado' ['unexpected fear'] (p. 62) that Eloísa feels as she first gathers her mother's letters from their hiding spot in the secret drawer foreshadows the inevitability of her experience in the Tower House as a 'terrible pesadilla' ['terrible nightmare'] (p. 135), contrary to the nostalgic images that her mother repeatedly paints for her in the stories she tells throughout the narrator's childhood and in the very letters that her daughter now holds in her hands.

The final letter of the novel, this time written by the uncles, is yet another instance in which the written word is ultimately censored for the preservation of the self. After reading the letter, in which her uncles express concern for her wellbeing after her quick departure and give her a check for the money her mother would have earned from her portion of the estate, Eloísa destroys both the letter and the check, tearing them to pieces that 'desaparecían revoloteando por la ventanilla . . . como si me desprendiera de otras muchas cartas, de recuerdos ajenos, de un desván con olor a cerrado, de arquillas y baúles, disfraces apolillados y bombillas de quince' ['disappeared fluttering through the window . . . as if I were ridding myself of many other letters, of other people's memories, of an attic with its smell of mustiness, of chests and trunks, moth-eaten costumes and 15-watt lightbulbs'] (p. 133). The metaphorical museum with its artefacts of memory is rendered obsolete as the scraps of paper fly through the train window. Fernández Cubas again repeats the symbolism of the swing in this closing scene when Eloísa recognises that now she is the one 'quien tenía la certeza de haber estado durante aquellos días balanceándome en un columpio, suspendida en el aire, ingrávida sobre un inmenso abismo. Hacia atrás, hacia delante [. . .] De nuevo hacia atrás' ['who had the certainty of having been, during those days, rocking on a swing, suspended in the air, weightless above an immense abyss. Backward, forward [. . .] Backward again'] (p. 134). The liminality of the Tower House and the valley with its nostalgic games and cyclical time has the dizzying effect of a swing on the narrator, who is constantly pushed between past and present, madness and sanity, denial and acceptance. In destroying the final words of her uncles, Eloísa effectuates a rupture with the past that allows her to move forward. This ultimate silencing, then, is the most important part of Eloísa's process of redefining herself, because it positions her subjectivity as independent from nostalgic desire.

Throughout *The Swing*, Fernández Cubas repeatedly brings our attention back to the dichotomous relationships between past and present, urban and rural, creating a Gothic landscape in which the pervasive presence of the unspeakable plays a fundamental role in the determination of the self. By portraying the isolated valley as existing outside the linear confines of time, Fernández Cubas invites a reading of her text as one that problematises the role of memory in the creation of the new national self – an especially relevant concept to a Spanish author writing during the memory boom of the 1990s. In this manner, Eloísa – the young woman from Paris – comes to represent the dual spectres of modernity and linear reality for her uncles, who prefer to censor the progression of time by immersing themselves in the spectral atmosphere of the past, much like the conservative insistence on amnesia through amnesty, which elevated forgetting as a national path toward healing. For Eloísa, however, the horror of seeing (and nearly being killed by) her mother's ghost shocks her into recognising that the prosthetic memories she has adopted during her stay in the Tower House are, in fact, fabrications based on a nostalgic version of the past that never did exist. To this extent, we can understand the narrator as a reflection of the individuals and communities who saw the post-dictatorial transition to democracy as upholding a flawed version of the historical past that was based on the cyclical repetitions of propagandistic nostalgia. As Eloísa's narrative demonstrates, silencing these fabricated memories allows the subject to access the unfiltered past, providing a space for closure and a path toward the formation of a new self-concept that is rooted in the truth.

Part III
Traumatic Memories

Introduction

Sigmund Freud, in *Beyond the Pleasure Principle*, first introduced the notion of the spectral nature of trauma when he said that the 'patient cannot remember the whole of what is repressed in him . . . He is obliged to *repeat* the repressed material as a contemporary experience instead of, as the physician would prefer to see, *remembering* it as something belonging to the past'.[1] These spectral returns – the latency of trauma itself – continue to cycle through the survivor's subconscious until the formerly unspeakable is voiced. Thus, Cathy Caruth characterises the state of being traumatised as being 'possessed by an image or event',[2] and explains that '[w]hat returns to haunt the victim, these stories tell us, is not only the reality of the violent event but also the reality of the way that its violence has not yet been fully known'.[3] Indeed, for Roger Luckhurst, '[g]hosts are the signals of atrocities, marking sites of untold violence, a traumatic past whose traces remain to attest to a lack of testimony',[4] and for María del Pilar Blanco and Esther Peeren, ghosts 'are part of a symptomatology of trauma, as they become both the objects of and metaphors for a wounded historical experience'.[5] Luckhurst also notes the transmissibility of trauma as it is often shared 'between victims and their listeners or viewers who are commonly moved to forms of overwhelming sympathy, even to the extent of claiming secondary victimhood',[6] a stance that echoes other spectral-adjacent theories of inherited trauma such as Nicholas Abraham and Maria Torok's transgenerational phantom and Marianne Hirsch's postmemory.

The Gothic, with its focus on repression and the unspeakable, is inherently intertwined with the concepts of trauma and memory; for these reasons, Steven Bruhm has called the Gothic 'a narrative of trauma'[7], noting in particular the contemporary Gothic's 'compulsive return to certain fixations, obsessions, and blockages'.[8] Likewise, for Ashlee Joyce '[t]he Gothic's emphasis on unspeakable anxieties and the casting off of these anxieties onto abject forms makes it an apt example of Luckhurst's argument that the conventions of genre are a privileged means of articulating the traumatic'.[9] Avril Horner sees inevitable interchanges between Gothic and trauma texts, where 'the Gothic mode feeds off the horror of traumatic situations for plot while trauma narratives are often structured through Gothic effects in order to convey a sense of haunting, of matters unresolved, of the past intruding into the present'.[10] Contemporary Gothic scholarship frequently examines trauma as an integral aspect of the genre's interpretation and portrayal of anxieties within both individual and collective experience.

In Spain, literary narratives often take on an undeniably spectral form as authors in the post-Franco era commonly underscore the latency of twentieth-century trauma in the socio-political anxieties of the present. For many of these authors, the Gothic is the mode that best addresses issues of memory and trauma related to Francoism and its legacy. Whereas in Part II of *Spectral Spain* I examined the effects of silence, forgetting and acts of censorship in Spanish Gothic narratives, in the present section I am interested in what happens when authors and their characters purposefully recall traumatic memories, giving a voice to the lingering ghosts of the past. These authors portray the act of remembering as invariably painful when related to trauma, but also as a necessary step to recovering one's own authorial voice from within an environment that seeks to repress memory.

Part III, 'Traumatic Memories', therefore examines the intersections of spectrality, childhood trauma, and national memory in several more recent texts by Espido Freire, Ana María Matute and Carlos Ruiz Zafón, employing memory and trauma theory to explain the resurgence of past trauma in present life. Childhood fantasy and imagination, which Francisco Ferrándiz has described as 'a toolbox full of powerful metaphors that act as vehicles for early experiences of fear and suffering',[11] will play a prominent role in our discussions of childhood trauma in Freire's *Irlanda* (1998) and Matute's *Uninhabited Paradise* (2008). Ruiz Zafón structures *The Prisoner of Heaven* (2011) as a testimonial text, bearing witness to horror through repeated references to historical figures and events that make use of Gothic excesses to highlight the contrasts between uncensored truths and the official narratives that seek to silence them. In each of these novels there is a sense of an underlying culture of violence and fear that penetrates the atmosphere in which the characters live, distorting the reality around them. For the child protagonists in particular, the spectres of trauma are an inescapable presence that comes to define – and, in some cases, disrupt – their progress toward adulthood. For the adult characters in these novels, haunting is both a palpable sign of trauma and an occasional symptom of disillusionment with life in an era that has inherited the unresolved ghosts of the past. Alison Ribeiro de Menezes, in her study of memory in contemporary Spain, reads trauma texts as a tool for authors 'to explore ways in which the assertion of agency over our pasts might also become the assertion of agency over our futures',[12] highlighting the appeal of these works as texts that recognise the potential to overcome trauma by giving it a voice. For all three of the authors studied in the following chapters, the ability to assert agency in the present is invariably connected to the voicing of trauma and the need to recognise its continued presence in the individual and collective experience. In these texts, the Gothic plays an integral role in the portrayal of trauma and the spectral nature of memory, emphasising darkness and monstrosity as an inevitable result of prolonged oppression and cyclical violence.

8

Violent Childhood: Dark Imagination and the Trauma of Progress in Espido Freire's Irlanda

☙

María Laura Espido Freire (1974–present), known by her pen name Espido Freire, is the youngest of the authors studied in this book and the only one to have grown up entirely in post-Franco Spain, forming part of what Montserrat Linares considers the group of Spanish 'women writers of the 1990s' and its intersection with Generation X.[1] Born in Bilbao (Basque Country), Freire spent her childhood summers in Galicia, where Celtic folklore and her grandmother's tales had a profound influence on the young author.[2] Freire's first novel, *Irlanda*, was published in 1998 when she was just twenty-three years old; the following year, she became the youngest author ever to receive the prestigious Premio Planeta de Novela literary award for her second novel, *Melocotones helados* [*Frozen Peaches*]. Freire has since published numerous adult and young adult novels, story collections, essays and translations, and she also works as a frequent columnist for Spanish newspapers. Her work has received both popular and critical acclaim, making her one of Spain's most well-known currently active writers. Despite Freire's success, however, the only one of her novels to be translated into English is *Irlanda*, leaving her virtually unknown to the English-language literary community.

In *Irlanda* (1998), teenage narrator Natalia relates her experiences on her family's country estate one summer, months after her younger sister, Sagrario, died from a long-term, debilitating illness. Natalia's mother sends her to spend the summer with her cousins, Irlanda and Roberto, with the hope that she will break free from her obsession with Sagrario's death and have the chance to live like a normal teenager. Natalia's first-person narrative is plagued with a series of out-of-sequence flashbacks that haunt the young girl, turning her sister's memory into a ghostly presence that pervades Natalia's mind and prevents her from normal interactions with her cousins and their friends. Through these flashbacks, we learn that Natalia is terrified of animals, and that she killed Sagrario's turtle years earlier (as she will eventually kill Irlanda's cat). Despite her seemingly innate violence, Natalia is extraordinarily ecologically minded, spending years learning about plants and collecting countless samples in her herbarium. Her interactions with the natural world are underscored by her use of superstition and fairy tales as a replacement for the reality around her, and she repeatedly mentions spirits of trees, rivers and other figures from Celtic mythology during her stay at the ancestral country house. As she spends more time with her cousin Irlanda, whose natural charm and beauty contrast sharply with the narrator's antisocial, brooding personality, Natalia becomes increasingly anxious and violent, and she progressively shares more details about Sagrario's death, eventually admitting that she smothered her sister with a pillow (presumably to stop the girl's suffering). Throughout the summer months, Irlanda's initial allure quickly transforms into manipulative and vindictive behaviour, which culminates when she purposefully seduces her friend Gabriel, sensing that her cousin is attracted to him but has no idea how to get his attention. This act is the final blow to Natalia's psyche, and she ends up pushing Irlanda off the crumbling tower to her death below. In the end, Natalia and her youngest sister, Nena, attend Irlanda's private school and Natalia continues to visit her cousin's grave, noting that she is no longer haunted by the ghosts that once dominated her life.

Freire has said that she is most inspired by 'the dark side of being human, the untold, the secret, and the innate need to communicate what I think and what I feel'.[3] Scholars have pointed to her self-professed love of the Brontës, Jane Austen and Edgar Allan Poe as key literary influences,[4] and her frequent themes of familial relationships, death and sexuality[5] within the dark, fairy-tale-like atmospheres that she portrays in her early narratives. Freire's lifelong consumption of folklore has had a clear impact on her writing, and she has explained that she especially relates to 'la versión original de los cuentos de hadas, la cruel, la que habla de las heroínas sacrificadas y de los errores bárbaramente castigados' ['the original version of the fairy tales, the cruel one, the one that talks of sacrificed heroines and of savagely punished errors'] because this 'se correspondía más a mi visión que la princesita rubia y alegre' ['corresponded more with my vision than the blond and happy little princess'].[6] Concha Alborg has studied Freire's works as part of a trend of the demythification of fairy tales seen in the literature of a number of contemporary Spanish women writers, here noting that instead of becoming Cinderella, Natalia rebukes the transformation into princess and adopts the role of witch.[7] Likewise, Mónica Poza Diéguez points to the role of magic and Galician superstition in Freire's works, reading Natalia as 'la druidesa que conoce, ama, colecciona y utiliza las plantas para llevar a cabo sus fines' ['the druidess who knows, loves, collects and utilises plants to carry out her plans'].[8] Myriam del Río Hernández sees Freire and Carmen Martín Gaite as literary successors of Carmen Laforet, noting that their literature 'proposes alternatives to realism through the creation of imaginary spaces that cohabit with reality. Both generate a literary space that works through subversion and the use of the symbolic and semantic potential of real spaces.'[9] Linares also sees the feminist potential of fantasy, asserting that Freire's use of it 'does not convert the female subject into something "unreal" or entirely implausible but rather presents the "self" in a more refined manner, truer to its essence. For Espido Freire, the use of fantasy in her work arises from a conscious awareness, from a feminist revindication.'[10] Maria T. Pao focuses specifically on Natalia's relationship with nature in an ecocritical reading of *Irlanda* that argues that 'the protagonist's moral development is predicated on notions of fairness, care, and other prosocial stances that ensue from her sensitivity to the natural environment',[11] explaining that the young girl views her violence as morally justified because of her intrinsic connection to the natural world. Samuel

Rodríguez Rodríguez, however, views Natalia's violence as stemming from what he considers Freire's obsessive theme of 'personajes femeninos, eternos protagonistas de sus relatos, [que] aparecen marcados por el trauma y la opresión, que les sumerge en un universo de perversión del cual les resulta imposible escapar' ['female characters, eternal protagonists of her tales, [who] appear marked by trauma and oppression, which submerges them in a universe of perversion from which it is impossible for them to escape'].[12] Although this understanding of Natalia's violent acts as a result of trauma is most consistent with my own reading of the novel, the aforementioned studies serve as a point of departure for my consideration of the treatment of the supernatural in Freire's text.

In this chapter, I analyse the ways in which Freire's *Irlanda* uses the psychological Gothic to provide a critical commentary on childhood trauma, class and sexuality in a small rural community in northern Spain. Folk tales and the natural landscape of the north blend with spirits of the dead that haunt the narrator, whose childhood trauma coupled with bullying related to class and gender lead to increasing violence and psychosis. Freire's narrative creates a notable tension between the outward desire for modernity and the inward pressure to conform to tradition, implying that the socio-economic divide and gender norms of Franco's Spain have not been resolved in the post-dictatorial era. I will therefore read *Irlanda* as a Gothic novel in which the portrayal of transgression becomes a commentary on the trauma of progress, understanding the repetitive acts of violence as an inevitable result of the liminal space between progress and stasis in which the narrator finds herself.

Irlanda is yet another example of the common mislabelling of Spanish Gothic texts; despite its clear adherence to Gothic themes and characteristics, scholars have most frequently considered it an example of fairy-tale-like fantasy (which, while true, also ignores the Gothic nature of many of the original fairy tales that Freire herself absorbed as a child). Freire immediately establishes a dark Gothic tone with the beginning lines of her novel, which tell of Sagrario's death and Natalia and Nena's obsessive visits to the cemetery. The opening paragraph also introduces the narrator's love of plants and acute knowledge of their potential poisons, the beginning of a number of striking parallels between *Irlanda* and American author Shirley Jackson's *We Have Always Lived in the Castle* (1962). Like Jackson's novel, Freire's text is also set in an ancestral home on the outskirts of a small town. The house, with its high arches and crumbling tower, is the focal point of the villagers' scorn because of the economic divide it represents. In Jackson's novel – also a first-person narrative – Merricat repeatedly remarks that '[t]he people of the village have always hated us',[13] a sentiment expressed on numerous occasions by Freire's Natalia, who asserts that '[t]he whole village had always hated us' (p. 20) because of the family's ostentatious generational wealth. In both novels, the narrator-protagonists experience reality through a deeply disturbing lens of superstition and death, prompting each of them to kill members of their own family while also clinging to their relationship with the one remaining sister (Merricat's Constance and Natalia's Nena) who encourages their continued child play and obsessions – traits that, in both cases, emphasise the narrators' search for safety through magic. The similarities between these two novels require more elaboration and commentary than what is feasible here, but their common features serve to highlight the undeniable Gothic tone of Freire's work, which follows Jackson's character and plot development in a way that underscores terror, transgression and the profound psychological effects of childhood trauma.

Spanish author Edurne Portela – like Freire, also born in 1974 in the Basque Country – has commented extensively on the 'herencia de violencia adquirida desde la infancia' ['inheritance of violence acquired since infancy'][14] among Basque citizens growing up in the post-Franco era. Portela asserts that 'para la mayoría de la ciudadanía vasca la violencia ha sido ordinaria, omnipresente y por lo tanto normalizada' ['for the majority of Basque citizens violence has been ordinary, omnipresent and therefore normalised'].[15] This violent inheritance has even manifested itself in the cultural upbringing of the post-Franco Basque generation, who 'se educó en la cotidianeidad y la convivencia con la violencia, si no directa, sí por lo menos con el discurso de la violencia: los juegos de niños muchas veces reproducían la violencia de los mayores' ['was educated in the everyday nature and coexistence of violence, if not direct, at least with the discourse of violence: the children's games often reproduced the violence of the adults'].[16] In similar recognition of this reality,

Freire herself has explained that her passion for folklore resulted from her early need to 'insuflar un poco de fantasía en un entorno tan real, tan dominado por la muerte' ['inject a bit of fantasy into an environment so real, so dominated by death'].[17] Although Freire's novel does not explicitly reference political and cultural violence, Natalia suffers from ongoing trauma whose root causes are not entirely explained; if she is, like Portela and Freire, a product of a generation of inherited violence, then her aggressive outbursts may potentially be seen as a reaction to the primary trauma of her sister's death exacerbated by the underlying situational trauma of growing up in a region plagued with violence resulting from decades of systematic cultural oppression and terror.

Regardless of the specific underlying causes of the trauma itself, Freire's text is punctuated with images of death and thoughts of violence that alternatingly haunt and provoke the narrator. Natalia is quick to see signs of darkness in other people and creatures: she tells Irlanda that Gabriel has 'demented eyes' (p. 40) that later seem to have 'the ghostly stare of those who have taken part in dark dances' (p. 63), Irlanda's cat has a 'wicked look' (p. 41), the cow is 'a red horned monster' (p. 86), and Natalia believes that she and Irlanda belong in the tower because it is a liminal space fit for 'demons' (p. 42). Her imagination often turns to violence, frequently wishing death or harm on those who pose a threat to her. Irlanda becomes the primary target of these thoughts, the first of which appears in chapter four when Natalia admits: 'I wished she would die, strangled with one of the ribbons she used to wear in her hair' (p. 44). Gabriel's traumatic past is especially provocative for Natalia, who envisions him 'with a frozen smile on the head he carried under his arm, leaving a trail of blood to alert someone to his death' (p. 70). He and Roberto together trigger Natalia's violent thoughts when she sees them working and thinks that 'they could tear me into pieces, that Roberto could turn and slap me at that moment, and that Gabriel could bash my head with the mallet and nobody could stop him' (p. 56). Freire's first-person narrative serves to underscore these dark thoughts, since we witness these events and images through Natalia's subjective lens, which distorts reality and emphasises darkness and terror.

Río Hernández notes that for Natalia, 'past experiences have their place in the present and are indispensable in the construction of identity'.[18] Natalia's subjectivity is largely based on the ongoing spectral presences that populate her alternate reality. This observation coincides with Cathy Caruth's notion of trauma as 'an overwhelming experience of sudden or catastrophic events in which the response to the event occurs in the often delayed, uncontrolled repetitive appearance of hallucinations and other intrusive phenomena'.[19] Natalia's constant visions of ghosts (most frequently those of Sagrario and her turtle) are thus the natural result of the trauma stemming from the deaths of both characters – family members whom Natalia killed. Problematising this relationship to trauma is the fact that Natalia's own self-concept is structured around death (counter-intuitive to her name, which comes from the Latin word meaning birth), making it impossible to stop her experience of trauma without also separating herself from the powerful bonds she shares with her sister in her after-death state.

Natalia's traumatic past is a spectral presence throughout the entire narrative, which features Sagrario's ghostly image and words (always appearing in italics in the text) that haunt Natalia daily. These 'intrusive phenomena' are especially problematic at night, when the narrator is plagued with repetitive nightmares in which she is 'haunted by the turtle that had tormented me since I was a little girl and by the last image of Sagrario's pale face among the pillows' (p. 10). She claims that '[d]ark spirits were all around me and I couldn't sleep' (p. 13), signs that Rodríguez Rodríguez reads as symptomatic of Natalia's 'sujeto traumatizado' ['traumatised subject'],[20] and an indication that the haunting is a manifestation of her conscience and recognition of guilt for the deaths she has caused. To this extent, we may also read these terror-inducing spectres as an example of what Donna Heiland considers 'ghosts of our own making' or, using Maturin's phrase, 'self-hauntings',[21] in that they result from past actions, the memory of which inevitably resurfaces in the subconscious as phantoms. For Natalia, this poses both a destabilising force to her psyche and, paradoxically, a comforting knowledge that her sister continues to exist alongside her, albeit in spectral form. If her nightmares are, as Rodríguez Rodríguez suggests, a product of guilt, then her reliance on superstition and dark magic can be explained as her attempt to maintain her sister's memory by blocking any form of progress that might permanently sever their relationship.

Galicia, where Freire spent childhood summers in her grandmother's home, is famous for its 'atmosphere of superstition, legend, mystery, and witchcraft',[22] all of which are featured in *Irlanda* as an integral part of Natalia's subjective worldview. Most of her interactions with nature at the country estate are based on a combination of local superstition and witchcraft, which Natalia frequently uses to draw circles around herself for protection from dark spirits. On one such occasion, she finds a meadow that she deems 'an enchanted place', claiming: 'no dark shadows would come near because I had drawn a circle with an ash wand. Besides, I had a stream, and the ghosts can't cross running water' (p. 62). Because of Gabriel's personal experiences with tragedy and darkness (embodied in his father's suicide), Natalia openly talks with him about these superstitions and folklore, explaining: 'The souls of the dead are hiding in chestnut trees. Also in oaks, service trees, and elders. Elder trees are witches, so you have to ask them for permission before you cut them. Otherwise they bleed and put a curse on you' (p. 63). This intimate connection – initiated out of shared trauma – becomes a catalyst for Natalia's budding affection for Gabriel, and she notes: 'Men always fall in love with beautiful girls, but Gabriel had told me about his father's blood and about being born and dying countless times in different worlds. If he rubbed fern seed into his eyes, he would see my sister leaning against my shoulder' (p. 80). Despite her clear attraction to Gabriel, Natalia's difficulty with advancing any form of a relationship with him is entirely due to her insistence on remaining in a world populated by ghosts.

For the young narrator, progress implies certain loss, whereas stasis means that the darkness and all of the ghosts – including that of her sister – remain. This trauma of progress, then, enters the text in two distinct ways: the tension between economy and ecology, and the competing pressures of sexual promiscuity and the need to maintain the gendered expectations of tradition. Both kinds of progress are embodied in the character of Irlanda, who comes to represent for Natalia the epitome of modernity and maturity, with their simultaneous allure and repulsion. The first of these tensions is introduced in Natalia's initial description of the country estate and her acknowledgement that the villagers have always hated the family; she explains that when she was very young, she and her cousins 'learned that the house had been the pride of the village at the beginning of the last century, and we had to look haughty and keep our backs straight before the envious eyes of the villagers, just as the house stood straight and arrogant despite its decrepitude' (p. 20). Even in death, Sagrario warns Natalia that their mother will likely 'sell her inheritance piece by piece, as she has started to do, and the rest of the family, leeches that they are, will take advantage of her' (p. 21). It is immediately clear that this capitalistic understanding of the world clashes with Natalia's own worldview; thus, her aunt's desire for Natalia to 'start meeting the right people' (p. 43) – implying the need to cultivate relationships based on economic and social gain – does not motivate the young narrator to interact with her cousin's friends. Similar to her mother, Irlanda, ever popular in her upper-class society at school, tells Natalia that she would like to be a banker or stockbroker because '[a]t least they have power in their hands, and money. I don't want to wait for some kings to show up at my tower window. Open your eyes, Natalia. There's nothing better in the world than having power' (p. 44). In saying this, Irlanda rejects the fairy-tale image of the damsel in distress, instead claiming agency through capital. In her reality, progress – and, thus, maturity – is defined in part by power, which is gained through money and material possessions. This explains Irlanda's obsession with the chests in the upper rooms of the house, which are filled with clothing and jewellery that form part of Natalia's inheritance from her grandmother. When her cousin insists on opening the chests and dividing the lot equally between them, Natalia initially balks at the idea, telling us:

> For a moment, I thought those chests were mine, that I would want to use them someday. But I was curious about the magic lamp, so I said nothing. Besides, the curtains by the open window swayed inward, and I was afraid Sagrario would come out of her tree and her tortured head would appear. (p. 55)

Natalia's constant return to her world of ghosts and superstition inhibits her entrance into Irlanda's society; her cousin, for her part, rebukes Natalia, telling her 'I've never known anyone so obsessed with fairy tales. You can be so childish sometimes' (p. 54), drawing a clear line between progress (Irlanda) and childlike stasis (Natalia).

In contrast to Irlanda's capitalistic drive for power, Natalia remains deeply connected to the land around her, which she envisions not as a parcel for profit (the clear interest of her cousin's family) but rather for its magical potential. The narrator's interactions with nature lead Pao to consider her 'a unique character whose entire moral development and sense of empathy emanate from ecocritical preoccupations, chief among them a non-aggressive relationship between the human and natural worlds'.[23] Here I would disagree with the characterisation of Natalia's relationship with nature as non-aggressive, given her clearly violent attitude toward animals and her purposeful use of plants as poisonous tools of death. While it is clear that she values plants and her time in the outdoors much more than interactions with people, I would contend that this relationship is based less on ecological empathy and more on the intrinsic connection between nature and the spirit world; that is, Natalia's deep appreciation of the natural (plant) world is both a product and catalyst of her continued insistence on existing solely within the liminal, spectral space between childhood and adulthood. In fact, even when Natalia expresses a desire to 'make a successful transition to the world of grown-ups', she immediately follows this assertion by saying: 'I thought about going up to the elder tree to ask its old spirit if I could cut a branch and place it under my pillow for protection' (p. 67). Her adherence to these superstitious beliefs and magical practices impedes her from undergoing the transition that Irlanda has already made.

Unfortunately, Natalia's acute awareness of the differences between herself and her cousin becomes intensified throughout the narrative, as Irlanda begins to act crueller and more vindictive toward her. After she sees herself forced to share her inherited chests with Irlanda, Natalia remarks: 'She had it all. She was beautiful and elegant. She had money and friends, a young mother and even a brother. I had nothing, nothing besides a sister who refused to stay in the cemetery and my nightmares about animals chasing me' (p. 60). This realisation fuels the second main source of tension in the text: the trauma of progress experienced in Natalia's burgeoning sexuality simultaneous to the impulsive need to repress her transition to adulthood. The narrator's entrance into the estate is also an entrance into the world of hastened sexual and emotional maturity. Natalia is astonished by her cousin's conversations with her friends, which most commonly focus on boys, their own physical beauty and even the illicit behaviour of a girl in their class who was expelled for possession of cocaine (a moment in the text that has the secondary effect of reminding the reader that the plot does, in fact, take place in post-Franco modernity – a fact that is easily forgotten due to the folkloric tone of the narrative). Natalia's interactions with her cousin constantly reinforce the dichotomous relationship between the two of them; while the narrator believes that 'growing up was terribly slow and painful', she notes that 'Irlanda leaned over the bed with so much grace that there was no doubt she had grown up. And the realization hurt me, which somehow made me grow up too' (p. 31). Given the importance Natalia places on stasis, the evidence of progress embodied in her cousin reminds her of her own inevitable transition into adulthood, a process that she equates with pain.

The idea of growing up becomes an obsessive notion for Natalia, who comes to view Irlanda's body as evidence of the existing standard of progress. After hearing Gabriel's ghostly voice and seeing a vision of 'the smug curve of his lips . . . together with the image of the snake crawling among the tight dresses' – a sexually-charged image that clearly denotes Natalia's own latent desires – she immediately thinks of Irlanda's body, noting that her 'waist was so small, you could wrap one hand around it' (p. 64), a thought that compels her to measure her own waist with her hands. Unsatisfied with her body, Natalia decides to stop eating altogether in order to lose weight so that she, too, can fit into the dresses that form part of her inheritance. When the teenagers throw a dinner party one evening, Irlanda wears one of the white dresses from the antique chests, looking 'like an antique doll', acting 'witty, smiling' and even singing songs at the request of the others at the table, with the result that '[a]ll eyes were on Irlanda that night' (p. 75). Her cousin's innate sexuality and charm sets an unattainable standard for Natalia, who again reverts to thoughts of witchcraft whenever she imagines being with Gabriel:

> I rehearsed what I would say to him. I could make him a magic salad with nasturtium leaves and oil from the roses growing against the wall facing east, and we would have a picnic in the meadow. There we would talk about the other worlds where we would be born, where beautiful blonde girls didn't exist. (p. 81)

Natalia's concept of romance – based entirely on a continuation of her ghostly realm – is incongruent with the reality of the other teenagers in the house, who are motivated by sexual impulses and who therefore look down upon Natalia as childish and odd. Irlanda takes advantage of her cousin's awkwardness and immaturity by purposefully seducing Gabriel, knowing that Natalia is attracted to him. After a series of scenes featuring Irlanda's wilful manipulation and cruelty, the narrator takes a handful of grapes and squeezes them, imagining that the juice dripping from them is actually Irlanda's blood and picturing 'the whole house flooding with blood, her white dresses, her spotless room soaked in blood' (p. 96). When Irlanda and Gabriel kiss in front of Natalia as Roberto lights fireworks from the tower several days later, a metaphorical fuse is lit inside the young narrator and from this moment on, thoughts of violence and death increasingly penetrate her mind, prompting her to act on them.

Within Freire's Gothic environment, the crumbling façade of the tower and the adults' and older children's repeated warnings of the dangers it poses foreshadow the narrator's own psychological collapse and return to violence. Natalia's ultimate psychotic breakdown is caused by these competing tensions that manifest themselves in her subconscious as the trauma of progress, invoking spectres and demons against whom Natalia must protect herself. When Natalia realises that Irlanda has manipulated Gabriel and taken him irrevocably away from her, she wishes all of them dead and asks Sagrario to help her to speed up time and bring them swiftly to their end. Her first step is to poison Irlanda's cat; in retaliation for her cat's murder, Irlanda sleeps with Gabriel, digging her nails into his skin in a visible sign of her ownership that Natalia cannot ignore. Even after seeing the red marks on his back, however, Natalia continues to interpret sexuality through the lens of dark magic, asserting that 'Gabriel, who had pressed his flesh against Irlanda's during those nights, was already possessed by another kind of magic from which he wouldn't be free, Irlanda's gravity field' (p. 114). Linares asserts that the overt signs of sexuality that Natalia sees in her cousin are what compels her to commit her final violent act: 'Sex has no place in her childish world of ghosts, dragons, spells and magic, so she decides to do away with Irlanda. Killing her cousin is a way of affirming her own will, of refusing to accept a world which she does not want to enter but which also denies her entry.'[24] Irlanda's final words are a reaffirmation of her dominance over Natalia: 'It's perfect, isn't it? . . . Everything. The world. The house at sunset. Birds flying. Life. Me' (p. 126). Her vanity is embellished by Gabriel's medallion, which she wears around her neck in purposeful provocation of Natalia's jealousy. After she removes the medallion, complaining of its weight, Natalia grabs it and then suddenly pushes Irlanda off the tower balcony, which crumbles and collapses underneath them. Natalia's sensorial experience of her cousin's death is further evidence of her existence in a liminal space, made obvious when she tells us: 'In my mind's ear, the chains tying her life to her body creaked. I heard them squeak and snap, the same sound as when my sister was smothered under the pillow and then was silent' (p. 126). The narrator's ability to not only see but also to hear death underscores her intimate connection with the darkness that results from a violent imagination and unresolved psychological trauma. Natalia then repeats this trauma in the retelling of the grisly scene with her parents, to whom she 'eagerly described how blood had oozed from Irlanda's shuttered body' (p. 127), a display of her insatiable appetite for the macabre despite the evident harm it causes her.

Irlanda's death is the culmination of the cyclical violence and terror propagated by the Gothic atmosphere of Natalia's alternate reality, and an inevitable result of the destabilising forces of incongruence and transgression that define the narrator's interactions in the world of progress around her. Sáez considers Natalia's odd behaviours (her obsession with dead plants, her childlike fantasies and her aggressive outbursts) to be 'válvulas de escape emocional' ['emotional escape valves'][25], allowing her to take control of her environment through her own repetitive, obsessive actions. Unfortunately for Natalia, these behaviours also clearly mark her difference among the other teenagers in the country estate, making her a target for bullying and the focal point of Irlanda's cruelty. Her death, however, has the unexpected effect of facilitating Natalia's transition into the world that her cousin has vacated, as evidenced when Natalia tells us: 'Nena and I were warmly received, as heirs to the affection Irlanda had inspired in everyone who knew her. There were birthday parties and a dance every spring and every fall, unexpected declarations of love, and inexorable refusals' (p. 128). In this manner, the inheritance that Irlanda once associated with capitalistic power becomes, for Natalia, an inheritance of social acceptance and maturity; without Irlanda for competition, Natalia now finds herself able to move freely within the world of progress, forming meaningful relationships and casting off the spectres that forever haunted her childhood. Indeed, she tells us that now Sagrario 'was happy dancing in the green fields around the country house' and that she had 'taken with her the turtle, the cat, and the baby magpies' who had all tormented Natalia in nightmares (p. 129). Moreover, Irlanda's burial marks a permanent end to her manipulation, as the narrator asserts that 'we buried her memory and her cold eyes. There she lived forever, never coming back, never visiting me in my dreams' (pp. 129–30). Thus, the cousins have permanently reversed roles: not only has Natalia entered the world of progress, but her cousin has retreated into a world of stasis in which even subconscious haunting is impossible.

It is worth noting that Freire's novel, like Jackson's, portrays this cycle of violence and dark fantasy through the lens of a first-person narrator who happens to be a female teenager, which not only raises questions of narrator reliability but also of the particular role of the female child in the Gothic narrative. Lucie Armitt has explained that the Gothic girl child is 'an enigma; a cipher for the appealing nature of things not always fully understood; one who is alluring, but potentially dangerous. In essence, one might argue that she, above all characters, best embodies the very attractiveness of Gothic literature itself.'[26] Female adolescents are especially charged with the tensions that dialogue with and reflect the Gothic environment they inhabit, as Armitt elaborates:

> Though magnetic attraction sometimes defines the bonds between girls in these narratives, such bonds are consistently fraught with danger, betrayal or loss. Repeatedly, the Gothic girl child must undergo trauma on her journey towards womanhood, and blood, that fluid especially associated with the female adolescent, plays a particularly horrific role in narratives such as *Carrie*. If Moers is right and the Gothic especially offers its heroines adventures they cannot find elsewhere, the price it seems they must pay for having them is learning to go it alone.[27]

Armitt's understanding of the archetypal girl child illuminates the relationship between Irlanda and Natalia as representative of the fundamental tensions that underlie the Gothic narrative, suggesting that the end result of that relationship – Irlanda's death at the hands of her cousin – was always an inevitable part of the narrator's own violent journey toward adulthood. The fact that the story itself is told to us by Natalia means that the scenes we 'witness' as readers are the by-product of the dark liminal space between childhood and adulthood – an unstable space populated with ghosts and shadows that distort reality and, therefore, memory. Natalia even acknowledges the problem of memory in the very beginning of her narrative when she comments on the stories her adult family members used to tell and remarks: 'you couldn't tell what had really happened from what had been made up each time those stories were told' (p. 16). It is rather telling that our narrator herself recognises the unreliability of memory, casting the narrative space as one in which reality and fantasy inevitably combine.

Espido Freire has stated that 'literature and its search for magical places tries to compensate for the loss of the ability that children possess to create worlds of their own'[28] and that *Irlanda* 'habla de la decisión ética que el ser adulto exige, y de qué les ocurre a quienes no eligen' ['speaks of the ethical decision that being an adult demands, and of what happens to those who do not choose'].[29] When read as a narrative of childhood trauma, her novel highlights the power of the imagination to create spaces that both encourage and repel darkness and violence. Whether *Irlanda* is interpreted as a story of individual trauma or as a commentary on the violent inheritance that Portela has acknowledged as part of post-Franco Basque society, Freire's use of haunting is key to the depiction of the painful return of memory and the trauma of progress. The resolution to this trauma by the end of the novel seems to indicate that transition is, indeed, possible, but not without first defeating the ghosts of memory – an act that problematises the ethical boundaries of good and evil, presenting violence as an occasionally necessary step on the path toward recovery.

9

The End of Innocence: Childhood Fantasy and Monstrous Reality in Ana María Matute's Uninhabited Paradise

༄

Ana María Matute's *Paraíso inhabitado* [hereafter translated as *Uninhabited Paradise*] (2008) is the last novel she published prior to her death and the inspiration for her unfinished *Family Demons* (the subject of our study in chapter four), which she conceived as a continued exploration of the themes from *Uninhabited Paradise*. Néstor Bórquez points to the prevalence of Matute's 'obsessive themes' in this novel, noting in particular 'el miedo a su madre y el amor a su padre . . . su estricta y controvertida educación religiosa . . . una persistente enfermedad de la niña . . . la referencia a lugares emblemáticos de la casa: la cocina – centro de felicidad y aventuras – y el cuarto oscuro de los castigos' ['the fear of her mother and the love for her father . . . her strict and controversial religious education . . . the girl's persistent illness . . . the reference to emblematic places in the house: the kitchen – centre of happiness and adventures – and the dark room of punishments'].[1] These themes, often referenced as influential aspects of Matute's own childhood, lead María Mercedes Pons Ballesteros to consider this novel 'una de sus obras más autobiográficas' ['one of her most autobiographical works'].[2]

In *Uninhabited Paradise*, narrator-protagonist Adriana recalls her memories as a young girl living with her upper-class family in a large, multi-family estate in Madrid in the 1930s. The youngest of four children, Adriana's childhood is a lonely one, marked by the almost complete absence of her parents and siblings and a stifling lack of love and affection. In compensation for her loneliness, Adriana immerses herself in a world of her own creation in which a unicorn in a tapestry on the wall in their house is a living creature that moves around the rooms and the grounds outside, the adults are 'giants' and the children are 'gnomes', and darkness is a welcome presence that contrasts sharply with the terrifying, monstrous world of adults. Her imagination and rebellious nature make her quite different from her peers at the religious school she attends, and she is considered a 'bad' girl by her teachers and her mother, who is exasperated with her for much of the novel. When Adriana becomes gravely ill after an outing with her father (the only day the two ever spend together), she is pulled from school for half of the year to convalesce in bed. She is lonely and the solitude is difficult for her, but finally she sees a young boy playing with his dog outside. The boy, Gavrila, quickly becomes Adriana's best friend and they spend most of their time immersed in their imaginary worlds and reading stories together. When Gavi becomes terribly ill with meningitis, his last words to Adriana shortly before his death are a promise that he will return for her. She then spends the remainder of the year waiting for his return, hearing his words always at the back of her mind, his absence turning into a phantom-like presence in her daily life. By the end of the novel, the civil war is beginning, coinciding with Gavi's death and Adriana's mother sending her back to school with the expectation that she will no longer act like a child; nevertheless, Adriana rebels once more and is expelled from school, so her mother sends her to live with her aunt Eduarda, where she will remain for the duration of the war.

Among the few studies that specifically examine this novel, the most common focal point is the blending of realities so typical of Matute's style. Bórquez considers the ways in which the narrator's memory of her youthful, innocent perspective contrasts with the adults' problematic relationship with reality in the context of the civil war era. For Bórquez, Matute's worlds nearly always end in one of two possible fates for the children who inhabit them: 'la desilusión o la muerte' ['disillusionment or death'].[3] Pons Ballesteros also points to the dichotomous worlds of Matute's fiction, noting: 'La infancia, sin duda alguna, es el núcleo en el que gravita toda su narrativa. Ya sean protagonistas, personajes o lectores, el niño siempre será parte activa de la historia' ['Childhood, without any doubt, is the nucleus around which her entire narrative gravitates. Whether they are protagonists, characters or readers, the child will always be an active part of the story'].[4] Maylis Santa-Cruz similarly studies the role of the child's perspective in the creation of multiple worlds in the text, which she labels as M1 (the actual world), M2 (the adult world of the 'Giants') and M3 (the child world of the 'Gnomes'), noting that it is in the second world (M2) where Matute injects a certain amount of realism that serves as the historical base of the novel.[5] Yannick Llored studies what he considers the novel's 'double perspective' by examining the relationship between adult narrator Adriana and the young Adriana of her memories, emphasising the role of the 'complejidad del lenguaje, sus múltiples temporalidades, los universos que concentra y crea en relación con diversos órdenes de realidad' ['complexity of the language, its multiple temporalities, the universes that it gathers and creates in relation to diverse orders of reality'].[6] Similarly, Murielle Borel asserts that through the depiction of this dual narrative voice (past and present), Matute performs a 'réécriture du réel' ['rewriting of the real'], in which personal memories come to represent collective memory from the era she portrays in this novel.[7]

Notably missing from the existing scholarship on *Uninhabited Paradise* is an examination of its Gothic qualities, and especially the fundamental role of monstrosity and spectrality in explaining young Adriana's image as 'bad girl'. Therefore, drawing on Juliann Fleenor's notion of the mother/daughter relationship at the centre of the Gothic plot, in this chapter I analyse Adriana's haunted, monstrous childhood, marked by absence, loss and her love of darkness as a way to compensate for the terrifying realm of the 'Giants' – the adults around her, whose bitterness and despair reflect the nightmarish reality of pre-civil war Madrid. By reading *Uninhabited Paradise* as a Gothic text, it becomes clear that Adriana's transgressive nature is a result both of the pressure to conform to the prevailing standards of the society in which she is raised and of the ongoing trauma of absence (that of her parents, siblings, friends and, in general, love). These absences act as spectral presences in the text that define and problematise Adriana's relationship with the adult world, which is a constant source of fear and anxiety for the young girl. By the end of the novel, her aunt's assertion that fantasy never returns marks the finality of disillusionment and leads to Adriana's abrupt, traumatic departure from childhood, just as the nation itself enters the harsh reality of war.

Absences underscore Matute's text as the main source of young Adriana's childhood trauma, evidenced by the now adult narrator's decision to begin her story by telling us: 'Nací cuando mis padres ya no se querían' ['I was born when my parents no longer loved each other'] (p. 7). The lack of love is accompanied by the physical absence of most of her immediate family members for the majority of her young life: she barely knows her father, her sister Cristina (already a teenager) has nothing to do with her and her twin brothers have very few interactions with her, leading Adriana to describe her early years as 'bastante solitarios' ['rather lonely'] (p. 7). Adriana's mother acknowledges the trauma that these absences have caused the young girl, confiding in her sister Eduarda that 'esta niña está pagando las consecuencias de una familia rota' ['this little girl is paying the consequences of a broken family'] (p. 50). Nevertheless, the mother's own absence dominates the text, with Adriana telling Eduarda '[t]ampoco a mamá la veo mucho' ['I don't see mom a lot either'] (p. 44), an admission that corresponds with Adriana's ever-diminishing affection for her mother that she blames principally on 'sus largas ausencias' ['her long absences'] (p. 35).

Fleenor has argued that the mother-daughter relationship is central to the female Gothic, which highlights the conflict at the centre of this relationship as fundamental to the process of identity formation. She explains:

> This maternal figure is also a double, a twin perhaps, to the woman herself. For the mother represents what the woman will become if she heeds her sexual self, if she heeds the self who seeks the power that comes with acting as the mother, and if she becomes pregnant.[8]

Fleenor suggests that the Gothic itself becomes a popular form with these readers 'not because it allows escape but because it expresses this confrontation with one of the central enigmas of female existence, the relationship of mother and daughter'.[9] Barbara Creed revisits this concept with Julia Kristeva's theory of abjection, which Creed applies to horror films of the 1970s and 1980s in which 'the child struggles to break away from the mother, representative of the archaic maternal figure, in a context in which the father is invariably absent (*Psycho, Carrie, The Birds*)' and in which the mother thus appears as the abject, 'monstrous-feminine'.[10] In these readings of the Gothic, the (m)other is only differentiated from the daughter (self) through a rejection of the former's imposed traditions. To this extent, although *Uninhabited Paradise* is not a horror text, its Gothic qualities serve to amplify the role of the mother-daughter relationship at the centre of the plot as one that problematises adherence to tradition and ultimately leads the young protagonist to challenge the inevitability of compliance. Nowhere is this rejection of the mother more obvious than the scene toward the end of the novel when Cristina reluctantly admits to Adriana that she wants to have a career but is unsure if she should, to which Adriana quickly responds: '¿Tú quieres ser como mamá?' ['Do you want to be like mom?'] (p. 305). As we will see, Adriana's continuous rebellion against her mother exemplifies this central conflict and illustrates what Ginette Carpenter describes as the Gothic's 'policing and transgressing the borders between ideological inscription and resistance'.[11]

In establishing the Gothic qualities of the narrative, it is important to note that Matute's portrayal of darkness subverts the traditional use of the motif: whereas darkness and night-time are most commonly associated with fear and evil in Gothic texts, here Adriana tells us that '[l]a noche era mi lugar, el que yo me había creado, o el que me había creado a mí, allí donde yo verdaderamente habitaba' ['night-time was my place, which I had created for myself, or which had created me, where I truly dwelled'].[12] In contrast with the safe familiarity of darkness, daytime is, for Adriana, the 'temible reino del sol' ['fearsome kingdom of the sun'] (p. 13), associated with the incomprehensible and terrifying adult world that she calls the land of the 'Giants'. The young protagonist experiences freedom from the strict confines of the adult-shaped daytime during her nightly adventures throughout the house, in which she creates imaginary worlds that serve as a safe haven – a 'paradise' – from the reality around her. In fact, Adriana credits her imaginary worlds as the sole source of happiness that 'me salvó de cosas como saber que nunca fui deseada, de haber nacido a destiempo en una familia que había ya perdido la ilusión y la práctica del amor' ['saved me from things such as knowing that I was never wanted, from having been born at the wrong time in a family that had already lost the illusion and the practice of love'] (p. 12). In this manner, darkness becomes an integral part of Adriana's survival in an adult world that repeatedly attempts to cast her as a monster, while the ongoing trauma of present absences lends the daytime a spectral quality that haunts the young girl and increasingly heightens her fear and anxiety.

These contrasts between night and day help to delineate Adriana's world as one in which the protagonist's imagination serves to filter the reality around her. Darkness, associated with blindness and distortion, here is a tool that allows Adriana to mould the landscape of shadows into a realm of fantasy where furniture transforms into 'animales o montañas, y hasta cascadas' ['animals or mountains, and even waterfalls'] (p. 13), and where the principal character is a unicorn who leaps from the tapestry and gallops around the house and gardens. This unicorn, a symbol of childhood fantasy, is reflected both in aunt Eduarda – who has 'grandes ojos azules de Unicornio' ['large blue Unicorn eyes'] (p. 38) – and in Gavrila, the only person in the text aside from Adriana who can actually see the magical creature. That Adriana allows these two people access to her world of darkness and fantasy indicates their status as marginalised characters in the narrative: Gavrila, like Adriana, is another lonely child whose only company is his imagination, and Eduarda, the opposite of her sister (Adriana's mother), rejects conservative tradition and instead embodies the freedoms of the Second Republic, wearing pants, driving a car and taking on romantic partners outside the institution of marriage. Their difference casts all three of them as monsters from the perspective of the world of Giants, where oppressive reality stifles creativity and demands conformity. Despite the adults' tendency to denigrate Adriana's constant imaginative play as immature and inappropriate for a girl of her age, Matute herself has reminded readers of the relevance of childhood fantasy in the real world: 'La crueldad, la ambición, la fragilidad del ser humano [. . .], todo se revela en estos cuentos aparentemente simples e indudablemente inocentes' ['Cruelty, ambition, the fragility of the human being [. . .], all is revealed in these apparently simple and undoubtedly innocent stories'].[13] We can therefore read Adriana's world of Gnomes as not only a counterpoint to the world of Giants, but also as a point of access to knowledge that allows her to better understand the adults' strange and often cruel reality.

The world of Giants, as perceived by young Adriana, quickly becomes a fearsome space of monstrous creation populated by 'aquellos altos y extraños seres Gigantes que me atemorizaban' ['those tall and strange Giant beings who terrified me'] (p. 13) and where her only concern is 'huir de ellos' ['to flee from them'] (p. 23). The brutality of this adult world overwhelms Adriana, who describes herself as simply 'intentando sobrevivir entre los Gigantes' ['trying to survive among the Giants'] (p. 53) – a description that paints her as a victim of a society in which, as Eduarda tells her, 'no somos mejores que los animales depredadores' ['we are no better than predatory animals'] (p. 54). For these reasons, Adriana repeatedly attempts to find ways to separate herself from the vicious daytime world through the use of imaginative play. When Eduarda buys her a small puppet theatre, the young protagonist claims a physical space in the house as the site of her imaginary creation, delighting in the thought that she now has complete control over these beings '[s]in que nadie metiera sus narices y castigos en el espacio que yo fabricaba al margen, siempre al margen' ['without anyone butting in and bringing their punishments into the space that I fabricated on the margin, always on the margin'] (p. 42). Later, during her sole outing with her father, a visit to the movie theatre becomes another fissure in the reality of the world of Giants where Adriana's imagination displaces her existing fear, allowing her to enter 'la tierra donde a mí me gustaba vivir, avanzar, imaginar' ['the world where I liked to live, advance, imagine'] (p. 128). The profound experience of being immersed in the images on the screen makes Adriana reluctant to leave the theatre, and she admits that 'sólo sabía una cosa: que no quería regresar al mundo de los Gigantes, de Saint Maur, de la casa' ['I only knew one thing: that I didn't want to return to the world of Giants, of Saint Maur, of home'] (p. 129). Adriana's reliance on imagination as both a physical and mental space highlights her suffering in the adult world, from which she constantly attempts to hide.

If the world of Giants is delineated in terms of the monstrosity of the adults who inhabit it, it soon becomes clear that the reverse is also true: from the perspective of the adults, Adriana's world of fantasy marks her inherent difference, and her rebellion against their strict rules and traditions turns her into a monstrous child. Much of Adriana's monstrosity is based on the gendered expectations within the patriarchal tradition to which her family belongs, which contrasts sharply with the liberal treatment of women during the Second Republic. Matute's portrayal of the mother as a steadfast proponent of tradition echoes the bourgeois atmosphere in the pre-war era and foreshadows the permanence of this tradition under the dictatorship, which gave the Catholic Church the power to construct 'models of gendered identity and behaviour' that became the basis for young girls' education.[14] Adriana's religious school, Saint Maur, replicates the era's educational standards, according to which 'una joven debía brillar por su capacidad de obediencia y de paciencia, aderezado todo ello con una dosis de belleza suficiente para hacer de ella una óptima candidata al matrimonio, fin primordial de su vida' ['a young girl should shine for her capacity for obedience and patience, all of this embellished with a dose of beauty sufficient enough to make her an optimal candidate for marriage, the fundamental purpose of her life'].[15] Saint Maur is a primary battleground between Adriana and the women (the nuns and her own mother) who see her disobedience as a sign of moral depravity. Adriana's sister Cristina is a recurring reference point for the nuns, who repeatedly compare Adriana to her older, better-behaved sister who was 'una alumna ejemplar, intachable, piadosa, aplicada y dulce' ['an exemplary alumna, impeccable, pious, diligent and sweet'] (p. 20). The school's emphasis on traditional femininity denotes Cristina as a model student and Adriana, therefore, as 'todo lo contrario' ['the complete opposite'], leading Adriana to the upsetting realisation that '[s]er como Cristina, ése era mi destino' ['being like Cristina, that was my destiny'] (p. 27). Cristina's physical absence throughout most of the text does not prevent her from having an impact on the young protagonist's life; as each of her classmates slowly becomes 'una pequeña Cristina' ['a little Cristina'] (p. 29) moulded in the image of the Catholic Church, and as her teachers use her sister's submissiveness as a reminder of her own rebellious nature, Cristina turns into a spectral presence that haunts Adriana with the threatening images of obedience and perfection – an encapsulation of the harsh reality of the adult world.

These ever-present hauntings at school and at home lead Adriana to view herself as a monster in the world of Giants. The women's characterisation of her in comparison to Cristina takes on the form of a word that becomes part of Adriana's identity for the remainder of the text: 'MALA. Yo era mala' ['BAD. I was bad'] (p. 29). In overhearing a conversation between her mother and Eduarda, Adriana learns that her mother thinks that she is 'muy rara' ['very strange'], that Nanny María and Isabel are both 'un poco asustadas' ['a little scared'] of her, and that Isabel even says that she has 'algo de bruja' ['something of a witch'] in her (p. 38). From their traditional perspective as women who comply with the patriarchal standard of their era, Adriana is a frightening, monstrous child who threatens to destabilise the structure they all adhere to and maintain. Adriana's mother even invites Eduarda to spend time with the girl, explaining to Adriana that her aunt 'intenta corregirte' ['is trying to correct you'] (p. 52), implying that there is something inherently wrong with her.

Despite her mother's admonitions, Adriana turns further toward monstrosity in defiance of the adults – the 'Giants' – around her. At the beginning of chapter five, she tells us:

> Poco a poco, sin apenas darme cuenta, adquirí la costumbre y el convencimiento de ser mala. Ya "mala" no era sólo una palabra pronunciada por Gigantes, era una realidad, porque si antes no la comprendía, ahora ya me había hecho una idea de lo que significaba: ser mala era no ser como ellos. Y yo no era como ellos – o como ellos querían que fuera.
>
> [Little by little, without even realising it, I acquired the habit and the conviction of being bad. "Bad" was no longer just a word pronounced by Giants, it was a reality, because if I didn't understand it before, now I had gotten the idea of what it meant: to be bad was to not be like them. And I wasn't like them – or how they wanted me to be.] (p. 76)

Adriana's new identification with wickedness bolsters her rebellious nature and prompts her to act out against the oppressive environment around her. When she takes the school bully's dessert at lunch, the nuns report the incident to her mother, who tells her 'eso es muy feo, eso es algo que no es propio de una señorita. Cristina se moría de vergüenza de ser acusada de algo semejante' ['that is very ugly, that is something that is inappropriate of a young lady. Cristina would die of embarrassment if she were accused of such a thing'] (p. 80). Here, the spectral invocation of Cristina, which the mother employs as a point of moral comparison, serves to heighten Adriana's anger and frustration, immediately leading her to muse that if Cristina 'se iba a morir de vergüenza, que se muriera de una vez, y me dejara en paz' ['was going to die of embarrassment, she should just die already, and leave me in peace'] (p. 81). As a form of punishment, her mother locks her in the 'Dark Room' (a storage room full of old clothes and items not on display), assuming that the darkness will scare Adriana into submission. What she does not realise, however, is that her daughter feels most comfortable away from the world of adults, immersed in the distorted reality of darkness, which the girl considers 'amable, podría decirse que protectora' ['kind, you could almost say protective'] (p. 83). Adriana, a true creature of the night, delights in this punishment and decides to do whatever it takes to be locked in the Dark Room again, in defiance of her mother and in a demonstration of the results of the woman's lack of attention and understanding, part of the trauma of absence that has defined Adriana's young life.

The combined presences of monstrosity and spectrality intensify as the narrative progresses, parallel to the onset of the civil war and the loss of Gavrila. What was initially a focus on Adriana's personal experiences in the dichotomous worlds of her imaginative creation soon becomes a commentary on the monstrous reality of Spanish society at the outbreak of the war. Adriana's lack of understanding of the adults' nuanced language here serves to shield her from much of the violence in the outside world while also inducing in her a baseline of fear and anxiety that she cannot explain nor avoid. Her father's strained actions on the day of their outing are what first make her aware of this fear: 'yo tenía miedo: y así supe que siempre lo había tenido, y que el miedo acababa apoderándose de todo lo que hacía, o decía, o escuchaba. Era un miedo sutil, frágil, y sin embargo, poderosamente destructor' ['I was afraid: and that is how I discovered that I had always been afraid, and that fear ended up overpowering everything I did, or said, or heard. It was a subtle, fragile, and yet, powerfully destructive fear'] (p. 124). This shared moment with her father, in which she compares them both to frightened birds, marks the beginning of what will become Adriana's permanent entry into the adult world.

The dismantling of Adriana's fantasy world of Gnomes is at first a gradual process, hastened by the adults who repeatedly draw her into their confidence and rely on her complicity. Isabel is the foremost of these: because she cannot read or write, she asks Adriana to help her to read the letters she receives in the mail and to send written responses that she dictates to the girl. These letters mystify Adriana because of the coded language they contain, with Isabel telling her brother '[y]a sé lo que le ha pasado a la vaca con lo de los lobos, he llorado mucho, deseo que la otra vaca esté bien, ojalá se muera el que dice que es culpa de los lobos' ['I already know what happened to the cow in reference to the wolves, I've cried a lot, I hope that the other cow is okay, I hope that the one who says it's the wolves' fault dies'] (pp. 189–90). The fairy-tale-like imagery here serves to avoid certain censorship while simultaneously masking reality from the young girl who acts as scribe. Although Adriana does not understand what is being said, she senses that the letters require the recipients to read between the lines to find the missing information, showing her awareness of the complexity of the adult language and the world it represents.

The young protagonist's fear increases yet again when she falls ill for a second time, requiring another period of convalescence that separates her from Gavrila and their imaginary world. The pain of this separation is accentuated by the total absence of her family: 'mamá no estaba. Ni papá. Ni los gemelos, ni Cristina' ['mom wasn't home. Nor dad. Nor the twins, nor Cristina'] (p. 205). In her feverish state, she realises that it is her mother's strictness that most upsets her, noting 'el temor de que, si despertaba del todo, algo me sería reprochado y rompería el bienestar recién descubierto. En aquel tiempo, vivía siempre con la vaga amenaza de arrastrar alguna o varias culpas. Aunque no lograba identificarlas, ni liberarme de ellas' ['the fear that, if I woke completely, I would be berated for something and it would break my recently uncovered wellbeing. At that time, I always lived with the vague threat of bearing some or various faults. Although I wasn't able to identify them, nor free myself from them'] (pp. 206–7). The fear of being punished becomes another spectral presence in Adriana's life, causing her to be constantly on guard against the overbearing attitude of her mother toward these perceived faults that Adriana herself describes as 'fantasmales' ['phantomlike'] (p. 207).

When she is finally able to rejoin Gavrila, her happy time with him is punctured by a notable increase in negative, disturbing input from the adult world, which is invariably portrayed as 'atroz' ['atrocious'] (p. 288) and full of 'gente muy mala' ['very bad people'] (p. 182) by the servants with whom she interacts daily. This is the world in which Teo, Gavrila's beloved caretaker and occasional participant in the children's games, is beaten and subsequently hospitalised for dressing in drag during Carnival, and where school bullies are allowed to continue terrorising their innocent victims. This is the world that Adriana suddenly perceives as 'acechante, devorador, desconocido' ['lurking, devouring, unknown'] (p. 288). The predatory nature of the outside world terrifies Adriana and destabilises the balance she had once achieved between the realms of darkness and daytime, giving increased access to the monstrous world of the Giants as it slowly infiltrates her everyday reality. Gavrila is the first to be consumed by the adult world, declaring that he hopes that the people who have beaten Teo 'se mueran' ['die'] (p. 242). This first act of violence to break into the children's consciousness coincides with the servants' concerns about the end of the Second Republic, echoed in the words of Joaquín, who wonders: '¿qué va a ser de nuestra Patria?' ['what will become of our homeland?'] (p. 242). As the skirmishes outside rage on, Adriana acknowledges that '[u]na amenaza incierta, pegajosa y flotante, parecía haberse adueñado tanto del patio interior como del piso . . . Un miedo casi irracional inundaba todo cuanto hacía o pensaba' ['an uncertain threat, sticky and floating, seemed to have taken over both the interior patio and the apartment . . . An almost irrational fear inundated everything I did or thought'] (p. 247). When the laundry woman comes with the news of the convents that the Republican troops are burning down, Adriana recalls hearing 'una risa oscura' ['a dark laugh'] (p. 254), further problematising her understanding of the events happening around her. Despite her confusion at this seemingly inexplicable reaction to the news, Adriana continues to glean nearly all her knowledge about the violence outside from the servants, with whom she clearly has a much deeper connection than her mostly absent family members. Llored notes the importance of this relationship between the narrator and the people who work for her family, asserting that Adriana 'se sintió y sigue sintiéndose próxima a los dominados y humildes cuya humanidad y relación con la vida le parecen más sinceras y despojadas de la artificialidad convencional característica de su grupo social y familiar' ['felt and continues feeling close to the dominated and poor people whose humanity and relationship with life seem more sincere and stripped of the conventional artificiality characteristic of her social and familial group'].[16] Thus, Adriana's entrance into the adult world is precipitated by her close relationships with the servants in her household, whose fears and anxieties about the uncertain political times provoke Adriana's own unease and hasten her loss of innocence.

Gavrila's death from meningitis occurs as Adriana's mother doubles down on her efforts to force the girl to act like a 'young lady' and to leave behind the world of childhood fantasy. The mother, concerned primarily with maintaining the image of tradition in her broken household, decides that not only will she no longer allow Adriana to play with boys (which she deems improper), but she will also forbid her to enjoy 'esos compadreos de la cocina' ['those companionships in the kitchen'] (p. 283), a direct reference to the socioeconomic divide between the family and staff that the woman will no longer permit Adriana to cross. She again invokes the spectral presence of Cristina, telling Adriana that she will have to 'imitar el comportamiento de tu hermana' ['imitate your sister's behaviour'] (p. 332). When Adriana refuses to abide by her mother's wishes, confessing her profound love for Gavrila, the woman quickly undergoes a final monstrous conversion in front of the young girl, becoming a vicious dragon: 'Levantó la cabeza, las garras aladas, lanzaba fuego por los ojos y la boca, fuego de infierno. Ya no era mamá, y me dio mucho miedo' ['She lifted her head, her winged talons, she shot fire from her eyes and mouth, fire from hell. She was no longer mom, and she scared me a lot'] (p. 332). No longer her mother, the creature slaps Adriana's face and tells her: 'El amor es una mentira' ['Love is a lie'] (p. 333), effectively destroying the foundation of desire and longing that defined Adriana's fantasy, replacing it instead with the stinging permanence of absence and disaffection. Adriana's final visit with Gavrila gives her a small amount of hope that she may be able to hang onto the illusion of childhood, embodied in the boy's assurance that he will return for her. The last three chapters of the novel see Adriana's increasing desperation to reunite with Gavrila, whose promise to return becomes a spectral voice that she carries within herself at all times. In her final return to Saint Maur, she rebels by hiding in a closet for several days, after which point the school finally expels her, leading her mother to send her to live with Eduarda for the duration of the war. Although this departure from the monstrous world of her family home might seem to indicate that Adriana has won the battle against her mother, the harsh reality of war gives one final, devastating blow to her imaginary realm when her aunt, in the last sentence of the novel, tells her: 'Los Unicornios nunca vuelven' ['Unicorns never return'] (p. 396). This assertion permanently shatters the imaginary worlds of Adriana's youth, leaving her with the bitter disillusion of their now shared adult reality.

Matute's Gothic portrayal of the dichotomous realms of childhood imagination purposefully centres on the brutality of the real, converting the mother into a monstrous villain who repeatedly attempts to dismantle Adriana's childhood, and transforming her other family members into spectral presences that emphasise absence while also reminding the girl of her own monstrosity in the face of tradition. The final, permanent end to Adriana's childhood is accompanied by the outbreak of the war and Eduarda's assertion that youthful fantasy never returns – a truth that is made even more painful from the narrator's current perspective as an adult, knowing what comes next: the deaths of her brothers, the loss of her father and the years of dictatorship, all of which continue the trauma of absence as the ongoing, profound trauma of loss. Thus, what young Adriana initially sees as the 'mundo sepultado' ['buried world'] (p. 382) of fantasy that results from Gavrila's death, becomes a symbol of the destruction of innocence associated with the war and the countless lives that will soon become part of the spectral realm of the past. Galdona Pérez has described Matute's authorial project as 'un grito de descontento que ya en su infancia le sirvió de refugio ante el horror de los adultos y que después, en plena madurez creadora, se concibe como una labor portadora de función social y como una herramienta de lucha contra la injusticia y la hipocresía' ['a shout of discontent that already in her childhood served as a refuge for her before the horror of the adults and that afterwards, in the height of her creative maturity, is conceived as a work of social function and as a weapon against injustice and hypocrisy'].[17] To this extent, we can return to the prior claims of the autobiographical nature of *Uninhabited Paradise* and acknowledge Adriana's rebellion as a symbolic shout of discontent in harmony with the author's own rejection of oppression and the monstrous forms of reality that Matute, as a child of the war, knew all too well. Thus, for Matute and her young protagonist alike, the possibility of such an 'uninhabited paradise' is marred by the knowledge that it will remain forever inaccessible to those who have experienced the sudden, traumatic loss of childhood innocence.

10

As the Ghost Speaks: Bearing Witness to Fascist Horror in Carlos Ruiz Zafón's The Prisoner of Heaven

ஒ

Carlos Ruiz Zafón (1964–2020) was a Spanish novelist and screenwriter, best known for his *Cemetery of Forgotten Books* series that debuted with *The Shadow of the Wind* in 2001. Born in Barcelona, Ruiz Zafón had an early love of literature and cinema, and after winning the Edebé Prize for his first young adult novel *The Prince of Mist* in 1994, he moved to Los Angeles, where he worked in film and as an author. With the publication of *The Shadow of the Wind*, Ruiz Zafón was an instant literary success, ultimately becoming contemporary Spain's most bestselling author and, internationally, the most-read Spanish author after Miguel de Cervantes. His novels, for which he has won numerous national and international awards, have been translated into more than fifty languages worldwide and have even inspired popular tours of Barcelona that trace the streets featured in his series. Ruiz Zafón passed away from cancer at the age of fifty-five in June of 2020, cutting short a career that put twentieth-century Spain – and Spanish history – on the international literary stage.

The Prisoner of Heaven (2011) is the third novel in Ruiz Zafón's *Cemetery of Forgotten Books* series, continuing the story of the Sempere family and Daniel's quest to uncover his family's connections to Spain's shadowy past. When a mysterious man enters the Sempere bookstore in Barcelona and leaves a cryptic message for Fermín Romero de Torres, the Sempere's friend and colleague, Daniel Sempere embarks on a mission to uncover the man's identity and his relationship to his own mother, who died when Daniel was just four years old. To protect Daniel and to explain the circumstances behind this apparition, Fermín opens up for the first time about his traumatic past, narrating the story of his imprisonment in Montjüic Castle after the war and his harrowing escape from the prison into the streets of the dispossessed – the survivors of the war who roam Barcelona without an identity, hiding from the power-hungry officials of the newly-minted Franco regime. While imprisoned in Montjüic, Fermín meets David Martín (author of the book *The Angel's Game*, the second novel in Ruiz Zafón's series). Martín, known to his fellow inmates as the 'Prisoner of Heaven' because of his downward spiral into madness, helps Fermín to come up with a plan to escape the prison, using *The Count of Monte Cristo* as inspiration. When Fermín's cellmate appears to have died, Fermín gets into the body bag, which the prison guards deposit into a mass grave on the outskirts of the castle. Once free, Fermín ultimately finds his way back onto the streets, carefully avoiding Inspector Fumero while searching for the Sempere family, whom he has promised Martín he would protect. As Fermín tells his story and describes the complicated web of corruption in the Franco government, acknowledging Governor Mauricio Valls's role in Isabella Sempere's death, Daniel becomes increasingly dark and brooding, and he swears to find Valls and seek revenge. The novel ends with Daniel's visit to his mother's tomb, where he finds a note that Martín has left inside an angel statue, giving him information about how to locate Valls.

Since Ruiz Zafón became a household name in the early 2000s, numerous scholars have studied his work, mostly focusing on *The Shadow of the Wind*. Part of Ruiz Zafón's undeniable impact on Spanish literature has been the widespread application of the term 'Gothic' to his work; until his literary success, few (if any) Spanish authors consistently had their works described as such. To this extent, we might consider Ruiz Zafón's entrance on the literary scene a turning point for the classification of Spanish literature that led to the increased acceptance and recognition of Gothic fiction in contemporary Spain. Indeed, Glennis and Gordon Byron consider him 'Spain's premier writer of gothic fictions'[1] and for Xavier Aldana Reyes, Ruiz Zafón 'has become synonymous with the Spanish Gothic as a mode'.[2] Many have asserted (as I have elsewhere[3]) that Ruiz Zafón's fiction employs the Gothic mode as a way to open a dialogue with the recent traumatic past. Ann Davies has argued that, at least in the case of *The Shadow of the Wind*, the historical background is less salient than the Gothic elements used to narrate it precisely because of the novel's position within the bestselling genre, which makes it 'self-consciously Gothic'[4] – a position that Aldana Reyes adopts in his view of Ruiz Zafón's writing as 'just the right amalgam of influence, revision and innovation, offering variations on a theme that feel nationally distinctive yet remain relatable to non-Spanish readers'.[5] Both of these critics note *The Prisoner of Heaven* as an exception to their understanding of the author's transnational form, but neither elaborates on this concept, nor on the importance of this novel in the trajectory of Ruiz Zafón's 'Barcelona Gothic'. Here I will argue that *The Prisoner of Heaven* is a pivotal text in the *Cemetery of Forgotten Books* series precisely because of its direct references to historical events, places and figures from the civil war era, all developed within the dark Gothic atmosphere characteristic of Ruiz Zafón's literature. This novel, the most disturbing and violent of the first three in the series, marks a shift in the tone of his narrative that culminates in his equally graphic *The Labyrinth of the Spirits* (2016), which also makes significant references to the specific history of Spain's dictatorial era.

Drawing on Derrida's notion of testimony, and trauma studies scholarship by Cathy Caruth and others, in this chapter I propose a reading of *The Prisoner of Heaven* as a testimonial of horror by protagonist Fermín Romero de Torres, in which Ruiz Zafón presents the trauma-induced anxieties of the Franco era while also implying the continued relevance of these anxieties in a turbulent socio-political present. Ruiz Zafón's Montjuïc Castle is the ominous Gothic fortress on the hill overlooking a war-torn Barcelona populated by dispossessed zombies; deep within, the tortured prisoners of the Republican army lie in the darkness, awaiting death. Spectrality is a fundamental aspect of this horrifying environment:

like ghosts, Fermín and the other banished prisoners are invisible to society at large, and their stories have been erased from the official narrative, effectively silencing them through their state-mandated rendering as (un)dead. As Fermín slowly reveals his own story, he bears witness to the lives of his fellow prisoners and victims of Franco's fascist regime, rupturing the silence and giving a voice to the 'ghosts' – both living and deceased – around whose stories the country's past and future converge. Given the current rise in fascist rhetoric in Spain and around the world, Ruiz Zafón's novel clearly demonstrates the important role of Gothic fiction in the collective act of remembering, in this case subverting the regime's official discourse by accepting the monstrous as part of the real and by voicing the formerly unspeakable.

Continuing the tradition of the first two novels in his series, in *The Prisoner of Heaven* Ruiz Zafón's Barcelona is a Gothic labyrinth of dark streets, ominous fortresses and malicious characters. The novel begins in December 1957, which Daniel describes as 'another long winter of shadows and ashes'.[6] Throughout the text, the dark and dreary streets give the narrative a constant foreboding tone, which is punctuated by occasional storms that in one scene streak the sky 'in a blanket of red clouds' (p. 154), making the city look 'dark, entwined with sharp, black silhouettes' (p. 156). Montjüic castle is the Gothic centrepiece of this post-war Barcelona, an imposing fortress with towers looming over the city below. Ruiz Zafón's description of the castle emphasises its importance as a space of terror in the text:

> The fortress was anchored at the highest point of the rocky mountain, suspended between the sea to the east, Barcelona's carpet of shadows to the north and, to the south, the endless city of the dead – the old Montjüic Cemetery whose stench rose up among the boulders and filtered through cracks in the stone and through the bars of the cells. In times past, the castle had been used for bombarding the city below, but only a few months after the fall of Barcelona, in January, and the final defeat in April, death came to dwell there in silence and Barcelonians, trapped in the longest night of their history, preferred not to look skywards and recognise the prison's outline crowning the hill. (p. 59)

By referencing historical fact and portraying this space through a Gothic lens, Ruiz Zafón establishes Montjüic as the prime setting of his narrative, foreshadowing the horrors that will occur within the castle walls and the terror that the building itself induces in the population living in the city below. The months and years after the Nationalist victory are one long, endless night for the defeated Barcelonians, and the cemetery with its putrid stench of death is a constant reminder of the magnitude of loss. Even years after the war, in 1958, the castle is a recurring spatial reference point in the text, and Daniel and Fermín both see it as a 'ghostly bird of prey scrutinising the city at its feet, expectant' (p. 259), thus acknowledging that the terror it represents is still ongoing.

In this manner, Ruiz Zafón's Barcelona shifts the Gothic focus from the rural countryside or outskirts of town to the city centre. José Colmeiro has noted a similar shift in debates about historical memory:

> La reconfiguración de la relación entre memoria e identidad cultural bajo la nueva dinámica establecida entre lo local y lo global, el centro y la periferia, tiene en la ciudad un marco privilegiado. No cabe duda que el *locus* definidor de la cultura contemporánea se encuentra en el espacio conflictivo de la ciudad, lugar de identificación y desidentificación, y también lugar de memoria y olvido.
>
> [The reconfiguration of the relationship between memory and cultural identity under the new dynamic established between the local and the global, the centre and the periphery, has a privileged setting in the city. There is no doubt that the defining *locus* of contemporary culture is found in the conflictive space of the city, a place of identification and disidentification, and also a place of memory and oblivion.][7]

That the city now acts as a symbolic space for modern cultural debates about memory also confirms the importance of Ruiz Zafón's Barcelona Gothic as more than just a transnational approach to Gothic form; the continued references to historical events, places and figures in this novel mark the narrative space as an intersection between Gothic fiction and historical trauma, both of which mutually define and shape the testimonial nature of the text itself.

As the Ghost Speaks

Beyond a mere symbolic presence, in *The Prisoner of Heaven* the Spanish civil war and its aftermath take on corporeal form, embodied in the streets and in the characters who are based on real people from the Franco regime. Ruiz Zafón references rubble in the streets resulting from bombings during the siege (p. 156), the 'skeletons of burned lorries and wrecked wagons' and the 'ruinous state of the plant, bombed during the war and abandoned like so many other buildings all over the city' (p. 129). Salgado, upon his return to Barcelona after being freed from Montjüic, notes that the city looks different 'without dead bodies in the streets' (p. 23). The entire metropolitan area is thus the complete opposite of the portrait of modernity that the Franco regime would tout as part of its success; instead, the city dwellers live in ruinous streets whose war-torn buildings reflect the unspeakable horrors that they have witnessed. These streets become the space where Daniel and Fermín quite literally walk through memory, retracing footsteps in order to uncover censored truths.

The process that Fermín goes through while recounting these truths is an act of testimony, in which he bears witness to the atrocities committed by the fascist regime at the beginning of the dictatorship. For Derrida, to testify is 'to render public',[8] a paradoxical act that requires the voicing of a secret that speaks to the past while also being physically present in a moment that breaks the condition of the past – the 'instant' – to which it speaks. Derrida considers testimony to be an act haunted by the possibility of a lie, and yet he acknowledges that it is only through accepting the potential untruths that truthful testimony is achieved, noting: 'without the *possibility* of this fiction, without the spectral virtuality of this simulacrum and as a result of this lie or this fragmentation of the true, no truthful testimony would be possible'.[9] Derrida's understanding of testimony highlights its inherently problematic nature while also accepting its intrinsic value in the reconstruction and sharing of memory, including when it is presented in the form of literary fiction. Fermín's testimony in Ruiz Zafón's novel appears in the third person, having been directly shared with Daniel who then shares it with us in his book, twice demonstrating the rupture of the instant that Derrida sees as part of the testimonial act. Although we might question the veracity of Fermín's testimony, the sequence of events leading up to and immediately following it corroborates everything he has said, giving his memories particular weight in the text and further illuminating the historical aspect of the fiction before us. That said, Ruiz Zafón clearly constructs his narrative in such a way that readers will understand Fermín's testimony as real within the confines of the book, while also recognising that the book itself is a work of fiction portraying certain aspects of historical truth – an awareness that is heightened by the Gothic excesses of the novel.

Although trauma has always been part of Ruiz Zafón's Barcelona Gothic, in this novel it takes on a more profound role as both deeply personal and undeniably collective because of its testimonial form. Fermín's part of the narrative, which details the horrific brutality and violence of the Civil Guard inside the walls of Montjüic, takes up half of Ruiz Zafón's novel, structuring the text – including all prior and subsequent scenes – around these traumatic memories. For Caruth, trauma 'is always the story of a wound that cries out, that addresses us in the attempt to tell us of a reality or truth that is not otherwise available'.[10] Due to the nature of trauma, which is associated with delayed response, Caruth explains that it is not 'linked only to what is known, but also to what remains unknown in our very actions and our language'.[11] An act that helps to recover the known and the unknown, testimony can therefore be understood 'not as a mode of *statement of*, but rather as a mode of *access to*'[12] the traumatic truth. In recognition of the collective nature of the memories he is recalling, Fermín begins his testimony by immediately describing the shared experience of the prisoners held at Montjüic: 'New prisoners were brought in by night, in cars or black vans that set off from the police station on Vía Layetana and crossed the city silently, nobody noticing or wishing to notice them' (p. 59). Already treated as ghosts by the world around them, once inside the fortress the prisoners are given a number, 'usually that of the cell they were going to occupy and where they were likely to die' (p. 59). The cells inside Montjüic are small and dark, the walls 'covered with crudely etched marks and messages left by previous tenants' (p. 63) – a reference to documented writings and drawings on the walls of Montjüic that can still be seen today in some of the former prison cells. Ruiz Zafón also mentions the dramatic increase in the prison population in the months following the war, when Fermín notes: 'The country's jails couldn't cope with the influx. The military authorities had instructed the Montjüic prison management to . . . absorb part of the torrent of convicts flooding that defeated, miserable Barcelona of 1940' (p. 88). These references to verifiable historical truths bolster Fermín's status as a reliable witness and as a representative of his former fellow prison inmates who can no longer speak for themselves.

Ruiz Zafón's portrait of trauma in post-war Barcelona also includes numerous references to Franco and his regime through Fermín's critical lens. The uncensored protagonist comments on the 'tyranny of the National-Catholic propaganda and its surreptitious indoctrination techniques' (p. 30), calls Spain 'a country that keeps producing beasts' like the fascist Valls (p. 100), and refers to women's lack of rights when he describes a radio program that recommends that a woman caller make amends with her neglectful husband through 'prayer, patience and to make use of her feminine wiles, but only within the strict limits of the Christian family' (p. 121). These criticisms (among others) are echoed in Daniel's later characterisation of Franco's government as 'a rotten, corrupt regime' (p. 209). When examined alongside the other references to historical acts and figures from dictatorial Spain, it is clear that Ruiz Zafón's project with this novel is much more specific to the case of twentieth-century Spain than the first two books in his series, and the testimonial form gives *The Prisoner of Heaven* a tone of urgency that is not as identifiable in his previous works.

The horrors that Fermín describes throughout his testimony also closely mirror documented cases of torture and executions in and outside of Franco's prisons and concentration camps. Outside the prison walls, corrupt politicians and agents of the regime work together to maintain the politics of terror among the civilians in the streets. Inspector Fumero, a central character in *The Shadow of the Wind*, is less physically present in this novel but still equally threatening, adding to the baseline of fear in Fermín's testimony. The violent and vindictive agent of law first appears as a memory in the form of scars all over Fermín's body, 'burns covering his torso, buttocks and much of his thighs', the sight of which prompts the prison guard to remark: 'It looks like our champion is an old acquaintance of Fumero's' (p. 61). Once he has escaped from the prison, Fermín is in constant fear of getting caught by Fumero and his men; the inspector, always searching for his old nemesis, continues to torture and kill suspects who he believes may be connected to Fermín and the Semperes, in one scene leaving behind mutilated bodies in a lodge that he has his agents burn to the ground (p. 144). Here, again, Ruiz Zafón references real historical figures: Fumero is an undeniable representation of some of the more notorious agents working for Franco's regime, most notably Antonio González Pacheco, known as 'Billy El Niño'. As an inspector with the Political-Social Brigade, González Pacheco was repeatedly accused of horrific acts of violence and torture throughout his career (charges that he never denied), but due to the 1977 Amnesty Law he was never prosecuted for his crimes and, in fact, he retained all of his regime-awarded medals and honours at the time of his death from COVID in May 2020[13] – a fact that turned the profound injustice of his violent acts into an ongoing trauma among the families of his victims. Much like the brutality of the streets outside, inside Ruiz Zafón's Montjüic prison, graphic scenes of torture and violence are an equally vivid part of Fermín's testimony. He recalls, for instance, that '[o]nce a fortnight a summary trial took place and those condemned were shot at dawn' (p. 71). Individual prisoners are frequently taken away for questioning, only to return beaten, bloodied, or – in Salgado's case – missing limbs entirely, coming back to the cell with 'a throbbing stump of purplish flesh cauterised with tar' (p. 99). Governor Valls does not deny the atrocities that occur inside the prison, even telling Fermín that Salgado is also 'missing some other key equipment he's lost along the way because of his stubborn refusal to cooperate' (p. 92). The prison tortures its inhabitants with an overwhelming atmosphere of horror, monstrosity and death, in which the inmates – 'teeming with nits and stinking of urine' (p. 100) – slowly spiral into madness as they await their inevitable execution.

One prisoner, David Martín, suffers from such serious delusions and psychotic episodes that the inmates call him 'The Prisoner of Heaven'. The governor has commissioned Martín to be the ghost writer for his memoirs, but instead Martín dedicates his time to writing what will become *The Angel's Game* (the second novel in Ruiz Zafón's series), in a frenzied process that emphasises the inherent connection between authorship and trauma. As Martín becomes less attached to the reality around him, his desperation to record his memories on paper increases dramatically. When Valls no longer permits him to have paper or ink as punishment for refusing to write his commissioned book, Martín 'would cut his hands and arms and use his own blood' (p. 182) to continue his work. The dire need to leave a record of the past – to bear witness to the trauma that he and others have suffered – leads him to write his text with his own bodily fluid, creating a narrative that is quite literally part of himself. In this case, authorship is paradoxically both an act of self-preservation and self-sacrifice, as the Derridean 'instant' necessarily becomes a catalyst for further trauma induced by the insatiable need to tell his secret. Dominick LaCapra describes this aspect of testimony in spectral terms, explaining that 'the survivor as witness often relives traumatic events and is possessed by the past'.[14] The lawyer Brians tells Fermín that he believes Martín 'has realised he's losing his mind, so he's trying to write down what he remembers before it's too late. It's as if he were writing himself a letter to find out who he is' (p. 175). Martín's madness is thus a result of the trauma he has experienced before and during his imprisonment but also, more importantly, of the fear that his story might not be told and that he, himself, may cease to exist; from within the liminal space that he inhabits between reality and the spectral realm of the past, Martín's authorial voice finally manages to reach its intended audience (Daniel, through Fermín), thus giving a symbolic ghost access to the present and hope of restoring memory through the living.

For Fermín as well, the act of retelling past trauma has an inevitably spectral connotation: not only is he invoking memories of his deceased fellow prisoners, he is also recognising his own ghostly nature as a man who no longer exists according to the official state narrative. Fermín's identification as a spectral presence begins with the title of part two of the novel: 'From Among the Dead'. With this title, Ruiz Zafón structures his text around spectrality and trauma, indicating that this man without documentation – a survivor of the atrocities of war – is representative of countless others like him who roam the streets in the post-war era. After he escapes

Montjüic, Fermín emerges from the body bag in a mass grave 'packed with rotting bodies and covered in quicklime . . . the open grave spreading at his feet like an ocean of tangled corpses' (p. 138). When he reaches a shanty town near the beach, he collapses in the street where two children discover him, a 'skeletal figure that seemed to be bleeding from every pore' (p. 140). His body, seemingly already that of a dead man, bears witness to the trauma he has suffered, and when asked where he has come from, Fermín replies: 'I've come back from among the dead' (p. 140).

Part three of the novel, titled 'Reborn', continues Fermín's testimony and elaborates on his self-identification as a spectral presence in the ominous streets of Barcelona. Spectrality quickly becomes a sign of difference for Fermín and the others living in the impoverished streets on the outskirts of the city, where a community of Roma people led by Armando (a self-described 'Gypsy') help Fermín to recover. Disgusted by the lack of truths in the local newspapers, which cover up the fact that a prisoner has escaped from Montjüic by instead declaring him dead, Armando acknowledges that he 'only existed in the invisible world of the poor and the untouchables', stating: 'There are times and places where not to be anyone is more honourable than to be someone' (p. 147). Here, ghostliness is a condition of a society that marginalises the poor and ethnic minorities, whose own stories of trauma are completely censored from official narratives. As Fermín explains to Daniel, '[a] law of silence made it plain that the city and the world ended at the gates of the shanty town' (p. 148), thereby marking the physical boundary between the urban, nationalist regime and the others it has pushed to the margins of society.

Fermín's 'rebirth' does not allow him to entirely return to the land of the living, instead relegating him to the liminal, ghostly status of the undocumented. In his dreams, he returns every night to the mass grave, where he sees a 'flood of ghostly bodies stirring like an eddy of eels. The dead bodies opened their eyes and climbed the walls, following him' (p. 149). In these recurring nightmares, Fermín realises that the terrifying undead 'only wanted to return to their homes, to their beds, and embrace the children, wives and lovers they had left behind. Yet nobody would open the door to them' (p. 149). The terror of these dreams is not the haunting, but the inescapable condition of spectrality itself: with no name and no official identity, none of these undocumented citizens can return to the lives they left behind without jeopardising the safety of their loved ones and themselves. When Fermín finally regains consciousness and is healed enough to leave the village, Armando informs him of his official death notice, saying: 'Fermín, you can do what you want, because you don't exist . . . you're now one of us, people who have no name and are not documented anywhere. We're ghosts. Invisible' (p. 153). After this point, Fermín is repeatedly ghosted by others around him, who tell him '[y]ou don't exist' (p. 174) and describe him as 'a beggar without a name' (p. 184). The trauma of his imprisonment and torture thus continues with the trauma of his own spectrality, a direct result of the Franco regime's marginalisation of all those who did not belong to the accepted categories of 'Spaniard' or adopt the new policy of silent obedience.

Silence, another distinctive feature of Ruiz Zafón's Barcelona Gothic, is also portrayed in spectral terms in direct relation to trauma, where the telling or not telling of one's story becomes an integral part of how survivors identify themselves and cope with the returns of the past. Fermín explains the torturous silence of trauma to Daniel as a widespread, collective phenomenon in the post-war era:

> Your father, like so many people who had to live through those years, swallowed everything and kept quiet. They just had to lump it. You pass them in the street every day and don't even see them. They've rotted away all these years with that pain inside them so that you, and others like you, could live. (p. 185)

The atmosphere of the first two decades of the dictatorship is permeated with silence, rendering all would-be dissenters ghostly. Theirs is a trauma that comes from mandated silence – from not speaking their truths, which continue to haunt them. Dori Laub has argued that in cases of traumatic incidents with potential testimonial witnesses, when the story is not told it 'serves as a perpetuation of its tyranny. The events become more and more distorted in their silent retention and pervasively invade and contaminate the survivor's daily life.'[15] Laub asserts that these survivors of trauma have 'an imperative need to *tell* and thus to come to *know* one's story, unimpeded by ghosts from the past against which one has to protect oneself. One has to know one's buried truth in order to be able to live one's life.'[16] Likewise, Zoë Crossland connects the testimonial act to 'the tangible materiality of the grave, and to its power to reveal past violence and to forcefully insert this spectacle into the present'.[17] Thus, we can read the collective pain of silence that Fermín describes above as a continuation of the politics of terror that defined the early stages of Francoism – a tyranny in perpetuation, mandated by censorship laws and the continual threat of violence against those who speak. To this extent, the act of giving testimony is therefore aligned with Ruiz Zafón's notion of rebirth: through telling their truths, survivors of trauma regain control of their own narratives, taking authorship of their own stories that recognise the ghosts of the past.

Testimony, then, is a powerful act that inherently binds the individual and the collective into an intertextual narrative of memory. Nevertheless, the act of bearing witness is often overwhelming for survivors, who may show signs of distress and even emotional breakdown during their testimony precisely because of the latency of trauma itself. We see these effects on Fermín, who becomes weak and 'so overcome with pain from remembering' (p. 97) as he tells Daniel his story. By the end of Fermín's testimony, Daniel notes that he 'was speaking in a feeble voice and looked disconsolate. Conjuring up those memories seemed to have left him lifeless' (p. 183). The psychological effects of telling the story are also passed on to Daniel as he relates Fermín's testimony to his wife, Bea: 'At first I felt anger swelling up inside me again, but as I advanced through the story I was overwhelmed by sadness and despair . . . I didn't know how I was going to be able to live with the secrets and implications of what Fermín had revealed to me' (p. 194). For Daniel, now a keeper of the traumatic secrets that Fermín has shared with him, the thought of silence is unbearable, and thus a new cycle of speaking the truth begins with Daniel's authorship of the very book that we are reading, thereby making us complicit in witnessing the trauma that unfolds in its pages.

Together, the repeated condemnations of the dictatorship and the graphic portrayal of brutality and violence make *The Prisoner of*

Heaven Ruiz Zafón's most undeniably political novel in his *Cemetery of Forgotten Books* series, and also the most clearly related to Spain's historical memory. Whereas the first two novels in the series could conceivably be interpreted on a broader scale as a representation of the general collective experience of twentieth-century trauma, this novel speaks directly to Spain's dictatorial past and ongoing fight to recover authorship of its own narrative. For Colmeiro, the testimonial act is a necessary process in contemporary Spain: 'Para superar esta crisis de la memoria, de carácter ya casi crónico en la sociedad española, es necesario superar el pasado; pero para ello sería preciso rehistorificar la memoria colectiva, deshacer los nudos del pasado atado y bien atado y abrirlo a la conciencia crítica' ['In order to overcome this crisis of memory, of an almost chronic character in Spanish society, it is necessary to overcome the past; but for that it would be necessary to rehistorify collective memory, to undo the very well-tied knots of the past and open it to the critical consciousness'].[18] Jo Labanyi likewise states: 'In a country that has emerged from forty years of cultural repression, the task of making reparation to the ghosts of the past – that is, to those relegated to the status of living dead, denied voice and memory – is considerable.'[19] By focusing his novel specifically on Spain's inherited trauma and by presenting it in testimonial form, Ruiz Zafón acknowledges this need to bear witness to the horrors of Francoism. Moreover, by crafting his trauma narrative as a Gothic novel, he emphasises the unspeakable nature of the atrocities committed by the regime, magnifying the contrast between the uncensored testimony and the politics of silence that control the official narratives.

Ruiz Zafón's conclusion is, at least in part, positive: Fermín takes over for Isaac as caretaker of the Cemetery of Forgotten Books, ensuring that the censored voices of the past and present will continue to be guarded and preserved into the as-yet unknown future. For Daniel, however, the new knowledge of these secrets is destructive, and he promises himself that he will seek revenge for the victims in Fermín's story, and especially for his mother, Isabella. It is not until the end of the fourth and final novel in the series, *The Labyrinth of the Spirits*, that Daniel will be able to uncover the whole truth and document it through his writing (which appears to us as these two novels). Authorship, then, is a fundamental aspect of Ruiz Zafón's literary project, demonstrating that the extent to which individual and collective voices are heard (or censored) determines a society's ability to process trauma and identity. Ruiz Zafón's Barcelona Gothic exemplifies the power of the Gothic form to transcend national and cultural boundaries while also remaining deeply personal and relevant to regional histories. As a Spanish Gothic author, Ruiz Zafón shows us time and again that terror comes from reality itself, and that in Spain, Gothic novels need not invent new monsters, because recent history is populated with them. Our takeaway, then, is to make sure that the stories of the victims are heard – not silenced – in order to foster a more inclusive national memory that acknowledges trauma, instead of pushing our ghosts to the margins of society where they will inevitably continue to haunt us.

Conclusion

While I was writing the final chapters of this book, Spanish Parliament passed the Democratic Memory Law, which went into effect on 21 October 2022. This law, a major part of the Pedro Sánchez government's platform to address historical memory and the Franco legacy, takes several significant steps in the ongoing battle for control of the memory narrative: the Franco dictatorship is officially declared illegal, the government will play an active role in the exhumations and identifications of remains in mass graves, and the existing symbols and honours associated with the regime will be dissolved (including the Francisco Franco Foundation and all titles of nobility). As part of these measures, the Valley of the Fallen has been renamed the 'Valley of Cuelgamuros' and José Antonio Primo de Rivera's remains (which have, until now, been in a prominent location inside the basilica) were removed to private burial in Madrid's San Isidro Cemetery on 24 April 2023.[1] Additionally, the law requires the removal of the remains of several other key figures in the Franco regime who are still buried in places of honour inside cathedrals and churches throughout the country.[2] The law also creates a dedicated office for the investigation of human rights violations during the period of the dictatorship, and defines more specifically the status of 'victim' and the rights they have, for the first time granting Spanish citizenship to the children of political exiles.

Not surprisingly, this law has provoked strong reactions from conservative leaders in Spain – among them representatives of the Partido Popular and Vox – who have long argued that the 1977 Pact of Forgetting should be left in place. Vowing to repeal this new law if they have a majority in the next national election cycle, the conservative opposition has declared it 'una traición a los españoles' ['a betrayal to Spaniards'], with Vox describing it as 'un ataque vil y miserable' ['a vile and miserable attack'] on the country's recent history.[3] This dramatic difference in opinion regarding the preservation of Spanish historical memory is symptomatic of the deep political divide that has only continued to grow in recent years, centred primarily on how the country views the past and what role that view can and will play in the imminent future. As Sebastiaan Faber has noted, 'Spanish democracy is anything but consolidated. If anything, it is dangerously fragile, with its longtime Francoist substratum on the rise rather than in retreat.'[4]

The Vox party's recent rise to power in Spain parallels significant political gains in adjacent far-right movements throughout Europe and in the United States. In fact, in his book on the origins of Vox, Miguel González points specifically to Donald Trump's 2016 presidential win as highly influential to Vox president Santiago Abascal's crafting of his own party's image; thus, Trump's 'Make America Great Again' (MAGA) slogan became Vox's 'Hacer España Grande Otra Vez' ['Make Spain Great Again'] and 'America First' became 'Los españoles primero' ['Spaniards first'].[5] The political platform is also strikingly similar to that of MAGA conservatives: Vox embraces nationalism, prioritises the traditional family rooted in Christian values, opposes abortion rights and same-sex marriage, fights against climate legislation, and advocates for strict, punitive measures to stop illegal immigration. Vox and MAGA – alongside other far-right movements like those led by France's Marine Le Pen, Italy's Giorgia Meloni and Hungary's Viktor Orbán – present to their constituents a political platform based on a nostalgic, mythologised view of the past that rejects progress and promotes authoritarianism. For Vox, much of that image of the past relies on the repudiation of historical memory and, in some cases, glorifies the image of the dictatorship. On 28 April 2019, as the spring election cycle began, Vox posted to their Twitter account: '¡Que comience la batalla!' ['Let the battle begin!'], with an image from *Lord of the Rings* showing Aragorn, as Spain, preparing for battle against the Mordor Orcs, whose faces are covered with the symbols and flags of various opposition groups including feminists, the Second Republic, anarchists, communists, LGBTQ+ rights and several news organisations.[6] After a successful election cycle, the Vox account followed up with the phrase 'Ya hemos pasao' ['We've already passed'], a direct reference to the song made famous by Celia Gámez after the Nationalists won the civil war in 1939, in which the Francoists made fun of the defeated Republicans' famous slogan 'No pasarán' ['They shall not pass'].[7] This contemporary invocation of the Franco dictatorship has also found its way to American politics, where Anthony Sabatini (a Republican member of the Florida House of Representatives) most recently tweeted a quote from Franco – 'I answer only to God and to History' – and then followed it with a photograph of the dictator standing with President Eisenhower, writing in response: 'Anyone who criticizes the above tweet is extremely un-American.'[8] The combination of far-right politics and Christian religious ideology that characterises the Vox and MAGA platforms inevitably recalls Franco's National Catholicism and other twentieth-century fascist movements, leading to the undeniable conclusion that the twenty-first-century political stage is primed for a repetition of the last century's struggles.

In *Spectral Spain*, we have seen how Spanish authors represent this national trauma through a spectral lens, making full use of Gothic conventions to illustrate the politics of terror, the oppressive feminine ideal, the marginalisation of ethnic minorities and the poor, the devastating economic and cultural effects of rural exodus, the widespread application of censorship, and the consequences on the children who grew up in this environment of fear and silence. Rendered ghostly because of a national pact that mandated forgetting, these traces of the past have continued to work their way into contemporary Spanish cultural production, seeking reparations for the collective trauma the country has endured. From a sociological perspective, as Avery Gordon asserts, '[g]hostly matters are part of social life. If we want to . . . contribute, in however small a measure, to changing it, we must learn how to identify hauntings and reckon with ghosts, must learn how to make contact with what is without doubt often painful, difficult, and unsettling.'[9] Part of the difficulty of dealing with these ghosts is, as we have seen, the inevitability of their return; Derrida, for example, insists that 'the future can only be for ghosts. And the past.'[10] These spectral returns transform our concept of linear chronology into a cyclical pattern that never fully rids itself of the traces of the past, especially where trauma is ongoing. In Spain, the landscape itself is dotted with mass graves that continue to serve as a symbol of the brutality of the regime and the pervasive silence of its aftermath. For Joan Ramon Resina, these bodies also represent the continuing failure of the government to fully reconcile with the past:

> The dead who are not granted passage into the cultural beyond remain politically active. Unable to go on living themselves, the survivors become permanent reminders of a past that no one wants to heed. Their broken lives are evidence that a state that does not bury the dead decomposes alongside the corpses.[11]

Like Resina, the authors we have studied here have all presented similar appeals to historical memory, recognising the need to acknowledge individual and collective trauma in a society that 'todavía vive de espaldas a sus fantasmas históricos' ['still lives with its back to its historical ghosts'].[12]

For all of the authors included in this book, the Gothic is the most appropriate form to represent the fractured national self that emerged from the darkness and terror of twentieth-century trauma. Using such conventions as the unspeakable, entrapment, duplicity, abjection, monstrosity, fragmentation and degeneration, our authors have demonstrated the transgressive power of the Gothic and its inherent ability to speak to fears that continue to be relevant today. In fact, Labanyi has argued in accordance with Bonnie Honig that 'the most appropriate genre for narrating the nation is not the romance but the gothic novel, for democracy does not mean living happily ever after with those you love, but learning to live nonviolently with those you would rather not live with and who may fill you with terror'.[13] Our authors, then, employ the Gothic as a means of narrating twentieth-century Spain, detailing collective experiences that resonate with their readers on a regional, national and, indeed, international level. Their narrative inevitably portrays the post-Franco nation as a house – and a landscape – haunted by the ghosts of the recent past; the increasing persistence of these ghosts corresponds with the growing need to recognise the flaws of the democratic structure itself, which was built around the figures and institutions of Francoism. The ongoing fear that Armengou and Belis have witnessed in their interviews with victims of the war is evidence of these failings, prompting them to ask: '¿Podemos hablar de democracia cuando todavía existe ese miedo?' ['Can we speak about democracy when that fear still exists?'].[14]

As authors writing in the post-Franco era, Mercè Rodoreda, Adelaida García Morales, Ana María Matute, Julio Llamazares, Cristina Fernández Cubas, Espido Freire and Carlos Ruiz Zafón allude to the recent historical past in their Gothic narratives; as readers of these texts in the twenty-first century, we cannot help but note the similarities between the authoritarianism portrayed in these novels and the current rise of the far-right throughout much of the world. No longer just a phenomenon of contemporary Spain, these widespread signs of neo-fascism once more beg the question: what will we do with the ghosts of the past? In Spain, as the continued popularity of Gothic literary and cultural production seems to indicate, there is a real need to come to terms with the haunting presences of twentieth-century national trauma. By reading and studying these texts, we can begin to understand the important work of Spain's historical memory activists who oversee the current exhumation of the mass graves scattered across the country, and the widespread fear of a return to the authoritarian policies of the not-so-distant past (as current Spanish politics once again returns to debate the rhetoric of the Franco regime frequently employed by the Vox party). Especially for women writers in the post-Franco period, there is a clear need to reclaim authorial voice through recognition of the recent injustices of an era that deprived them of agency; these ghosts, rooted in the oppressive policies of National Catholicism, serve as a reminder of the fragility of democracy and the precarious balance of human rights. As Spain continues to grapple with its political treatment of historical memory, these authors – speaking from the margins – bear witness to a Gothicised national past and warn us of its potential spectral return in the imminent future.

Notes

Introduction

1. Javier Marías, *Tomorrow in the Battle Think on Me*, trans. Margaret Jull Costa (New York: Harcourt Brace & Company, 1996), pp. 66–7.
2. Jo Labanyi has noted, similarly, that the term 'post-Franco' 'defines it as a period haunted by a spectral Francoist past'. See: 'History and Hauntology; or, What Does One Do with the Ghosts of the Past? Reflections on Spanish Film and Fiction of the Post-Franco Period', in J. R. Resina (ed.), *Disremembering the Dictatorship: The Politics of Memory in the Spanish Transition to Democracy* (Amsterdam: Editions Rodopi B. V., 2000), p. 68.
3. Sebastiaan Faber, *Exhuming Franco: Spain's Second Transition* (Nashville: Vanderbilt University Press, 2021).
4. See Jo Labanyi, *Spanish Culture from Romanticism to the Present: Structures of Feeling* (Cambridge: Legenda, 2019), p. 8: Cultural historians of Spain have in fact noted that Spain has the most mass graves of any country in the world except Cambodia.
5. Even in cases where these street names have been changed, these changes have been fiercely contested, as noted most recently in a controversial March 2021 decision in Oviedo (capital of the northern community of Asturias) to return the names of several streets to their Franco-era names honouring nationalist war heroes and the coup of 19 July 1936, after they had been changed in 2019 to honour the

memory of people who were not associated with the regime (or those who actively fought and spoke out against it).

6 The transition to democracy, known among Hispanists simply as the 'Transition', is a period that historians generally place in a range of years from the late 1970s to the late 1980s. Teresa Vilarós, however, extends this period to a twenty-year span starting before Franco's death, in 1973, and ending roughly in 1993.

7 Jacques Derrida, *Specters of Marx: The State of the Debt, the Work of Mourning, & the New International*, trans. Peggy Kamuf (New York: Routledge, 1994).

8 Jo Labanyi, *Constructing Identity in Contemporary Spain: Theoretical Debates and Cultural Practice* (New York: Oxford University Press, 2002), p. 1.

9 Jo Labanyi, 'Memory and Modernity in Democratic Spain: The Difficulty of Coming to Terms with the Spanish Civil War', *Poetics Today*, 28/1 (2007), 109.

10 Eloy E. Merino and H. Rosi Song (eds), *Traces of Contamination: Unearthing the Francoist Legacy in Contemporary Spanish Discourse* (Lewisburg: Bucknell University Press, 2005), p. 17.

11 José Colmeiro, 'Nation of Ghosts?: Haunting, Historical Memory and Forgetting in Post-Franco Spain', *452°F*, 4 (2011), 28.

12 Patricia Keller, *Ghostly Landscapes: Film, Photography, and the Aesthetics of Haunting in Contemporary Spanish Culture* (Toronto: University of Toronto Press, 2016), p. 15.

13 Antonio Córdoba and Daniel García-Donoso (eds), *Rite, Flesh, and Stone: The Matter of Death in Contemporary Spanish Culture* (Nashville: Vanderbilt University Press, 2021), p. 10.

14 See, for instance, articles on spectrality in Spanish film by Anne Hardcastle (2005), Isabel Alvarez-Sancho (2016), María Gil Poisa (2016), Sarah Thomas (2016), as well as monographs on Spanish Gothic by Ann Davies (2016) and Xavier Aldana Reyes (2017).

15 Fred Botting, *Gothic* (London: Routledge, 1996), p. 1.

16 Labanyi, *Constructing Identity*, p. 1.

17 Labanyi, *Constructing Identity*, p. 7.

18 Xavier Aldana Reyes, *Spanish Gothic: National Identity, Collaboration and Cultural Adaptation* (London: Palgrave MacMillan, 2017), pp. 17–22.

19 Jo Labanyi, 'History and Hauntology; or, What Does One Do with the Ghosts of the Past? Reflections on Spanish Film and Fiction of the Post-Franco Period', in J. R. Resina (ed.), *Disremembering the*

Dictatorship: The Politics of Memory in the Spanish Transition to Democracy (Amsterdam: Editions Rodopi B. V., 2000), pp. 65–82.

20   Janet Pérez, 'Contemporary Spanish Women Writers and the Feminine Neo-Gothic', *Romance Quarterly*, 51/2 (2004), 125–40.

21   Miriam López Santos, *La novela gótica en España (1788–1833)* (Pontevedra: Editorial Academia del Hispanismo, 2010).

22   Abigail Lee Six, *The Gothic Fiction of Adelaida García Morales: Haunting Words* (Woodbridge: Tamesis, 2006).

23   See *Gothic Terrors: Incarceration, Duplication, and Bloodlust in Spanish Narrative* (Lewisburg: Bucknell University Press, 2010); and *Spanish Vampire Fiction Since 1900: Blood Relations* (London: Routledge, 2019).

24   Ann Davies, *Contemporary Spanish Gothic* (Edinburgh: Edinburgh University Press, 2016), p. 175.

25   Aldana Reyes, *Spanish Gothic*, p. 23.

26   Teresa M. Vilarós, *El mono del desencanto: Una crítica de la transición española (1973–1993)* (Madrid: Siglo XXI Editores, 1998), p. 244.

27   Michael Richards, 'Grand Narratives, Collective Memory, and Social History: Public Uses of the Past in Postwar Spain', in C. Jerez-Farrán and S. Amago (eds), *Unearthing Franco's Legacy: Mass Graves and the Recovery of Historical Memory in Spain* (Notre Dame: University of Notre Dame, 2010), p. 141.

28   Paul Ricoeur, *Memory, History, Forgetting*, trans. Kathleen Blamey and David Pellauer (Chicago: University of Chicago Press, 2004).

29   Nicholas Abraham and Maria Torok, *The Shell and the Kernel: Renewals of Psychoanalysis*, ed. and trans. Nicholas T. Rand (Chicago: University of Chicago Press, 1994).

30   Richard J. Golsan (ed.), *Fascism's Return: Scandal, Revision, and Ideology Since 1980* (Lincoln: University of Nebraska Press, 1998), p. 6.

31   Joan Ramon Resina, *The Ghost in the Constitution: Historical Memory and Denial in Spanish Society* (Liverpool: Liverpool University Press, 2017), p. 2.

32   Avery Gordon, *Ghostly Matters: Haunting and the Sociological Imagination* (Minneapolis: University of Minnesota Press, 2008), p. 7.

33   Carlos Jerez-Farrán and Samuel Amago (eds), *Unearthing Franco's Legacy: Mass Graves and the Recovery of Historical Memory in Spain* (Notre Dame: University of Notre Dame Press, 2010), p. 1.

34   George E. Haggerty, *Gothic Fiction/Gothic Form* (University Park: The Pennsylvania State University Press, 1989), p. 3.

35   Carmen Moreno Nuño, 'The Ghosts of Javier Marías: The Trauma of a Civil War Unforgotten', in E. Merino and H. Rosi Song (eds),

Notes

Traces of Contamination: Unearthing the Francoist Legacy in Contemporary Spanish Discourse (Lewisburg: Bucknell University Press, 2005), p. 129.

36. Joan Ramon Resina, 'Short of Memory: The Reclamation of the Past Since the Spanish Transition to Democracy', in J. R. Resina (ed.), *Disremembering the Dictatorship: The Politics of Memory in the Spanish Transition to Democracy* (Amsterdam: Editions Rodopi B. V., 2000), p. 112.
37. Fiona Schouten, *A Diffuse Murmur of History: Literary Memory Narratives of Civil War and Dictatorship in Spanish Novels After 1990* (Brussels: Peter Lang, 2010), p. 16.
38. María del Pilar Blanco and Esther Peeren (eds), *The Spectralities Reader: Ghosts and Haunting in Contemporary Cultural Theory* (New York: Bloomsbury, 2013), p. 16.
39. Vilarós, *El mono*, p. 31.

Part I: Introduction

1. Ellen Moers, *Literary Women* (New York: Anchor Books, 1977), p. 203.
2. Sandra M. Gilbert and Susan Gubar, *The Madwoman in the Attic: The Woman Writer and the Nineteenth-Century Literary Imagination* (New Haven: Yale University Press, 1979), p. 17.
3. Maggie Kilgour, *The Rise of the Gothic Novel* (New York: Routledge, 1995), p. 9.
4. Kate Ferguson Ellis, *The Contested Castle: Gothic Novels and the Subversion of Domestic Ideology* (Urbana: University of Illinois Press, 1989), p. 219.
5. Gina Wisker, *Contemporary Women's Gothic Fiction* (London: Palgrave, 2016), p. 14.
6. Diana Wallace, 'A Woman's Place', in A. Horner and S. Zlosnik (eds), *Women and the Gothic: An Edinburgh Companion* (Edinburgh: Edinburgh University Press, 2016), p. 75.
7. Dara Downey, *American Women's Ghost Stories in the Gilded Age* (New York: Palgrave, 2014), p. 13.
8. Rosario Ruiz Franco, *¿Eternas menores? Las mujeres en el franquismo* (Madrid: Biblioteca Nueva, 2007), p. 28.
9. Rosa Isabel Galdona Pérez, *Discurso femenino en la novela española de posguerra: Carmen Laforet, Ana María Matute y Elena Quiroga* (La Laguna: Universidad de La Laguna, 2001), p. 126.
10. Galdona Pérez, *Discurso femenino*, p. 347.

Notes

11 Hélène Cixous, 'The Laugh of the Medusa', *Signs*, 1/4 (1976), 880.
12 Donna Heiland, *Gothic & Gender: An Introduction* (Oxford: Blackwell Publishing, 2004), p. 158.

Chapter 1

1 Kathleen McNerney, 'Introduction', in K. McNerney and N. Vosburg (eds), *The Garden Across the Border: Mercè Rodoreda's Fiction* (Selinsgrove: Susquehanna University Press, 1994), p. 7.
2 María Isidra Mencos, 'Mercè Rodoreda and the Criticism of Her Works: Analysis and Selected Bibliography', in K. McNerney (ed.), *The Voices and Visions: The Words and Works of Mercè Rodoreda* (Selinsgrove: Susquehanna University Press, 1999), p. 241.
3 Joan Ramon Resina, *The Ghost in the Constitution: Historical Memory and Denial in Spanish Society* (Liverpool: Liverpool University Press, 2017), p. 156.
4 Lisa Vollendorf, 'Exchanging Terms: Toward the Feminist Fantastic in *Mirall trencat*', in K. McNerney (ed.), *Voices and Visions: The Words and Works of Mercè Rodoreda* (Selinsgrove: Susquehanna University Press, 1999), p. 158.
5 Eva Bru, 'Between the Abject and the Sublime: Excessive Bodies in Mercè Rodoreda's *El Carrer de les Camèlies* and *Mirall trencat*', *Catalan Review*, 24 (2010), 321.
6 Resina, *The Ghost in the Constitution*, p. 147.
7 Christine R. Arkinstall, *Gender, Class, and Nation: Mercè Rodoreda and the Subjects of Modernism* (Lewisburg: Bucknell University Press, 2004), p. 139.
8 Gonzalo Navajas, 'Normative Order and the Catalan *Heimat* in Mercè Rodoreda's *Mirall trencat*', in K. McNerney and N. Vosburg (eds), *The Garden Across the Border: Mercè Rodoreda's Fiction* (Selinsgrove: Susquehanna University Press, 1994), p. 99.
9 Bru, 'Between the Abject and the Sublime', 314.
10 Elizabeth Scarlett, '"Vinculada a les flors": Flowers and the Body in *Jardí vora el mar* and *Mirall trencat*', in K. McNerney and N. Vosburg (eds), *The Garden Across the Border: Mercè Rodoreda's Fiction* (Selinsgrove: Susquehanna University Press, 1994), p. 74.
11 Josefina González, '*Mirall trencat*: un umbral autobiográfico en la obra de Mercè Rodoreda', *Revista de Estudios Hispánicos*, 30/1 (1996), 109.
12 Arkinstall, *Gender, Class, and Nation*, p. 119.

Notes

[13] Vollendorf, 'Exchanging Terms', p. 157.
[14] Janet Pérez, 'Gothic Spaces, Transgressions, and Apparitions in *Mirall trencat*: Rodoreda's Adaptation of the Paradigm', in K. McNerney and N. Vosburg (eds), *The Garden Across the Border: Mercè Rodoreda's Fiction* (Selinsgrove: Susquehanna University Press, 1994), p. 95.
[15] Mercè Rodoreda, *A Broken Mirror*, trans. Josep Miquel Sobrer (Lincoln: University of Nebraska Press, 2006), p. 24.
[16] González, '*Mirall trencat*', 106.
[17] Pérez, 'Gothic Spaces', p. 89.
[18] Scarlett, '"Vinculada a les flors"', p. 78.
[19] Dara Downey, *American Women's Ghost Stories in the Gilded Age* (New York: Palgrave, 2014), p. 37.
[20] Arkinstall, *Gender, Class, and Nation*, p. 149.
[21] Bru, 'Between the Abject and the Sublime', 316.
[22] Vollendorf, 'Exchanging Terms', p. 165.
[23] Downey, *American Women's Ghost Stories*, p. 78.
[24] Pérez, 'Gothic Spaces', p. 92.
[25] Vollendorf, 'Exchanging Terms', p. 164.
[26] Vollendorf, 'Exchanging Terms', p. 164.
[27] Navajas, 'Normative Order', p. 102.
[28] Navajas, 'Normative Order', p. 101.
[29] Resina, *The Ghost in the Constitution*, p. 120.
[30] Vollendorf, 'Exchanging Terms', p. 162.
[31] Vollendorf, 'Exchanging Terms', p. 171.
[32] McNerney, 'Introduction', p. 8.
[33] Pérez, 'Gothic Spaces', p. 95.

Chapter 2

[1] Currie K. Thompson, 'Adelaida García Morales's *Bene* and That Not-so-obscure Object of Desire', *Revista de Estudios Hispánicos*, 22/1 (Jan 1988), 100–1.
[2] Elizabeth J. Ordóñez, *Voices of Their Own: Contemporary Spanish Narrative by Women* (Cranbury: Associated University Press, 1991), p. 174.
[3] Abigail Lee Six, *The Gothic Fiction of Adelaida García Morales: Haunting Words* (Woodbridge: Tamesis, 2006), p. 21.
[4] Epicteto José Díaz, 'Imágenes de la soledad en *El Sur* y *Bene* de Adelaida García Morales', *Revista de Literatura*, 70/139 (Jan–June 2008), 231.

Notes

5 Thomas G. Deveny, 'Preface', in A. García Morales, *The South and Bene: Two Novellas*, trans. Thomas G. Deveny (Lincoln: University of Nebraska Press, 1999), p. ix.
6 Carolina García Sanz, '"Disciplinando al gitano" en el siglo XX: regulación y parapenalidad en España desde una perspectiva europea', *Historia y Política*, 40 (2019), 127.
7 García Sanz, 'Disciplinando al gitano', 127.
8 David Corkill, 'Race, Immigration and Multiculturalism in Spain', in B. Jordan and R. Morgan-Tamosunas (eds), *Contemporary Spanish Cultural Studies* (London: Arnold, 2000), pp. 52–3.
9 Jo Labanyi, 'Postmodernism and the Problem of Cultural Identity', in H. Graham and J. Labanyi (eds), *Spanish Cultural Studies: An Introduction* (Oxford: Oxford University Press, 1995), p. 397.
10 Paul Julian Smith, *The Moderns: Time, Space, and Subjectivity in Contemporary Spanish Culture* (Oxford: Oxford University Press, 2000), p. 162.
11 Julia Kristeva, *Powers of Horror: An Essay on Abjection* (New York: Columbia University Press, 1982), p. 4.
12 Kristeva, *Powers of Horror*, p. 4.
13 Kristeva, *Powers of Horror*, p. 7.
14 Barbara Creed, *The Monstrous Feminine: Film, Feminism, Psychoanalysis* (New York: Routledge, 1993), p. 29.
15 Eugenia C. DeLamotte, *Perils of the Night: A Feminist Study of Nineteenth-Century Gothic* (New York: Oxford University Press, 1990), p. 20.
16 Marie Mulvey-Roberts, *Dangerous Bodies: Historicising the Gothic Corporeal* (Manchester: Manchester University Press, 2016), p. 221.
17 Maisha Wester, 'The Gothic in and as Race Theory', in J. E. Hogle and R. Miles (eds), *The Gothic and Theory: An Edinburgh Companion* (Edinburgh: Edinburgh University Press, 2020), p. 53.
18 George E. Haggerty, *Gothic Fiction/Gothic Form* (University Park: The Pennsylvania State University Press, 1989), p. 20.
19 Adelaida García Morales, *The South and Bene*, trans. Sarah Marsh (Manchester: Carcanet, 1992), p. 60.
20 Ordóñez, *Voices of Their Own*, p. 185.
21 Díaz, 'Imágenes de la soledad', 232.
22 Thompson, 'Adelaida García Morales's *Bene*', 102.
23 Katherine Henry, 'Slavery and Civic Recovery: Gothic Interventions in Whitman and Weld', in R. Bienstock Anolik and D. L. Howard

(eds), *The Gothic Other: Racial and Social Constructions in the Literary Imagination* (Jefferson: McFarland & Co., 2004), p. 38.
24. Ruth Bienstock Anolik and Douglas L. Howard (eds), *The Gothic Other: Racial and Social Constructions in the Literary Imagination* (Jefferson: McFarland & Co., 2004), p. 1.
25. Thompson, 'Adelaida García Morales's *Bene*', 103.
26. Mario Praz, *The Romantic Agony* (London: Oxford University Press, 1954), p. 192.
27. Eve Kosofsky Sedgwick, *The Coherence of Gothic Conventions* (New York: Arno Press, 1980), p. 11.
28. Judith Halberstam, *Skin Shows: Gothic Horror and the Technology of Monsters* (Durham: Duke University Press, 1995), p. 20.
29. Angela Curran, 'Aristotelian Reflections on Horror and Tragedy in *An American Werewolf in London* and *The Sixth Sense*', in S. J. Schneider and D. Shaw (eds), *Dark Thoughts: Philosophic Reflections on Cinematic Horror* (Lanham: Scarecrow Press, 2003), p. 49.
30. Fred Botting, *Gothic Romanced: Consumption, Gender and Technology in Contemporary Fictions* (New York: Routledge, 2008), p. 195.

Chapter 3

1. Janet Pérez, 'Contemporary Spanish Women Writers and the Feminine Neo-Gothic', *Romance Quarterly*, 51/2 (2004), 133.
2. Abigail Lee Six, *The Gothic Fiction of Adelaida García Morales: Haunting Words* (Woodbridge: Tamesis, 2006), p. 71.
3. Carlos Vadillo Buenfil, '*La tía Águeda*, de Adelaida García Morales: Entre la novela de iniciación y la escritura confesional', *Castilla. Estudios de Literatura*, 6 (2015), 407.
4. Dulce Chacón, 'La mujer y la construcción del olvido', in E. Silva, A. Esteban, J. Castán and P. Salvador (eds), *La memoria de los olvidados: Un debate sobre el silencio de la represión franquista* (Valladolid: Ámbito Ediciones, 2004), p. 76.
5. Emilio Silva, Asunción Esteban, Javier Castán and Pancho Salvador (eds), *La memoria de los olvidados: Un debate sobre el silencio de la represión franquista* (Valladolid: Ámbito Ediciones, 2004).
6. Eider de Dios Fernández, 'Domesticidad y familia: Ambigüedad y contradicción en los modelos de feminidad en el franquismo', *Feminismo/s*, 23 (2014), 25.
7. Dios Fernández, 'Domesticidad y familia', 26–7.

[8] Beatriz Onandia Ruiz, 'Entre el pecado y la lujuria: la inmoralidad pública durante el franquismo', *Raudem, Revista de Estudios de las Mujeres*, 6 (2018), 174.
[9] Adelaida García Morales, *La tía Águeda* (Barcelona: Editorial Anagrama, 1995), p. 12.
[10] Alejandro Camino Rodríguez, 'Entre el hogar y la profesión: Los manuales de conducta de Francisca Bohigas durante el primer franquismo (1939–1950)', *Revista Travessias*, 12/1 (2018), 232.
[11] David D. Gilmore, 'Men and Women in Southern Spain: "Domestic Power" Revisited', *American Anthropologist*, 92/4 (1990), 958.
[12] Diana Wallace, 'The Ghost Story and Feminism', in S. Brewster and L. Thurston (eds), *The Routledge Handbook to the Ghost Story* (New York: Routledge, 2018), p. 432.
[13] Wallace, 'The Ghost Story and Feminism', p. 434.
[14] Lourdes Albuixech, 'Recurring Themes and Techniques in Adelaida García Morales's Narrative', *Hispanófila*, 151 (2007), 99.
[15] Albuixech, 'Recurring Themes', 100.
[16] Beatriz Trigo, 'El conflicto íntimo: la recuperación de la identidad a través de lo fantástico en *El secreto de Elisa* de Adelaida García Morales', *Letras Femeninas*, 31/1 (2005), 181.
[17] Trigo, 'El conflicto íntimo', 190.
[18] Laura Edith Ponce Romo, 'Ecos de un pasado, elementos neo-góticos en la narrativa de Adelaida García Morales' (PhD thesis, Texas Tech University, Lubbock, 2012), 145.
[19] Ponce Romo, 'Ecos de un pasado', 146.
[20] Ponce Romo, 'Ecos de un pasado', 148.
[21] Ponce Romo, 'Ecos de un pasado', 150.
[22] Ponce Romo, 'Ecos de un pasado', 149.
[23] Adelaida García Morales, *El secreto de Elisa* (Madrid: Editorial Debate, 1999), p. 5.
[24] Juliann E. Fleenor (ed.), *The Female Gothic* (Montréal: Eden Press Inc., 1983), p. 233.
[25] John Hooper, *The New Spaniards* (2nd edn, New York: Penguin Group, 2006), p. 126.
[26] Darcie D. Rives, 'Haunted by Violence: Edith Wharton's "The Decoration of Houses" and Her Gothic Fiction', *Edith Wharton Review*, 22/1 (2006), 10.
[27] Rives, 'Haunted by Violence', p. 10.
[28] Marianne Hirsch, *Family Frames: Photography, Narrative, and Postmemory* (Cambridge: Harvard University Press, 1997), p. 23.

Notes

[29] Hirsch, *Family Frames*, p. 6.
[30] Hirsch, *Family Frames*, p. 5.
[31] Hirsch, *Family Frames*, p. 22.
[32] Patricia Keller, *Ghostly Landscapes: Film, Photography, and the Aesthetics of Haunting in Contemporary Spanish Culture* (Toronto: University of Toronto Press, 2016), p. 22.
[33] Emma Liggins, *The Haunted House in Women's Ghost Stories: Gender, Space and Modernity, 1850–1945* (Cham: Palgrave MacMillan, 2020), p. 218.
[34] S. L. Varnado, *Haunted Presence: The Numinous in Gothic Fiction* (Tuscaloosa: University of Alabama Press, 1987), p. 2.
[35] Mary Nash, 'La construcción de una cultura política desde la legitimidad feminista durante la transición política democrática', in A. Aguado and T. M. Ortega (eds), *Feminismos y antifeminismos: culturas políticas e identidades de género en la España del siglo XX* (Valencia: Universitat de Valencia, 2011), p. 301.
[36] Hooper, *The New Spaniards*, p. 130.
[37] Judith Halberstam, *Skin Shows: Gothic Horror and the Technology of Monsters* (Durham: Duke University Press, 1995), p. 125.
[38] Susanne Becker, 'Postmodern Feminine Horror Fictions', in V. Sage and A. L. Smith (eds), *Modern Gothic: A Reader* (Manchester: Manchester University Press, 1996), p. 72.
[39] Rives, 'Haunted by Violence', p. 8.

Chapter 4

[1] Marie-Lise Gazarian-Gautier, *Ana María Matute: La voz del silencio* (Madrid: Espasa Calpe, 1997), p. 37.
[2] María Paz Ortuño, 'Menos es más: Notas sobre la escritura de una novela inacabada', in A. M. Matute, *Demonios familiares* (Barcelona: Editorial Planeta, 2014), p. 175.
[3] Paz Ortuño, 'Menos es más', p. 176.
[4] Natalie Noyaret, 'Formes et enjeux du silence dans *Demonios familiares* d'Ana María Matute', in N. Noyaret and C. Orsini-Saillet (eds), *L'expression du silence dans le récit de fiction espagnol contemporain* (Binges: Orbis Tertius, 2018), p. 203.
[5] Noyaret, 'Formes et enjeux', p. 203.

Notes

6. Concepción Torres Begines, 'Espacios de la infancia y la memoria en Ana María Matute: *Paraíso inhabitado* y *Demonios familiares*', *Dicenda*, 37 (2019), 132.
7. Silvia Bermúdez, 'Novels as History Lessons in Ana María Matute's *Primera memoria* (1960) and *Demonios familiares* (2014): From Betrayal to Solidarity', in M. Bieder and R. Johnson (eds), *Spanish Women Writers and Spain's Civil War* (New York: Routledge, 2017), p. 146.
8. Pere Gimferrer, 'Prólogo', in A. M. Matute, *Demonios familiares* (Barcelona: Editorial Planeta, 2014), p. 7.
9. Paz Ortuño, 'Menos es más', p. 174.
10. Fred Botting, *Gothic* (London: Routledge, 1996), p. 3.
11. Ana María Matute, *Demonios familiares* (Barcelona: Editorial Planeta, 2014), p. 28.
12. Torres Begines, 'Espacios', p. 143.
13. Nick Freeman, 'Haunted Houses', in S. Brewster and L. Thurston (eds), *The Routledge Handbook to the Ghost Story* (New York: Routledge, 2018), p. 328.
14. Bermúdez, 'Novels as History', p. 148.
15. Juliann E. Fleenor (ed.), *The Female Gothic* (Montréal: Eden Press Inc., 1983), p. 27.
16. Diana Wallace and Andrew Smith (eds), *The Female Gothic: New Directions* (New York: Palgrave, 2009), p. 3.
17. Emma Liggins, *The Haunted House in Women's Ghost Stories: Gender, Space and Modernity, 1850–1945* (Cham: Palgrave MacMillan, 2020), p. 227.
18. Guadalupe Cabedo-Timmons, 'La orfandad matutiana: Entrevista con María Paz Ortuño, autora del epílogo de *Demonios familiares*, la novela póstuma de Ana María Matute', *L'Érudit Franco-Espagnol*, 16 (2022), 61.
19. Cabedo-Timmons, 'La orfandad matutiana', 50.
20. Abigail Lee Six, *Gothic Terrors: Incarceration, Duplication, and Bloodlust in Spanish Narrative* (Lewisburg: Bucknell University Press, 2010), p. 147.
21. Cabedo-Timmons, 'La orfandad matutiana', 66–7.
22. Jacques Derrida, *Specters of Marx: The State of the Debt, the Work of Mourning, & the New International*, trans. Peggy Kamuf (New York: Routledge, 1994), p. 11.
23. Liggins, *The Haunted House*, p. 11.
24. Gazarian-Gautier, *Ana María Matute*, p. 11.

Notes

Part II: Introduction

1. Eve Kosofsky Sedgwick, *The Coherence of Gothic Conventions* (New York: Arno Press, 1980), p. 15.
2. David Punter, 'The English Ghost Story', in S. Brewster and L. Thurston (eds), *The Routledge Handbook to the Ghost Story* (New York: Routledge, 2018), p. 183.
3. Nicolas Abraham and Nicholas Rand, 'Notes on the Phantom: A Complement to Freud's Metapsychology', *Critical Inquiry*, 13/2 (1987), 287.
4. Joan Ramon Resina, 'The Weight of Memory and the Lightness of Oblivion: The Dead of the Spanish Civil War', in C. Jerez-Farrán and S. Amago (eds), *Unearthing Franco's Legacy: Mass Graves and the Recovery of Historical Memory in Spain* (Notre Dame: University of Notre Dame Press, 2010), p. 227.
5. Enrique Gavilán, 'De la imposibilidad y de la necesidad de la 'memoria histórica', in E. Silva, A. Esteban, J. Castán and P. Salvador (eds), *La memoria de los olvidados: Un debate sobre el silencio de la represión franquista* (Valladolid: Ámbito Ediciones, 2004), p. 55.
6. Felipe González and Juan Luis Cebrián, *El futuro no es lo que era: una conversación* (Madrid: Grupo Santillana de Ediciones, S. A., 2001), p. 30.
7. Carmen Moreno Nuño, 'The Ghosts of Javier Marías: The Trauma of a Civil War Unforgotten', in E. Merino and H. Rosi Song (eds), *Traces of Contamination: Unearthing the Francoist Legacy in Contemporary Spanish Discourse* (Lewisburg: Bucknell University Press, 2005), p. 130.
8. Sergio del Molino, *La España vacía* (Madrid: Penguin Random House, 2022).
9. Emilio Gancedo, *Palabras mayores: un viaje por la memoria rural* (Logroño: Pepitas de Calabaza, 2017).
10. Javier Cercas, *El monarca de las sombras* (New York: Penguin Random House, 2017), p. 279.
11. Raymond Williams, *The Country and the City* (New York: Oxford University Press, 1973), p. 1.
12. Dominick LaCapra, *Writing History, Writing Trauma* (Baltimore: Johns Hopkins University Press, 2001), p. 66.

Notes

Chapter 5

1. Julio Llamazares, *Wolf Moon*, trans. Simon Deefholts and Kathryn Phillips-Miles (London: Peter Owen, 2017), p. 187.
2. Jo Labanyi, 'Memory and Modernity in Democratic Spain: The Difficulty of Coming to Terms with the Spanish Civil War', *Poetics Today*, 28/1 (2007), 99.
3. José Manuel López de Abiada and Augusta López Bernasocchi, 'Gramáticas de la memoria. Variaciones en torno a la transición española en cuatro novelas recientes (1985–2000): "Luna de lobos, Beatus ille, Corazón tan blanco y La caída de Madrid"', *Iberoamericana*, 4/15 (2004), 124.
4. López de Abiada and López Bernasocchi, 'Gramáticas de la memoria', 99.
5. Dorothée te Riele, 'The Metaphorical Landscape of the Spanish Author Julio Llamazares', in L. Korthals Altes and M. van Montfrans (eds), *The New Georgics: Rural and Regional Motifs in the Contemporary European Novel* (Amsterdam: Rodopi, 2002), pp. 199–213.
6. Li-Jung Tseng, 'El espacio imaginario y la memoria en tres novelas de Julio Llamazares: *Luna de lobos, La lluvia amarilla y El cielo de Madrid*', *Siglo XXI*, 11 (2013), 143.
7. Susan L. Martin-Márquez, 'Vision, Power and Narrative in *Luna de lobos*: Julio Llamazares' Spanish Panopticon', *Revista Canadiense de Estudios Hispánicos*, 19/2 (1995), 380.
8. John B. Margenot, 'Imaginería demoníaca en "Luna de lobos y La lluvia amarilla"', *Hispanic Journal*, 22/2 (2001), 495–509.
9. Labanyi, 'Memory and Modernity', 99.
10. Cristina Ruiz Serrano, '"Traigo la camisa roja de sangre de un compañero": la mujer en la guerrilla antifranquista', *Revista Canadiense de Estudios Hispánicos*, 36/1 (2011), 169.
11. López de Abiada and López Bernasocchi, 'Gramáticas de la memoria', 128.
12. Julián Casanova, 'The Faces of Terror: Violence During the Franco Dictatorship', in C. Jerez-Farrán and S. Amago (eds), *Unearthing Franco's Legacy: Mass Graves and the Recovery of Historical Memory in Spain* (Notre Dame: University of Notre Dame, 2010), p. 101.
13. Carmen Moreno Nuño, 'The Ghosts of Javier Marías: The Trauma of a Civil War Unforgotten', in E. Merino and H. Rosi Song (eds), *Traces of Contamination: Unearthing the Francoist Legacy in Contemporary Spanish Discourse* (Lewisburg: Bucknell University Press, 2005), p. 131.

Notes

14. Margenot, 'Imaginería', 496.
15. Riele, 'Metaphorical Landscape', p. 210.
16. Margenot, 'Imaginería', 500.
17. López de Abiada and López Bernasocchi, 'Gramáticas de la memoria', 127.
18. Inge Beisel, 'La memoria colectiva en las obras de Julio Llamazares', in A. de Toro and D. Ingenschay (eds), *La novela española actual: autores y tendencias* (Kassel: Edition Reichenberger, 1995), p. 196.
19. Julián Casanova, *La iglesia de Franco* (Madrid: Ediciones Temas de Hoy, 2001), p. 51.
20. Jo Labanyi, *Spanish Culture from Romanticism to the Present: Structures of Feeling* (Cambridge: Legenda, 2019), p. 303.
21. Andrew Smith, *The Ghost Story 1840–1920: A Cultural History* (Manchester: Manchester University Press, 2010), p. 4.
22. Avery Gordon, *Ghostly Matters: Haunting and the Sociological Imagination* (Minneapolis: University of Minnesota Press, 2008), p. 63.
23. Montse Armengou and Ricard Belis, *Las fosas del silencio: ¿Hay un holocausto español?* (Barcelona: Televisió de Catalunya, 2004), p. 89.
24. Paloma Aguilar Fernández, *Memoria y olvido de la guerra civil española* (Madrid: Alianza Editorial, 1996), p. 43.
25. Cristina Moreiras Menor, *Cultura herida: literatura y cine en la España democrática* (Madrid: Ediciones Libertarias, 2002), p. 28.
26. Timothy C. Baker, *Contemporary Scottish Gothic: Mourning, Authenticity, and Tradition* (New York: Palgrave Macmillan, 2014), p. 18.
27. Labanyi, 'Memory and Modernity', 100.
28. Riele, 'Metaphorical Landscape', p. 202.

Chapter 6

1. Ellen Mayock, 'Determinismo y libre albedrío en "La lluvia amarilla" de Julio Llamazares', *Hispania*, 93/4 (2010), 587.
2. Rosa María Díez Cobo, 'Páramos humanos: retóricas del espacio vacío en *La lluvia amarilla* de Julio Llamazares y en la novela neorrural española', *Siglo XXI*, 15 (2017), 17.
3. Jo Labanyi, 'History and Hauntology; or, What Does One Do with the Ghosts of the Past? Reflections on Spanish Film and Fiction of the Post-Franco Period', in J. R. Resina (ed.), *Disremembering the Dictatorship: The Politics of Memory in the Spanish Transition to Democracy* (Amsterdam: Editions Rodopi B. V., 2000), p. 67.

Notes

[4] José Antonio Llera, 'Memoria, duelo y melancolía en *La lluvia amarilla*, de Julio Llamazares', *Revista de Literatura*, 81/162 (2019), 540.
[5] Llera, 'Memoria', 537.
[6] Robert Nana Baah, 'Constructing a Stylistics of Compassion: Julio Llamazares and the Poetry of Abandonment, Loneliness, and Death in "La lluvia amarilla"', *Hispanófila*, 124 (1998), 36.
[7] Li-Jung Tseng, 'El espacio imaginario y la memoria en tres novelas de Julio Llamazares: *Luna de lobos*, *La lluvia amarilla* y *El cielo de Madrid*', *Siglo XXI*, 11 (2013), 147.
[8] Michael Richards, 'From War Culture to Civil Society: Francoism, Social Change and Memories of the Spanish Civil War', *History and Memory*, 14/1–2 (Special Issue: Images of a Contested Past, 2002), 106.
[9] John Hooper, *The New Spaniards* (2nd edn, New York: Penguin Group, 2006), p. 3.
[10] Sergio del Molino, *La España vacía* (Madrid: Penguin Random House, 2022), p. 36.
[11] Molino, *La España*, p. 37.
[12] Molino, *La España*, p. 37.
[13] Molino, *La España*, p. 42.
[14] Julio Llamazares, *The Yellow Rain*, trans. Margaret Jull Costa (Orlando: Harcourt, 2003), p. 1.
[15] Julio Ángel Olivares Merino, 'La sobreimpresión febril: modalidades de la espectralidad en *La lluvia amarilla*, de Julio Llamazares', in N. Álvarez Méndez and A. Abello Verano (eds), *Realidades fracturadas: estéticas de lo insólito en la narrativa en lengua española (1980–2018)* (Madrid: Visor Libros, 2019), p. 209.
[16] Llera, 'Memoria', 538.
[17] Mayock, 'Determinismo', 590.
[18] Joanne Watkiss, *Gothic Contemporaries: The Haunted Text* (Cardiff: University of Wales Press, 2012), p. 25.
[19] Baah, 'Constructing', 35.
[20] Baah, 'Constructing', 40.
[21] Llera, 'Memoria', 536.
[22] Olivares Merino, 'La sobreimposición', p. 209.
[23] Pere Ysàs, 'El franquismo: de la victoria a una larga supervivencia', in A. Esteban Recio, D. Etura and M. Tomasoni (eds), *La alargada sombra del franquismo: Naturaleza, mecanismos de pervivencia y huellas de la dictadura* (Granada: Editorial Comares, 2019), p. 6.
[24] Montse Armengou and Ricard Belis, *Las fosas del silencio: ¿Hay un holocausto español?* (Barcelona: Televisió de Catalunya, 2004), p. 169.

[25] Francisco Ferrándiz, 'Cries and Whispers: Exhuming and Narrating Defeat in Spain Today', *Journal of Spanish Cultural Studies*, 9/2 (2008), 177.
[26] Richards, 'From War', 108.
[27] Emma Liggins, *The Haunted House in Women's Ghost Stories: Gender, Space and Modernity, 1850–1945* (Cham: Palgrave MacMillan, 2020), p. 158.
[28] Díez Cobo, 'Páramos', 20.
[29] Olivares Merino, 'La sobreimposición', p. 232.
[30] Timothy C. Baker, *Contemporary Scottish Gothic: Mourning, Authenticity, and Tradition* (New York: Palgrave Macmillan, 2014), p. 22.
[31] Baker, *Contemporary Scottish Gothic*, p. 17.
[32] Baker, *Contemporary Scottish Gothic*, p. 19.
[33] Tseng, 'El espacio', 145.
[34] Jeffrey Andrew Weinstock (ed.), *Spectral America: Phantoms and the National Imagination* (Madison: University of Wisconsin Press, 2004), p. 6.
[35] Llera, 'Memoria', 534.

Chapter 7

[1] Jessica Folkart, *Angles on Otherness in Post-Franco Spain: The Fiction of Cristina Fernández Cubas* (Lewisburg: Bucknell University Press, 2002), p. 13.
[2] See Kathleen M. Glenn and Cristina Fernández Cubas, 'Conversación con Cristina Fernández Cubas', *Anales de la literatura española contemporánea*, 18/1–2 (1993), 355–63; and Janet Pérez, 'Contemporary Spanish Women Writers and the Feminine Neo-Gothic', *Romance Quarterly*, 51/2 (2004), 125–40.
[3] Glenn and Fernández Cubas, 'Conversación', p. 359.
[4] Kathleen M. Glenn, 'Gothic Indecipherability and Doubling in the Fiction of Cristina Fernández Cubas', *Monographic Review/Revista Monográfica*, 8 (1992), 125.
[5] Glenn and Fernández Cubas, 'Conversación', p. 360.
[6] Folkart, *Angles*, p. 15.
[7] Kathleen M. Glenn and Janet Pérez (eds), *Mapping the Fiction of Cristina Fernández Cubas* (Newark: University of Delaware Press, 2005), p. 11.
[8] Glenn, 'Gothic Indecipherability', 125.

Notes

9   Xavier Aldana Reyes, *Spanish Gothic: National Identity, Collaboration and Cultural Adaptation* (London: Palgrave MacMillan, 2017), p. 162.
10 Janet Pérez, 'Contemporary Spanish Women Writers and the Feminine Neo-Gothic', *Romance Quarterly*, 51/2 (2004), 135.
11 Folkart, *Angles*, p. 27.
12 John B. Margenot, 'The Metafictional Metaphor in *El columpio*', in K. Glenn and J. Pérez (eds), *Mapping the Fiction of Cristina Fernández Cubas* (Newark: University of Delaware Press, 2005), p. 168.
13 Catherine G. Bellver, 'Spectators and Spectacle: The Theatrical Dimension in the Works of Cristina Fernández Cubas', *Hispania*, 90/1 (2007), 57.
14 See Silvia Bermúdez, 'Looking for Mom in All the Wrong Places: The Mother-Daughter Bond and the Evolution of Identity in *El columpio*'; and Akiko Tsuchiya, 'Repetition, Remembrance, and the Construction of Subjectivity in the Works of Cristina Fernández Cubas', in K. Glenn and J. Pérez (eds), *Mapping the Fiction of Cristina Fernández Cubas* (Newark: University of Delaware Press, 2005).
15 Cristina Fernández Cubas, *El columpio* (Barcelona: Tusquets Editores, 1995), p. 11.
16 Folkart, *Angles*, p. 21.
17 Tsuchiya, 'Repetition', p. 108.
18 Alison Landsberg, *Prosthetic Memory: The Transformation of American Remembrance in the Age of Mass Culture* (New York: Columbia University Press, 2004), p. 2.
19 Landsberg, *Prosthetic Memory*, p. 4.
20 Bermúdez, 'Looking', p. 153.
21 Margenot, 'The Metafictional', p. 177.
22 Folkart, *Angles*, p. 128.
23 Bellver, 'Spectators', 57.
24 David L. Eng and David Kazanjian (eds), *Loss: The Politics of Mourning* (Berkeley: University of California Press, 2003), p. 3.
25 Eng and Kazanjian, *Loss*, p. 4.
26 Tsuchiya, 'Repetition', p. 111.

Part III: Introduction

1   Sigmund Freud, *Beyond the Pleasure Principle*, ed. and trans. James Strachey (New York: W. W. Norton & Company, 1961), p. 12.

Notes

2. Cathy Caruth (ed.), *Trauma: Explorations in Memory* (Baltimore: The Johns Hopkins University Press, 1995), p. 5.
3. Cathy Caruth, *Unclaimed Experience: Trauma, Narrative, and History* (Baltimore: Johns Hopkins University Press, 2016), p. 6.
4. Roger Luckhurst, *The Trauma Question* (New York: Routledge, 2008), p. 93.
5. María del Pilar Blanco and Esther Peeren (eds), *Popular Ghosts: The Haunted Spaces of Everyday Culture* (New York: Continuum, 2010), p. 12.
6. Luckhurst, *The Trauma Question*, p. 3.
7. Steven Bruhm, 'The Contemporary Gothic: Why We Need It', in J. Hogle (ed.), *The Cambridge Companion to Gothic Fiction* (Cambridge: Cambridge University Press, 2002), p. 268.
8. Bruhm, 'The Contemporary Gothic', p. 261.
9. Ashlee Joyce, *The Gothic in Contemporary British Trauma Fiction* (Cham: Palgrave, 2019), p. 20.
10. Avril Horner, 'Apocalypses Now: Collective Trauma, Globalisation and the New Gothic Sublime', in M. Nadal and M. Calvo (eds), *Trauma in Contemporary Literature: Narrative and Representation* (New York: Routledge, 2014), p. 36.
11. Francisco Ferrándiz, 'Cries and Whispers: Exhuming and Narrating Defeat in Spain Today', *Journal of Spanish Cultural Studies*, 9/2 (2008), 186.
12. Alison Ribeiro de Menezes, *Embodying Memory in Contemporary Spain* (New York: Palgrave MacMillan, 2014), p. 5.

Chapter 8

1. Montserrat Linares, 'Fragmented Identities: The Narrative World of Espido Freire', in K. A. Kietrys and M. Linares (eds), *Women in the Spanish Novel Today: Essays on the Reflection of Self in the Works of Three Generations* (Jefferson: McFarland & Company, 2009), p. 205.
2. Espido Freire, *Irlanda*, trans. Toshiya Kamei (Tuscaloosa: Fairy Tale Review Press, 2011), p. 135.
3. Isabel Asensio, 'Remapping Contemporary Spanish Literature: A Conversation with Espido Freire', *Weber: The Contemporary West*, 36/2 (2020), 45.
4. Maria T. Pao, 'Justified: Ecocriticism and Moral Development in Espido Freire's *Irlanda* (1998)', *Neophilologus*, 101 (2017), 568.

5 Consuelo Barrera García, 'Fantasía, onirismo y muerte en las novelas de Espido Freire', *Huerto de San Juan. Filología y Didáctica de la Lengua*, 7 (2004), 48.

6 Christine Henseler, 'Del bien y del mal: una entrevista con Espido Freire', *Letras Peninsulares*, 17/2–3 (2004–5), 256.

7 Concha Alborg, 'Espido Freire: (Re)Lectura y (Sub)Versión de los cuentos de hadas', in K. Glenn and A. Encinar (eds), *La pluralidad narrativa: escritores españoles contemporáneos (1984–2004)* (Madrid: Editorial Biblioteca Nueva, 2005), p. 251.

8 Mónica Poza Diéguez, 'La sugerencia de la trama o la magia narrativa de Espido Freire', *Espéculo*, 20 (2002), https://webs.ucm.es/info/especulo/numero20/freire.html, accessed 12 Oct 2022.

9 Myriam del Río Hernández, 'Shadowing LaForet: Memory and the Imaginary in the Worlds of Espido Freire and Carmen Martín Gaite', in A. Walsh (ed.), *Telling Tales: Storytelling in Contemporary Spain* (Newcastle upon Tyne: Cambridge Scholars Publishing, 2015), p. 139.

10 Linares, 'Fragmented Identities', p. 206.

11 Pao, 'Justified', 561.

12 Samuel Rodríguez Rodríguez, 'Trauma y perversión en *Irlanda*, de Espido Freire', in R. de la Fuente Ballesteros, J. Pérez-Magallón and J. Manuel Goñi Pérez (eds), *El trauma en la literatura hispánica* (Valladolid: Universitas Castellae, 2016), p. 177.

13 Shirley Jackson, *We Have Always Lived in the Castle* (New York: Penguin Books, 2006), p. 4.

14 Edurne M. Portela, *El eco de los disparos: cultura y memoria de la violencia* (Barcelona: Galaxia Gutenberg, 2016), p. 18.

15 Portela, *El eco de los disparos*, p. 18.

16 Portela, *El eco de los disparos*, p. 17.

17 Henseler, 'Del bien y del mal', 256.

18 Río Hernández, 'Shadowing LaForet', p. 135.

19 Cathy Caruth, *Unclaimed Experience: Trauma, Narrative, and History* (Baltimore: Johns Hopkins University Press, 2016), pp. 11–12.

20 Rodríguez Rodríguez, 'Trauma y perversión', p. 178.

21 Donna Heiland, *Gothic & Gender: An Introduction* (Oxford: Blackwell Publishing, 2004), p. 77.

22 Janet Pérez, 'Contemporary Spanish Women Writers and the Feminine Neo-Gothic', *Romance Quarterly*, 51/2 (2004), 131.

23 Pao, 'Justified', 572.

24 Linares, 'Fragmented Identities', p. 211.

Notes

25 Iñaki Beti Sáez, 'El universo emocional en la narrativa de Espido Freire', *Sancho el Sabio: Revista de cultura e investigación vasca*, 13 (2000), 189.
26 Lucie Armitt, 'The Gothic Girl Child', in A. Horner and S. Zlosnik (eds), *Women and the Gothic* (Edinburgh: Edinburgh University Press, 2016), p. 60.
27 Armitt, 'The Gothic Girl Child', p. 72.
28 Río Hernández, 'Shadowing LaForet', p. 142.
29 Henseler, 'Del bien y del mal', p. 255.

Chapter 9

1 Néstor Bórquez, 'Memoria, infancia y guerra civil: el mundo narrativo de Ana María Matute', *Olivar*, 16 (2011), 160.
2 María Mercedes Pons Ballesteros, 'El paraíso inhabitado de Ana María Matute: entre la realidad y la fantasía', *Tavira*, 25 (2009), 211.
3 Bórquez, 'Memoria', 167.
4 Pons Ballesteros, 'El paraíso inhabitado', 215.
5 Maylis Santa-Cruz, 'Un autre monde est-il possible?: Paraíso inhabitado d'Ana María Matute', *Bulletin hispanique*, 116/2 (Dec 2014), 554.
6 Yannick Llored, '*Paraíso inhabitado* de Ana María Matute: Un singular estilo tardío desde la infancia como origen', *Cuadernos de Investigación Filológica*, 46 (2019), 63.
7 Murielle Borel, 'De la mémoire intime à la mémoire collective : représentations et influence dans Paraíso inhabitado d'Ana María Matute', *Cahiers d'Etudes Romanes, Centre aixois d'études romanes*, 39 (2019). Doi : 10.4000/etudesromanes.10031.
8 Juliann E. Fleenor (ed.), *The Female Gothic* (Montréal: Eden Press Inc., 1983), p. 16.
9 Fleenor, *The Female Gothic*, p. 16.
10 Barbara Creed, *The Monstrous Feminine: Film, Feminism, Psychoanalysis* (New York: Routledge, 1993), p. 12.
11 Ginette Carpenter, 'Mothers and Others', in A. Horner and S. Zlosnik (eds), *Women and the Gothic* (Edinburgh: Edinburgh University Press, 2016), p. 46.
12 Ana María Matute, *Paraíso inhabitado* (Barcelona: Editorial Planeta, 2018), p. 11.
13 Quoted in Bórquez, 'Memoria', p. 165.

Notes

14 Elvira Antón, 'Gendered Images: Constructions of Masculinity and Femininity in Television Advertising', in B. Jordan and R. Morgan-Tamosunas (eds), *Contemporary Spanish Cultural Studies* (London: Arnold, 2000), p. 206.
15 Rosa Isabel Galdona Pérez, *Discurso femenino en la novela española de posguerra: Carmen Laforet, Ana María Matute y Elena Quiroga* (La Laguna: Universidad de La Laguna, 2001), p. 135.
16 Llored, '*Paraíso inhabitado*', 68.
17 Galdona Pérez, '*Discurso femenino*', p. 108.

Chapter 10

1 Glennis Byron and Gordon Byron, 'Barcelona gothic: Carlos Ruiz Zafón's *La sombra del viento* and the omnipresent past', *Journal of Romance Studies*, 12/1 (2012), 73.
2 Xavier Aldana Reyes, *Spanish Gothic: National Identity, Collaboration and Cultural Adaptation* (London: Palgrave MacMillan, 2017), p. 27.
3 See Heidi Backes, 'Shared Trauma: Historical Memory and the *Doppelgänger* in Carlos Ruiz Zafón's *The Shadow of the Wind*', *Aeternum: Journal of Contemporary Gothic Studies*, 6/1 (June 2019), 49–63; and 'Rehistoricizing the Gothic in Modern Spanish Fiction: Adelaida García Morales, Carlos Ruiz Zafón and Post-Franco Spain' (PhD thesis, University of Wisconsin, Madison, 2011).
4 Ann Davies, *Contemporary Spanish Gothic* (Edinburgh: Edinburgh University Press, 2016), p. 67.
5 Aldana Reyes, *Spanish Gothic*, p. 179.
6 Carlos Ruiz Zafón, *The Prisoner of Heaven*, trans. Lucia Graves (New York: HarperCollins Publishers, 2012), p. 5.
7 José F. Colmeiro, *Memoria histórica e identidad cultural: de la postguerra a la postmodernidad* (Barcelona: Anthropos Editorial, 2005), p. 152.
8 Jacques Derrida, *The Instant of My Death (Blanchot) and Demeure: Fiction and Testimony (Derrida)*, trans. Elizabeth Rottenberg (Stanford: Stanford University Press, 2000), p. 30.
9 Derrida, *The Instant of My Death*, p. 72.
10 Cathy Caruth, *Unclaimed Experience: Trauma, Narrative, and History* (Baltimore: Johns Hopkins University Press, 2016), p. 4.
11 Caruth, *Unclaimed Experience*, p. 4.

Notes

12. Shoshana Felman, 'Education and Crisis, or the Vicissitudes of Teaching', in C. Caruth (ed.), *Trauma: Explorations in Memory* (Baltimore: The Johns Hopkins University Press, 1995), p. 24.
13. El Nacional, 'Coronavirus death of alleged Francoist torturer Billy el Niño inflames social media' (7 May 2020), https://www.elnacional.cat/en/news/coronavirus-death-torturer-billy-nino-twitter_500811_102.html, accessed 20 Oct 2022.
14. Dominick LaCapra, *Writing History, Writing Trauma* (Baltimore: Johns Hopkins University Press, 2001), p. 97.
15. Dori Laub, 'Truth and Testimony: The Process and the Struggle', in C. Caruth (ed.), *Trauma: Explorations in Memory* (Baltimore: Johns Hopkins University Press, 1995), p. 64.
16. Laub, 'Truth and Testimony', p. 63.
17. Zoë Crossland, 'Epilogue', in F. Ferrándiz, A. C. G. M. Robbern and R. Wilson (eds), *Necropolitics: Mass Graves and Exhumations in the Age of Human Rights* (Philadelphia: University of Pennsylvania Press, 2015), p. 249.
18. Colmeiro, *Memoria histórica*, p. 25.
19. Jo Labanyi, *Spanish Culture from Romanticism to the Present: Structures of Feeling* (Cambridge: Legenda, 2019), p. 315.

Conclusion

1. El País, 'Así le hemos contado la exhumación de José Antonio Primo de Rivera' (24 Apr 2023), https://elpais.com/espana/2023-04-24/la-exhumacion-de-primo-de-rivera-del-valle-de-los-caidos-ultimas-noticias-en-directo.html, accessed 25 Apr 2023.
2. RTVE, 'Así es la Ley de Memoria Democrática que entra en vigor: mapa de desaparecidos y anulación de condenas franquistas' (20 Oct 2022), https://www.rtve.es/noticias/20221020/asi-ley-memoria-democratica-entra-hoy-vigor-del-mapa-desaparecidos-anulacion-condenas-franquistas/2406472.shtml, accessed 28 Oct 2022.
3. El Mundo, 'Aprobada la Ley de Memoria Democrática con el rechazo del PP, Vox y Cs: "Es una traición a los españoles"' (5 Oct 2022), https://www.elmundo.es/espana/2022/10/05/633d8252fdddff15618b45aa.html, accessed 28 Oct 2022.
4. Sebastiaan Faber, *Exhuming Franco: Spain's Second Transition* (Nashville: Vanderbilt University Press, 2021), p. 3.

5 Miguel González, *Vox S. A.: El negocio del patriotismo español* (Barcelona: Península, 2022), p. 121.
6 Vox, '¡Qué comience la batalla!' [Twitter post], 4:09 a.m., 28 Apr 2019, *https://twitter.com/vox_es/status/1122427641750011904?s=20&t=sexxxhHsm2lKLsmAYSMT6g*, accessed 28 Apr 2019.
7 Vox, 'Ya hemos pasao' [Twitter post], 6:26 p.m., 26 May 2019, *https://twitter.com/vox_es/status/1132790111551348736?s=20&t=kBlhaoCxs4eV6jUOzVwb_Q*, accessed 26 May 2019.
8 Rep. Anthony Sabatini, 'I answer only to God and to History. – Francisco Franco' [Twitter post], 11:09 p.m., 19 Oct 2022, *https://twitter.com/AnthonySabatini/status/1582947194780323841?s=20&t=3pDgVls1etN6B9tUOs2tEA*, accessed 19 Oct 2022.
9 Avery Gordon, *Ghostly Matters: Haunting and the Sociological Imagination* (Minneapolis: University of Minnesota Press, 2008), p. 23.
10 Jacques Derrida, *Specters of Marx: The State of the Debt, the Work of Mourning, & the New International*, trans. Peggy Kamuf (New York: Routledge, 1994), p. 37.
11 Joan Ramon Resina, *The Ghost in the Constitution: Historical Memory and Denial in Spanish Society* (Liverpool: Liverpool University Press, 2017), p. 177.
12 Montse Armengou and Ricard Belis, *Las fosas del silencio: ¿Hay un holocausto español?* (Barcelona: Televisió de Catalunya, 2004), p. 69.
13 Jo Labanyi, 'Testimonies of Repression: Methodological and Political Issues', in C. Jerez-Farrán, Carlos and S. Amago (eds), *Unearthing Franco's Legacy: Mass Graves and the Recovery of Historical Memory in Spain* (Notre Dame: University of Notre Dame Press, 2010), p. 193.
14 Armengou and Belis, *Las fossa del silencio*, p. 250.

Bibliography

Abraham, Nicolas and Nicholas Rand, 'Notes on the Phantom: A Complement to Freud's Metapsychology', *Critical Inquiry*, 13/2 (1987), 287–92.

Abraham, Nicolas and Maria Torok, *The Shell and the Kernel: Renewals of Psychoanalysis*, ed. and trans. Nicholas T. Rand (Chicago: University of Chicago Press, 1994).

Aguilar Fernández, Paloma, *Memoria y olvido de la guerra civil española* (Madrid: Alianza Editorial, 1996).

Alborg, Concha, 'Espido Freire: (Re)Lectura y (Sub)Versión de los cuentos de hadas', in K. Glenn and A. Encinar (eds), *La pluralidad narrativa: escritores españoles contemporáneos (1984–2004)* (Madrid: Editorial Biblioteca Nueva, 2005), pp. 243–54.

Albuixech, Lourdes, 'Recurring Themes and Techniques in Adelaida García Morales's Narrative', *Hispanófila*, 151 (2007), 93–103.

Aldana Reyes, Xavier, *Spanish Gothic: National Identity, Collaboration and Cultural Adaptation* (London: Palgrave Macmillan, 2017).

Alvarez-Sancho, Isabel, '"Pa Negre" y los otros fantasmas de la postmemoria: El "phantom" y los intertextos con "La plaça del Diamant, El espíritu de la colmena y El laberinto del fauno"', *MLN*, 131/2 (Hispanic Issue, 2016), 517–35.

Antón, Elvira, 'Gendered Images: Constructions of Masculinity and Femininity in Television Advertising', in B. Jordan and

R. Morgan-Tamosunas (eds), *Contemporary Spanish Cultural Studies* (London: Arnold, 2000), pp. 205–13.

Arkinstall, Christine R., *Gender, Class, and Nation: Mercè Rodoreda and the Subjects of Modernism* (Lewisburg: Bucknell University Press, 2004).

Armengou, Montse and Ricard Belis, *Las fosas del silencio: ¿Hay un holocausto español?* (Barcelona: Televisió de Catalunya, 2004).

Armitt, Lucie, 'The Gothic Girl Child', in A. Horner and S. Zlosnik (eds), *Women and the Gothic* (Edinburgh: Edinburgh University Press, 2016), pp. 60–73.

Asensio, Isabel, 'Remapping Contemporary Spanish Literature: A Conversation with Espido Freire', *Weber: The Contemporary West*, 36/2 (2020), 43–51.

Baah, Robert Nana, 'Constructing a Stylistics of Compassion: Julio Llamazares and the Poetry of Abandonment, Loneliness, and Death in "La lluvia amarilla"', *Hispanófila*, 124 (1998), 35–49.

Bachelard, Gaston, *The Poetics of Space*, trans. Maria Jolas (Boston: Beacon Press, 1969).

Backes, Heidi, 'Rehistoricizing the Gothic in Modern Spanish Fiction: Adelaida García Morales, Carlos Ruiz Zafón and Post-Franco Spain' (PhD thesis, University of Wisconsin, Madison, 2011).

Backes, Heidi, 'Shared Trauma: Historical Memory and the *Doppelgänger* in Carlos Ruiz Zafón's *The Shadow of the Wind*', *Aeternum: Journal of Contemporary Gothic Studies*, 6/1 (June 2019), 49–63.

Baker, Timothy C., *Contemporary Scottish Gothic: Mourning, Authenticity, and Tradition* (New York: Palgrave Macmillan, 2014).

Barrera García, Consuelo, 'Fantasía, onirismo y muerte en las novelas de Espido Freire', *Huerto de San Juan. Filología y Didáctica de la Lengua*, 7 (2004), 21–58.

Becker, Susanne, 'Postmodern Feminine Horror Fictions', in V. Sage and A. L. Smith (eds), *Modern Gothic: A Reader* (Manchester: Manchester University Press, 1996), pp. 71–80.

Beisel, Inge, 'La memoria colectiva en las obras de Julio Llamazares', in A. de Toro and D. Ingenschay (eds), *La novela española actual: autores y tendencias* (Kassel: Edition Reichenberger, 1995), pp. 193–229.

Bellver, Catherine G., 'Spectators and Spectacle: The Theatrical Dimension in the Works of Cristina Fernández Cubas', *Hispania*, 90/1 (2007), 52–61.

Bermúdez, Silvia, 'Looking for Mom in All the Wrong Places: The Mother-Daughter Bond and the Evolution of Identity in *El columpio*', in K. Glenn and J. Pérez (eds), *Mapping the Fiction of Cristina Fernández Cubas* (Newark: University of Delaware Press, 2005), pp. 151–66.

Bermúdez, Silvia, 'Novels as History Lessons in Ana María Matute's *Primera memoria* (1960) and *Demonios familiares* (2014): From Betrayal to Solidarity', in M. Bieder and R. Johnson (eds), *Spanish Women Writers and Spain's Civil War* (New York: Routledge, 2017), pp. 144–54.

Bienstock Anolik, Ruth and Douglas L. Howard (eds), *The Gothic Other: Racial and Social Constructions in the Literary Imagination* (Jefferson: McFarland & Co., 2004).

Blanco, María del Pilar and Esther Peeren (eds), *Popular Ghosts: The Haunted Spaces of Everyday Culture* (New York: Continuum, 2010).

Blanco, María del Pilar and Esther Peeren (eds), *The Spectralities Reader: Ghosts and Haunting in Contemporary Cultural Theory* (New York: Bloomsbury, 2013).

Borel, Murielle, 'De la mémoire intime à la mémoire collective: représentations et influence dans Paraíso inhabitado d'Ana María Matute', *Cahiers d'Etudes Romanes, Centre aixois d'études romanes*, 39 (2019). Doi: 10.4000/etudesromanes.10031.

Bórquez, Néstor, 'Memoria, infancia y guerra civil: el mundo narrativo de Ana María Matute', *Olivar*, 16 (2011), 159–77.

Botting, Fred, *Gothic* (London: Routledge, 1996).

Botting, Fred, *Gothic Romanced: Consumption, Gender and Technology in Contemporary Fictions* (New York: Routledge, 2008).

Bru, Eva, 'Between the Abject and the Sublime: Excessive Bodies in Mercè Rodoreda's *El Carrer de les Camèlies* and *Mirall trencat*', *Catalan Review*, 24 (2010), 311–28.

Bruhm, Steven, 'The Contemporary Gothic: Why We Need It', in J. Hogle (ed.), *The Cambridge Companion to Gothic Fiction* (Cambridge: Cambridge University Press, 2002), pp. 259–76.

Byron, Glennis and Gordon Byron, 'Barcelona gothic: Carlos Ruiz Zafón's *La sombra del viento* and the omnipresent past', *Journal of Romance Studies*, 12/1 (2012), 72–84.

Cabedo-Timmons, Guadalupe, 'La orfandad matutiana: Entrevista con María Paz Ortuño, autora del epílogo de *Demonios familiares*, la novela póstuma de Ana María Matute', *L'Érudit Franco-Espagnol*, 16 (2022), 50–68.

Camino Rodríguez, Alejandro, 'Entre el hogar y la profesión: Los manuales de conducta de Francisca Bohigas durante el primer franquismo (1939–1950)', *Revista Travessias*, 12/1 (2018), 224–42.

Carpenter, Ginette, 'Mothers and Others', in A. Horner and S. Zlosnik (eds), *Women and the Gothic* (Edinburgh: Edinburgh University Press, 2016), pp. 46–59.

Caruth, Cathy (ed.), *Trauma: Explorations in Memory* (Baltimore: The Johns Hopkins University Press, 1995).

Caruth, Cathy, *Unclaimed Experience: Trauma, Narrative, and History* (Baltimore: Johns Hopkins University Press, 2016).

Casanova, Julian, 'The Faces of Terror: Violence During the Franco Dictatorship', in C. Jerez-Farrán and S. Amago (eds), *Unearthing Franco's Legacy: Mass Graves and the Recovery of Historical Memory in Spain* (Notre Dame: University of Notre Dame, 2010), pp. 90–120.

Cercas, Javier, *El monarca de las sombras* (New York: Penguin Random House, 2017).

Chacón, Dulce, 'La mujer y la construcción del olvido', in E. Silva, A. Esteban, J. Castán and P. Salvador (eds), *La memoria de los olvidados: Un debate sobre el silencio de la represión franquista* (Valladolid: Ámbito Ediciones, 2004), pp. 75–8.

Cixous, Hélène, 'The Laugh of the Medusa', *Signs*, 1/4 (1976), 875–93.

Colmeiro, José F., *Memoria histórica e identidad cultural: de la postguerra a la postmodernidad* (Barcelona: Anthropos Editorial, 2005).

Colmeiro, José, 'Nation of Ghosts?: Haunting, Historical Memory and Forgetting in Post-Franco Spain', *452ºF*, 4 (2011), 17–34.

Córdoba, Antonio and Daniel García-Donoso (eds), *Rite, Flesh, and Stone: The Matter of Death in Contemporary Spanish Culture* (Nashville: Vanderbilt University Press, 2021).

Corkill, David, 'Race, Immigration and Multiculturalism in Spain', in B. Jordan and R. Morgan-Tamosunas (eds), *Contemporary Spanish Cultural Studies* (London: Arnold, 2000), pp. 48–57.

Creed, Barbara, *The Monstrous Feminine: Film, Feminism, Psychoanalysis* (New York: Routledge, 1993).

Crossland, Zoë, 'Epilogue', in F. Ferrándiz, A. C. G. M. Robbern and R. Wilson (eds), *Necropolitics: Mass Graves and Exhumations in the Age of Human Rights* (Philadelphia: University of Pennsylvania Press, 2015), pp. 240–52.

Curran, Angela, 'Aristotelian Reflections on Horror and Tragedy in *An American Werewolf in London* and *The Sixth Sense*', in S. J. Schneider and D. Shaw (eds), *Dark Thoughts: Philosophic Reflections on Cinematic Horror* (Lanham: Scarecrow Press, 2003), pp. 47–64.

Davies, Ann, *Contemporary Spanish Gothic* (Edinburgh: Edinburgh University Press, 2016).

DeLamotte, Eugenia C., *Perils of the Night: A Feminist Study of Nineteenth-Century Gothic* (New York: Oxford University Press, 1990).

Derrida, Jacques, *Specters of Marx: The State of the Debt, the Work of Mourning, & the New International*, trans. Peggy Kamuf (New York: Routledge, 1994).

Derrida, Jacques, *The Instant of My Death (Blanchot) and Demeure: Fiction and Testimony (Derrida)*, trans. Elizabeth Rottenberg (Stanford: Stanford University Press, 2000).

Deveny, Thomas G., 'Preface', in A. García Morales, *The South and Bene: Two Novellas*, trans. Thomas G. Deveny (Lincoln: University of Nebraska Press, 1999).

Díaz, Epicteto José, 'Imágenes de la soledad en *El Sur* y *Bene* de Adelaida García Morales', *Revista de Literatura*, 70/139 (Jan–June 2008), 223–37.

Díez Cobo, Rosa María, 'Páramos humanos: retóricas del espacio vacío en *La lluvia amarilla* de Julio Llamazares y en la novela neorrural española', *Siglo XXI*, 15 (2017), 13–25.

Dios Fernández, Eider de, 'Domesticidad y familia: Ambigüedad y contradicción en los modelos de feminidad en el franquismo', *Feminismo/s*, 23 (2014), 23–46.

Downey, Dara, *American Women's Ghost Stories in the Gilded Age* (New York: Palgrave, 2014).

El Mundo, 'Aprobada la Ley de Memoria Democrática con el rechazo del PP, Vox y Cs: "Es una traición a los españoles"' (5 Oct 2022), https://www.elmundo.es/espana/2022/10/05/633d8252fdddff15618b45aa.html, accessed 28 Oct 2022.

El Nacional, 'Coronavirus death of alleged Francoist torturer Billy el Niño inflames social media' (7 May 2020), https://www.elnacional.cat/en/news/coronavirus-death-torturer-bill y-nino-twitter_500811_102.html, accessed 20 Oct 2022.

El País, 'Así le hemos contado la exhumación de José Antonio Primo de Rivera' (24 Apr 2023), https://elpais.com/espana/2023-04-24/la-exhumacion-de-primo-de-rivera-del-valle-de-los-caidos-ultimas-noticias-en-directo.html, accessed 25 Apr 2023.

Ellis, Kate Ferguson, *The Contested Castle: Gothic Novels and the Subversion of Domestic Ideology* (Urbana: University of Illinois Press, 1989).

Eng, David L. and David Kazanjian (eds), *Loss: The Politics of Mourning* (Berkeley: University of California Press, 2003).

Faber, Sebastiaan, *Exhuming Franco: Spain's Second Transition* (Nashville: Vanderbilt University Press, 2021).

Felman, Shoshana, 'Education and Crisis, or the Vicissitudes of Teaching', in C. Caruth (ed.), *Trauma: Explorations in Memory* (Baltimore: The Johns Hopkins University Press, 1995), pp. 13–60.

Fernández Cubas, Cristina, *El columpio* (Barcelona: Tusquets Editores, 1995).

Ferrándiz, Francisco, 'Cries and Whispers: Exhuming and Narrating Defeat in Spain Today', *Journal of Spanish Cultural Studies*, 9/2 (2008), 177–92.

Fleenor, Juliann E. (ed.), *The Female Gothic* (Montréal: Eden Press Inc., 1983).

Folkart, Jessica, *Angles on Otherness in Post-Franco Spain: The Fiction of Cristina Fernández Cubas* (Lewisburg: Bucknell University Press, 2002).

Freeman, Nick, 'Haunted Houses', in S. Brewster and L. Thurston (eds), *The Routledge Handbook to the Ghost Story* (New York: Routledge, 2018), pp. 328–37.

Freire, Espido, *Irlanda*, trans. Toshiya Kamei (Tuscaloosa: Fairy Tale Review Press, 2011).

Freud, Sigmund, *Beyond the Pleasure Principle*, ed. and trans. James Strachey (New York: W. W. Norton & Company, 1961).

Galdona Pérez, Rosa Isabel, *Discurso femenino en la novela española de posguerra: Carmen Laforet, Ana María Matute y Elena Quiroga* (La Laguna: Universidad de La Laguna, 2001).

Gancedo, Emilio, *Palabras mayores: un viaje por la memoria rural* (Logroño: Pepitas de Calabaza, 2017).

García Morales. Adelaida, *The South and Bene*, trans. Sarah Marsh (Manchester: Carcanet, 1992).

García Morales, Adelaida, *La tía Águeda* (Barcelona: Editorial Anagrama, 1995).

García Morales, Adelaida, *El secreto de Elisa* (Madrid: Editorial Debate, 1999).

García Sanz, Carolina, '"Disciplinando al gitano" en el siglo XX: regulación y parapenalidad en España desde una perspectiva europea', *Historia y Política*, 40 (2019), 115–46.

Gavilán, Enrique, 'De la imposibilidad y de la necesidad de la 'memoria histórica', in E. Silva, A. Esteban, J. Castán and P. Salvador (eds), *La memoria de los olvidados: Un debate sobre el silencio de la represión franquista* (Valladolid: Ámbito Ediciones, 2004), pp. 55–68.

Gazarian-Gautier, Marie-Lise, *Ana María Matute: La voz del silencio* (Madrid: Espasa Calpe, 1997).

Gil Poisa, María, '¿Qué es un fantasma? Trauma pasado y fantasía en el cine contemporáneo sobre la Guerra Civil española: El cine de Guillermo del Toro', *Hispania*, 99/1 (2016), 128–36.

Gilbert, Sandra M. and Susan Gubar, *The Madwoman in the Attic: The Woman Writer and the Nineteenth-Century Literary Imagination* (New Haven: Yale University Press, 1979).

Gilmore, David D., 'Men and Women in Southern Spain: "Domestic Power" Revisited', *American Anthropologist*, 92/4 (1990), 953–70.

Glenn, Kathleen M., 'Gothic Indecipherability and Doubling in the Fiction of Cristina Fernández Cubas', *Monographic Review/ Revista Monográfica*, 8 (1992), 125–41.

Glenn, Kathleen M. and Cristina Fernández Cubas, 'Conversación con Cristina Fernández Cubas', *Anales de la literatura española contemporánea*, 18/1–2 (1993), 355–63.

Glenn, Kathleen M. and Janet Pérez (eds), *Mapping the Fiction of Cristina Fernández Cubas* (Newark: University of Delaware Press, 2005).
Golsan, Richard J. (ed.), *Fascism's Return: Scandal, Revision, and Ideology Since 1980* (Lincoln: University of Nebraska Press, 1998).
González, Felipe and Juan Luis Cebrián, *El futuro no es lo que era: una conversación* (Madrid: Grupo Santillana de Ediciones, S. A., 2001).
González, Josefina, '*Mirall trencat*: un umbral autobiográfico en la obra de Mercè Rodoreda', *Revista de Estudios Hispánicos*, 30/1 (1996), 103–19.
González, Miguel, *Vox S. A.: El negocio del patriotismo español* (Barcelona: Península, 2022).
Gordon, Avery, *Ghostly Matters: Haunting and the Sociological Imagination* (Minneapolis: University of Minnesota Press, 2008).
Haggerty, George E., *Gothic Fiction/Gothic Form* (University Park: The Pennsylvania State University Press, 1989).
Halberstam, Judith, *Skin Shows: Gothic Horror and the Technology of Monsters* (Durham: Duke University Press, 1995).
Hardcastle, Anne E., 'Ghosts of the Past and Present: Hauntology and the Spanish Civil War in Guillermo del Toro's "The Devil's Backbone"', *Journal of the Fantastic in the Arts*, 15/2 (2005), 119–31.
Heiland, Donna, *Gothic & Gender: An Introduction* (Oxford: Blackwell Publishing, 2004).
Henry, Katherine, 'Slavery and Civic Recovery: Gothic Interventions in Whitman and Weld', in R. Bienstock Anolik and D. L. Howard (eds), *The Gothic Other: Racial and Social Constructions in the Literary Imagination* (Jefferson: McFarland & Co., 2004), pp. 32–53.
Henseler, Christine, 'Del bien y del mal: una entrevista con Espido Freire', *Letras Peninsulares*, 17/2–3 (2004–5), 249–58.
Hirsch, Marianne, *Family Frames: Photography, Narrative, and Postmemory* (Cambridge: Harvard University Press, 1997).
Hooper, John, *The New Spaniards* (2nd edn, New York: Penguin Group, 2006).
Horner, Avril, 'Apocalypses Now: Collective Trauma, Globalisation and the New Gothic Sublime', in M. Nadal and M. Calvo (eds),

Trauma in Contemporary Literature: Narrative and Representation (New York: Routledge, 2014), pp. 35–50.

Isidra Mencos, María, 'Mercè Rodoreda and the Criticism of Her Works: Analysis and Selected Bibliography', in K. McNerney (ed.), *The Voices and Visions: The Words and Works of Mercè Rodoreda* (Selinsgrove: Susquehanna University Press, 1999), pp. 240–65.

Jackson, Shirley, *We Have Always Lived in the Castle* (New York: Penguin Books, 2006).

Jerez-Farrán, Carlos and Samuel Amago (eds), *Unearthing Franco's Legacy: Mass Graves and the Recovery of Historical Memory in Spain* (Notre Dame: University of Notre Dame Press, 2010).

Joyce, Ashlee, *The Gothic in Contemporary British Trauma Fiction* (Cham: Palgrave, 2019).

Keller, Patricia, *Ghostly Landscapes: Film, Photography, and the Aesthetics of Haunting in Contemporary Spanish Culture* (Toronto: University of Toronto Press, 2016).

Kilgour, Maggie, *The Rise of the Gothic Novel* (New York: Routledge, 1995).

Kristeva, Julia, *Powers of Horror: An Essay on Abjection* (New York: Columbia University Press, 1982).

Labanyi, Jo, 'Postmodernism and the Problem of Cultural Identity', in H. Graham and J. Labanyi (eds), *Spanish Cultural Studies: An Introduction* (Oxford: Oxford University Press, 1995), pp. 396–406.

Labanyi, Jo, 'History and Hauntology; or, What Does One Do with the Ghosts of the Past? Reflections on Spanish Film and Fiction of the Post-Franco Period', in J. R. Resina (ed.), *Disremembering the Dictatorship: The Politics of Memory in the Spanish Transition to Democracy* (Amsterdam: Editions Rodopi B. V., 2000), pp. 65–82.

Labanyi, Jo, *Constructing Identity in Contemporary Spain: Theoretical Debates and Cultural Practice* (New York: Oxford University Press, 2002).

Labanyi, Jo, 'Memory and Modernity in Democratic Spain: The Difficulty of Coming to Terms with the Spanish Civil War', *Poetics Today*, 28/1 (2007), 89–116.

Labanyi, Jo, 'Testimonies of Repression: Methodological and Political Issues', in C. Jerez-Farrán, Carlos and S. Amago (eds),

Unearthing Franco's Legacy: Mass Graves and the Recovery of Historical Memory in Spain (Notre Dame: University of Notre Dame Press, 2010), pp. 192–205.

Labanyi, Jo, *Spanish Culture from Romanticism to the Present: Structures of Feeling* (Cambridge: Legenda, 2019).

LaCapra, Dominick, *Writing History, Writing Trauma* (Baltimore: Johns Hopkins University Press, 2001).

Landsberg, Alison, *Prosthetic Memory: The Transformation of American Remembrance in the Age of Mass Culture* (New York: Columbia University Press, 2004).

Laub, Dori, 'Truth and Testimony: The Process and the Struggle', in C. Caruth (ed.), *Trauma: Explorations in Memory* (Baltimore: Johns Hopkins University Press, 1995), pp. 61–75.

Lee Six, Abigail, *The Gothic Fiction of Adelaida García Morales: Haunting Words* (Woodbridge: Tamesis, 2006).

Lee Six, Abigail, *Gothic Terrors: Incarceration, Duplication, and Bloodlust in Spanish Narrative* (Lewisburg: Bucknell University Press, 2010).

Lee Six, Abigail, *Spanish Vampire Fiction Since 1900: Blood Relations* (London: Routledge, 2019).

Liggins, Emma, *The Haunted House in Women's Ghost Stories: Gender, Space and Modernity, 1850–1945* (Cham: Palgrave Macmillan, 2020).

Linares, Montserrat, 'Fragmented Identities: The Narrative World of Espido Freire', in K. A. Kietrys and M. Linares (eds), *Women in the Spanish Novel Today: Essays on the Reflection of Self in the Works of Three Generations* (Jefferson: McFarland & Company, 2009), pp. 205–18.

Llamazares, Julio, *The Yellow Rain*, trans. Margaret Jull Costa (Orlando: Harcourt, 2003).

Llamazares, Julio, *Wolf Moon*, trans. Simon Deefholts and Kathryn Phillips-Miles (London: Peter Owen, 2017).

Llera, José Antonio, 'Memoria, duelo y melancolía en *La lluvia amarilla*, de Julio Llamazares', *Revista de Literatura*, 81/162 (2019), 533–48.

Llored, Yannick, '*Paraíso inhabitado* de Ana María Matute: Un singular estilo tardío desde la infancia como origen', *Cuadernos de Investigación Filológica*, 46 (2019), 59–76.

López de Abiada, José Manuel and Augusta López Bernasocchi, 'Gramáticas de la memoria. Variaciones en torno a la transición española en cuatro novelas recientes (1985–2000): "Luna de lobos, Beatus ille, Corazón tan blanco y La caída de Madrid"', *Iberoamericana*, 4/15 (2004), 123–41.

López Santos, Miriam, *La novela gótica en España (1788–1833)* (Pontevedra: Editorial Academia del Hispanismo, 2010).

Luckhurst, Roger, *The Trauma Question* (New York: Routledge, 2008).

Marías, Javier, *Tomorrow in the Battle Think on Me*, trans. Margaret Jull Costa (New York: Harcourt Brace & Company, 1996).

Margenot, John B., 'Imaginería demoníaca en "Luna de lobos y La lluvia amarilla"', *Hispanic Journal*, 22/2 (2001), 495–509.

Margenot, John B., 'The Metafictional Metaphor in *El columpio*', in K. Glenn and J. Pérez (eds), *Mapping the Fiction of Cristina Fernández Cubas* (Newark: University of Delaware Press, 2005), pp. 167–83.

Martin-Márquez, Susan L., 'Vision, Power and Narrative in *Luna de lobos*: Julio Llamazares' Spanish Panopticon', *Revista Canadiense de Estudios Hispánicos*, 19/2 (1995), 379–87.

Matute, Ana María, *Paraíso inhabitado* (Barcelona: Editorial Planeta, 2018).

Matute, Ana María, *Demonios familiares* (Barcelona: Editorial Planeta, 2014).

Mayock, Ellen, 'Determinismo y libre albedrío en "La lluvia amarilla" de Julio Llamazares', *Hispania*, 93/4 (2010), 587–93.

McNerney, Kathleen and Nancy Vosburg (eds), *The Garden Across the Border: Mercè Rodoreda's Fiction* (Selinsgrove: Susquehanna University Press, 1994).

Merino, Eloy E. and H. Rosi Song (eds), *Traces of Contamination: Unearthing the Francoist Legacy in Contemporary Spanish Discourse* (Lewisburg: Bucknell University Press, 2005).

Moers, Ellen, *Literary Women* (New York: Anchor Books, 1977).

Molino, Sergio del, *La España vacía* (Madrid: Penguin Random House, 2022).

Moreiras Menor, Cristina, *Cultura herida: literatura y cine en la España democrática* (Madrid: Ediciones Libertarias, 2002).

Moreno Nuño, Carmen, 'The Ghosts of Javier Marías: The Trauma of a Civil War Unforgotten', in E. Merino and H. Rosi Song (eds), *Traces of Contamination: Unearthing the Francoist Legacy in Contemporary Spanish Discourse* (Lewisburg: Bucknell University Press, 2005), pp. 124–46.

Mulvey-Roberts, Marie, *Dangerous Bodies: Historicising the Gothic Corporeal* (Manchester: Manchester University Press, 2016).

Nash, Mary, 'La construcción de una cultura política desde la legitimidad feminista durante la transición política democrática', in A. Aguado and T. M. Ortega (eds), *Feminismos y antifeminismos: culturas políticas e identidades de género en la España del siglo XX* (Valencia: Universitat de Valencia, 2011), pp. 283–306.

Navajas, Gonzalo, 'Normative Order and the Catalan *Heimat* in Mercè Rodoreda's *Mirall trencat*', in K. McNerney and N. Vosburg (eds), *The Garden Across the Border: Mercè Rodoreda's Fiction* (Selinsgrove: Susquehanna University Press, 1994), pp. 98–109.

Noyaret, Natalie, 'Formes et enjeux du silence dans *Demonios familiares* d'Ana María Matute', in N. Noyaret and C. Orsini-Saillet (eds), *L'expression du silence dans le récit de fiction espagnol contemporain* (Binges: Orbis Tertius, 2018), pp. 201–15.

Olivares Merino, Julio Ángel, 'La sobreimpresión febril: modalidades de la espectralidad en *La lluvia amarilla*, de Julio Llamazares', in N. Álvarez Méndez and A. Abello Verano (eds), *Realidades fracturadas: estéticas de lo insólito en la narrativa en lengua española (1980–2018)* (Madrid: Visor Libros, 2019), pp. 207–38.

Onandia Ruiz, Beatriz, 'Entre el pecado y la lujuria: la inmoralidad pública durante el franquismo', *Raudem, Revista de Estudios de las Mujeres*, 6 (2018), 172–97.

Ordóñez, Elizabeth J., *Voices of Their Own: Contemporary Spanish Narrative by Women* (Cranbury: Associated University Press, 1991).

Pao, Maria T., 'Justified: Ecocriticism and Moral Development in Espido Freire's *Irlanda* (1998)', *Neophilologus*, 101 (2017), 561–73.

Pérez, Janet, 'Gothic Spaces, Transgressions, and Apparitions in *Mirall trencat*: Rodoreda's Adaptation of the Paradigm', in K. McNerney and N. Vosburg (eds), *The Garden Across the Border: Mercè Rodoreda's Fiction* (Selinsgrove: Susquehanna University Press, 1994), pp. 85–97.

Pérez, Janet, 'Contemporary Spanish Women Writers and the Feminine Neo-Gothic', *Romance Quarterly*, 51/2 (2004), 125–40.

Ponce Romo, Laura Edith, 'Ecos de un pasado, elementos neo-góticos en la narrativa de Adelaida García Morales' (PhD thesis, Texas Tech University, Lubbock, 2012).

Pons Ballesteros, María Mercedes, 'El paraíso inhabitado de Ana María Matute: entre la realidad y la fantasía', *Tavira*, 25 (2009), 209–23.

Portela, M. Edurne, *El eco de los disparos: cultura y memoria de la violencia* (Barcelona: Galaxia Gutenberg, 2016).

Poza Diéguez, Mónica, 'La sugerencia de la trama o la magia narrativa de Espido Freire', *Espéculo*, 20 (2002), https://webs.ucm.es/info/especulo/numero20/freire.html, accessed 12 Oct 2022.

Praz, Mario, *The Romantic Agony* (London: Oxford University Press, 1954).

Punter, David, 'The English Ghost Story', in S. Brewster and L. Thurston (eds), *The Routledge Handbook to the Ghost Story* (New York: Routledge, 2018), pp. 179–87.

Resina, Joan Ramon, 'Short of Memory: the Reclamation of the Past Since the Spanish Transition to Democracy', in J. R. Resina (ed.), *Disremembering the Dictatorship: The Politics of Memory in the Spanish Transition to Democracy* (Amsterdam: Editions Rodopi B. V., 2000), pp. 83–126.

Resina, Joan Ramon, 'The Weight of Memory and the Lightness of Oblivion: The Dead of the Spanish Civil War', in C. Jerez-Farrán and S. Amago (eds), *Unearthing Franco's Legacy: Mass Graves and the Recovery of Historical Memory in Spain* (Notre Dame: University of Notre Dame Press, 2010), pp. 221–42.

Resina, Joan Ramon, *The Ghost in the Constitution: Historical Memory and Denial in Spanish Society* (Liverpool: Liverpool University Press, 2017).

Ribeiro de Menezes, Alison, *Embodying Memory in Contemporary Spain* (New York: Palgrave Macmillan, 2014).

Richards, Michael, 'From War Culture to Civil Society: Francoism, Social Change and Memories of the Spanish Civil War', *History and Memory*, 14/1–2 (Special Issue: Images of a Contested Past, 2002), 93–120.

Richards, Michael, 'Grand Narratives, Collective Memory, and Social History: Public Uses of the Past in Postwar Spain', in C. Jerez-Farrán and S. Amago (eds), *Unearthing Franco's Legacy: Mass Graves and the Recovery of Historical Memory in Spain* (Notre Dame: University of Notre Dame Press, 2010), pp. 121–45.

Ricoeur, Paul, *Memory, History, Forgetting*, trans. Kathleen Blamey and David Pellauer (Chicago: University of Chicago Press, 2004).

Riele, Dorothée te, 'The Metaphorical Landscape of the Spanish Author Julio Llamazares', in L. Korthals Altes and M. van Montfrans (eds), *The New Georgics: Rural and Regional Motifs in the Contemporary European Novel* (Amsterdam: Rodopi, 2002), pp. 199–213.

Río Hernández, Myriam del, 'Shadowing LaForet: Memory and the Imaginary in the Worlds of Espido Freire and Carmen Martín Gaite', in A. Walsh (ed.), *Telling Tales: Storytelling in Contemporary Spain* (Newcastle upon Tyne: Cambridge Scholars Publishing, 2015), pp. 128–45.

Rives, Darcie D., 'Haunted by Violence: Edith Wharton's "The Decoration of Houses" and Her Gothic Fiction', *Edith Wharton Review*, 22/1 (2006), 8–15.

Roas, David and Ana Casas (eds), *La realidad oculta: cuentos fantásticos españoles del siglo XX* (Palencia: Menoscuarto Ediciones, 2008).

Rodoreda, Mercè, *A Broken Mirror*, trans. Josep Miquel Sobrer (Lincoln: University of Nebraska Press, 2006).

Rodríguez Rodríguez, Samuel, 'Trauma y perversión en *Irlanda*, de Espido Freire', in R. de la Fuente Ballesteros, J. Pérez-Magallón and J. Manuel Goñi Pérez (eds), *El trauma en la literatura hispánica* (Valladolid: Universitas Castellae, 2016), pp. 177–85.

RTVE, 'Así es la Ley de Memoria Democrática que entra en vigor: mapa de desaparecidos y anulación de condenas franquistas' (20 Oct 2022), *https://www.rtve.es/noticias/20221020/asi-ley-memoria-democratica-entra-hoy-vigor-del-mapa-desaparecidos-anulacion-condenas-franquistas/2406472.shtml*, accessed 28 Oct 2022.

Ruiz Franco, Rosario, *¿Eternas menores? Las mujeres en el franquismo* (Madrid: Biblioteca Nueva, 2007).

Ruiz Serrano, Cristina, '"Traigo la camisa roja de sangre de un compañero": la mujer en la guerrilla antifranquista', *Revista Canadiense de Estudios Hispánicos*, 36/1 (2011), 169–85.

Ruiz Zafón, Carlos, *The Prisoner of Heaven*, trans. Lucia Graves (New York: HarperCollins Publishers, 2012).

Sáez, Iñaki Beti, 'El universo emocional en la narrativa de Espido Freire', *Sancho el Sabio: Revista de cultura e investigación vasca*, 13 (2000), 185–94.

Santa-Cruz, Maylis, 'Un autre monde est-il possible?: Paraíso inhabitado d'Ana María Matute', *Bulletin hispanique*, 116/2 (Dec 2014), 549–61.

Scarlett, Elizabeth, '"Vinculada a les flors": Flowers and the Body in *Jardí vora el mar* and *Mirall trencat*', in K. McNerney and N. Vosburg (eds), *The Garden Across the Border: Mercè Rodoreda's Fiction* (Selinsgrove: Susquehanna University Press, 1994), pp. 73–84.

Schouten, Fiona, *A Diffuse Murmur of History: Literary Memory Narratives of Civil War and Dictatorship in Spanish Novels After 1990* (Brussels: Peter Lang, 2010).

Sedgwick, Eve Kosofsky, *The Coherence of Gothic Conventions* (New York: Arno Press, 1980).

Silva, Emilio, Asunción Esteban, Javier Castán and Pancho Salvador (eds), *La memoria de los olvidados: Un debate sobre el silencio de la represión franquista* (Valladolid: Ámbito Ediciones, 2004).

Smith, Andrew, *The Ghost Story 1840–1920: A Cultural History* (Manchester: Manchester University Press, 2010).

Smith, Paul Julian, *The Moderns: Time, Space, and Subjectivity in Contemporary Spanish Culture* (Oxford: Oxford University Press, 2000).

Thomas, Sarah, 'Phantom Children: Spectral Presences and the Violent Past in Two Films of Contemporary Spain', in A. Ribas-Casasayas and A. L. Petersen (eds), *Espectros: Ghostly Hauntings in Contemporary Transhispanic Narratives* (Lanham: Bucknell University Press, 2016), pp. 101–15.

Thompson, Currie K., 'Adelaida García Morales's *Bene* and That Not-so-obscure Object of Desire', *Revista de Estudios Hispánicos*, 22/1 (Jan 1988), 99–106.

Torres Begines, Concepción, 'Espacios de la infancia y la memoria en Ana María Matute: *Paraíso inhabitado* y *Demonios familiares*', *Dicenda*, 37 (2019), 123–40.

Trigo, Beatriz, 'El conflicto íntimo: la recuperación de la identidad a través de lo fantástico en *El secreto de Elisa* de Adelaida García Morales', *Letras Femeninas*, 31/1 (2005), 180–94.

Tseng, Li-Jung, 'El espacio imaginario y la memoria en tres novelas de Julio Llamazares: *Luna de lobos*, *La lluvia amarilla* y *El cielo de Madrid*', *Siglo XXI*, 11 (2013), 133–68.

Tsuchiya, Akiko, 'Repetition, Remembrance, and the Construction of Subjectivity in the Works of Cristina Fernández Cubas', in K. Glenn and J. Pérez (eds), *Mapping the Fiction of Cristina Fernández Cubas* (Newark: University of Delaware Press, 2005), pp. 99–117.

Vadillo Buenfil, Carlos, '*La tía Águeda*, de Adelaida García Morales: Entre la novela de iniciación y la escritura confesional', *Castilla. Estudios de Literatura*, 6 (2015), 402–22.

Varnado, S. L., *Haunted Presence: The Numinous in Gothic Fiction* (Tuscaloosa: University of Alabama Press, 1987).

Vilarós, Teresa M., *El mono del desencanto: Una crítica de la transición española (1973–1993)* (Madrid: Siglo XXI Editores, 1998).

Vollendorf, Lisa, 'Exchanging Terms: Toward the Feminist Fantastic in *Mirall trencat*', in K. McNerney (ed.), *Voices and Visions: The Words and Works of Mercè Rodoreda* (Selinsgrove: Susquehanna University Press, 1999), pp. 156–74.

Wallace, Diana, 'The Ghost Story and Feminism', in S. Brewster and L. Thurston (eds), *The Routledge Handbook to the Ghost Story* (New York: Routledge, 2018), pp. 427–35.

Wallace, Diana, 'A Woman's Place', in A. Horner and S. Zlosnik (eds), *Women and the Gothic: An Edinburgh Companion* (Edinburgh: Edinburgh University Press, 2016), pp. 74–88.

Wallace, Diana and Andrew Smith (eds), *The Female Gothic: New Directions* (New York: Palgrave, 2009).

Watkiss, Joanne, *Gothic Contemporaries: The Haunted Text* (Cardiff: University of Wales Press, 2012).

Weinstock, Jeffrey Andrew (ed.), *Spectral America: Phantoms and the National Imagination* (Madison: University of Wisconsin Press, 2004).

Wester, Maisha, 'The Gothic in and as Race Theory', in J. E. Hogle and R. Miles (eds), *The Gothic and Theory: An Edinburgh*

Companion (Edinburgh: Edinburgh University Press, 2020), pp. 53–70.

Williams, Raymond, *The Country and the City* (New York: Oxford University Press, 1973).

Wisker, Gina, *Contemporary Women's Gothic Fiction* (London: Palgrave, 2016).

Ysàs, Pere, 'El franquismo: de la victoria a una larga supervivencia', in A. Esteban Recio, D. Etura and M. Tomasoni (eds), *La alargada sombra del franquismo: Naturaleza, mecanismos de pervivencia y huellas de la dictadura* (Granada: Editorial Comares, 2019), pp. 5–24.

Index

A
Abascal, Santiago 206
abjection 13, 42, 44, 50, 55, 71, 157, 179, 208
  see also Kristeva, Julia
abortion 98, 206
Abraham, Nicholas and Maria Torok 10, 14, 107–8, 157
  see also phantoms, transgenerational
absence 21, 108, 126, 131, 133, 135, 138, 176–8, 184–5, 188
  maternal 95, 102, 179
  present absences 2–3, 16, 38, 102–3, 120, 129, 180
Aldana Reyes, Xavier 5, 6, 143, 192
alterity *see* otherness
amnesia 11, 108, 122, 154
  see also forgetting; oblivion; Pact of Forgetting
Amnesty Law 3, 108, 154, 198
  see also Pact of Forgetting
Angel in the House 13, 19, 63
  see also femininity; gender, traditional roles

animalisation 117–19
anxiety 15, 47, 76, 83, 85, 115, 137, 144, 157
  domestic 19–21, 38, 61, 74, 102
  future 5, 13, 28
  socio-political 8, 91, 134, 158, 187, 192
  race-related 49–50, 59
  see also fear; horror; sublime; terror
Aragon 14, 125, 130
Association for the Recovery of Historical Memory 3, 15
Asturias 14, 112
authoritarianism 20, 96–7, 101, 206, 209
authorship 19, 84, 86, 112, 124, 158, 188, 199, 202–3, 209
autonomy 20–1, 23–4, 27, 33–4, 37, 39, 97

B
Bachelard, Gaston 89, 113
Barcelona 23–6, 31, 128, 190–4, 197
  see also Gothic, Barcelona Gothic

Index

barriers 46–7, 49, 53, 55–7, 93, 99, 143
  see also borders; boundaries
Basque Country 160, 164, 174
bedrooms 34, 55–6, 71, 81–2, 142, 148
Billy El Niño *see* González Pacheco, Antonio
blood 28–9, 82, 116, 130–1, 165, 167, 171–3, 198–9
body 2, 44–5, 71, 127, 131, 133, 191, 197, 200
  female 20, 22, 26, 31–3, 38, 49, 59, 72, 75, 82–3, 90, 170, 172
borders 22, 26, 43–5
  see also barriers; boundaries
boundaries 13, 19, 42, 44–7, 49, 52, 57–9, 75, 99–100, 174, 204
  see also barriers; borders
burial 2–3, 9, 69, 115–16, 121, 135, 139, 173, 202, 205

C

Cantabria 14, 112
capitalism 31–2, 168–9, 173
Caruth, Cathy 14, 158, 166, 196
Catalonia 23–6, 36, 45
  see also Barcelona
Catholic Church 64, 66, 70, 119, 182
  see also clergy; National Catholicism
cemeteries 8, 11, 67, 77, 126, 128, 130, 134–5, 163, 169, 193–4, 205
censorship 113, 121–2, 134, 148, 153, 158, 185
  literary 87, 102
  metaphorical 37
  political tool 10, 114, 195, 200, 202–3, 207
  see also silence
Cercas, Javier 109

Cervantes, Miguel de 43, 190
childhood 100, 144–8, 150–3, 163, 169, 174, 176–8, 180, 188–9
  see also innocence
circularity (cyclical) 80, 109–10, 117, 134, 146, 149, 153–4, 159
Civil Guard 57, 112–13, 116–19, 121, 123, 196
civil war 1–3, 7–8, 11, 87, 94, 122, 128, 134, 140, 207
  representation in literature 24–5, 27, 35, 88–90, 98, 109, 111, 125, 127, 132–3, 176, 184, 192, 195
class (socioeconomic) 13, 24, 30–3, 43, 45, 47, 49, 53, 58–9, 163, 168
claustrophobia 19, 49, 62, 77–8, 80, 85, 91, 127
clergy 118–19
  see also Catholic Church; National Catholicism
Colmeiro, José 3, 194, 203
concentration camps 24, 114, 197
conservatism 10, 41, 154, 180, 206
countryside (rural) 8, 73, 76, 85, 88, 107, 109–11, 113, 117, 120, 126–8, 131–2, 140, 145
  see also landscape
curriculum (school) 64–5, 67, 182

D

darkness 55, 159, 165, 167, 172, 174, 176, 184, 186
  interior 70, 83, 93, 145
  night 113, 115–18, 179–80
Davies, Ann 6, 192
death 4, 38, 42, 49, 52, 115–16, 121, 123–4, 128, 133, 137–8, 165–6
  atmosphere 29, 57, 77, 81, 120, 131–2, 136, 193–4

Index

characters 29, 32, 34, 37, 49, 58, 69–72, 96–7, 118, 135, 152, 161, 172, 176, 188
  see also living dead; revenants; undead; zombies
decay 29, 121, 127, 130–1, 136
degeneration 14, 121, 136, 208
democracy 3, 6–11, 60–1, 114, 121–2, 154, 206, 208–9
  see also Transition (political era)
Democratic Memory Law 2, 205
Derrida, Jacques 3, 7, 28, 102, 192, 195, 208
  see also hauntology
devil (diabolical) 21, 42, 46, 50–2, 54, 57–8, 67, 70, 116
  see also evil; Fatal Woman
disillusionment 3, 10, 12, 159, 176, 178, 188
divorce 61, 76
  see also marriage
domesticity 19–21, 27, 30, 34, 38, 61, 64, 67, 71, 75–7, 85, 91–2
  see also space (physical), domestic
doubles 141, 143–4, 149, 178

E

entrapment 19, 21, 42, 48–9, 52, 56–8, 60–1, 63, 84, 86, 91, 96, 208
  see also imprisonment
evil 45–6, 51–6, 66, 174, 179
  see also devil (diabolical)
exhumation 2, 123, 134, 139–40, 205, 209
exodus (rural) 14, 109, 128, 146, 207
  see also Great Trauma; urban-rural divide
Extremadura 46

F

fairy tales 161–3, 168, 185
  see also fantasy
Falange 63, 66, 72
  see also fascism; Women's Section
fantastic (literary) 5, 9, 27, 29, 41–2, 55, 73–4, 142–4
fantasy 84, 152, 165, 173–4
  childhood 15, 158, 178, 180, 182, 185, 187–8
  see also fairy tales
fascism 10, 15, 21, 63, 119, 193, 207, 209
  see also Falange; National Catholicism; Women's Section
Fatal Woman 52, 58
  see also devil (diabolical); sexuality, female
fear 45, 62, 66, 69–71, 80–1, 91–2, 95, 107–8, 127, 131, 136–7, 153, 184–6
  atmosphere 28–9, 133, 159, 207, 209
  of difference 50–1, 53–4, 59
  politics of 114–15, 117, 121, 134, 140
  women's 21, 83–4
  see also anxiety; horror; sublime; terror
femininity 19, 26–7, 30, 32, 34, 63, 66, 72, 74–5, 82, 96, 179, 182, 197, 207
  see also Angel in the House; gender, traditional roles
Fernández Arias, Casimiro 112
Fernández Cubas, Cristina (biography and criticism) 141–4
flashbacks 125, 133, 137, 161
Fleenor, Juliann 75, 94, 177–8
folklore 26, 119, 161–2, 165, 167, 170
  see also mythology

Index

forgetting 3, 10, 79, 134–6, 140, 154
   see also amnesia; oblivion; Pact of Forgetting
fragmentation 11, 13, 35–8, 195, 208
Franco, Francisco 1, 94
   death 1–2, 140
   Francisco Franco Foundation 2, 206
   legacy 2–3, 5, 205–7, 209
   policies 23, 37, 39, 43–5, 86, 109, 114–15, 119, 134, 138, 195, 197, 201–3
   post-Franco era 3, 8, 10, 15–16, 75, 82, 108, 121–2, 144, 158, 164, 174
Freire, Espido (biography and criticism) 160–3
Freud, Sigmund 151, 157
   see also psychoanalysis

G

Galicia 45, 160, 162, 167
García Morales, Adelaida (biography and criticism) 40–2, 60–3, 73–4
gaze 54, 93, 96, 102, 136
   male 21, 38, 73, 79, 83–5
gender 12, 73
   traditional roles 12, 34, 61, 63, 67, 69, 71–2, 74, 85, 97, 163, 167, 182
   see also Angel in the House; femininity
Generation of '68 141
ghosts 1, 20, 51, 81, 109, 157
   figures 35–6, 41, 55–6, 58, 70, 75, 82–5, 92–3, 95, 125–6, 135–7, 150, 166–7
   metaphorical 2–3, 10–12, 79, 102, 115, 119–20, 133, 193, 199–202, 207–9

ghost stories 3, 30, 38, 42, 71, 81, 93, 102, 107, 135
ghost towns 8, 127, 140
   see also haunting; hauntology; phantoms; seance; spectrality; spirits
González Pacheco, Antonio 198
Gothic
   atmosphere 4, 11, 14, 28–9, 46–7, 116, 128, 130, 132, 140, 145, 154, 164, 171, 193
   Barcelona Gothic 192, 194, 196, 201, 204
   Female Gothic 13, 19–20, 75, 78, 91, 94, 178
   Spanish Gothic 4–6, 8–9, 12, 16, 27, 143, 158, 163, 191–2, 204
Great Trauma 109, 128–9, 132, 138, 140
   see also exodus (rural); urban-rural divide
gypsies *see* Roma

H

haunting 1, 7–8, 15–16, 30, 37, 97–8, 101, 107, 110, 119–20, 150, 157–9, 173–4, 195, 201
   aesthetics of 3–4
   haunted house motif 7, 12–13, 19–22, 37–8, 42, 59, 61, 63, 71–2, 76, 90–1, 93, 102
   in marriage 62, 69, 71
   of people 28, 35–6, 50, 81, 84–6, 94, 161, 165–6, 183
   see also ghosts; hauntology; phantoms; seance; spectrality; spirits
hauntology 3, 28
   see also Derrida, Jacques
Hirsch, Marianne *see* postmemory

Index

historical memory 7, 10, 12, 89, 108, 112, 114, 194, 203, 205–6, 208–9
   Historical Memory Law 10
   see also memory
home *see* space (physical), domestic
horror 15, 20, 41, 45, 50, 58, 83, 93, 153–4, 158, 179, 189, 192, 194–5, 197–8, 203
   see also anxiety; fear; sublime; terror

I

identity 44–5, 115–16, 127, 137, 164–5, 191, 201, 204
   cultural 128
   female 71, 94, 178, 182
   loss of 20
   national 37, 43, 45, 59, 128, 138, 194
   personal 36, 124
imprisonment 46, 75, 78, 83, 97, 191, 199, 201
   see also entrapment
innocence 62, 67–8, 88, 98, 100, 176, 181, 186–9
   see also childhood; purity
isolation 29, 83, 118
   geographical 46, 72–3, 77, 109, 113, 116, 125, 128, 145, 154
   self-imposed 48, 56, 97
   solitude 42, 123, 126–7, 129, 132, 138

J

Jackson, Shirley 164, 173, 179

K

Kristeva, Julia 44, 52
   see also abjection

L

Labanyi, Jo 3, 5, 44, 112, 119, 124, 127, 203, 208
LaCapra, Dominick 110, 199
Landsberg, Alison 146–7
   see also memory, prosthetic
landscape 3, 109–10, 112, 115–17, 119–21, 124, 125–7, 129–33, 136, 139, 163, 208
   memory landscape 11, 107, 113, 137–9, 146
   see also countryside (rural)
Le Pen, Marine 206
Lee Six, Abigail 5–6, 42, 62, 98
León (province) 111–12, 114, 126, 128, 140
letters (correspondence) 73, 78–80, 142–4, 148–9, 152–3, 185, 199
liminality 10–11, 19, 137, 139, 141, 144–6, 154, 163, 165, 169, 172, 174, 199–200
linearity 109, 149–50, 154, 208
living dead 49, 54, 116, 119, 203
   see also revenants; undead; zombies
Llamazares, Julio (biography and criticism) 111–13, 125–7
loss 102, 124, 131, 138, 140, 144, 151–2, 167, 188, 194
   of community 129
   of family 41, 57, 63, 125, 135, 142
   see also silence, of loss

M

madness 62, 70, 72, 85, 109, 133–4, 136–7, 144, 150, 152, 154, 191, 198–9
   see also psychosis
MAGA (political movement) 206–7
magic 162, 164, 166, 168–71, 174, 180

maquis (historical background) 113–15
marginalisation 4, 7, 42–4, 50, 58, 77, 119, 180, 200–1, 207
Marías, Javier 1
marriage 32–3, 36, 65, 71, 75–7, 98, 180, 182
   see also divorce
mass graves 2–3, 11, 125, 133–5, 140, 191, 200, 205, 208–9
maternity 19–20, 26, 33–4, 38, 64–5, 71, 75–6, 82, 94–6, 152, 178–9
   see also motherhood
matricide 33–4
Matute, Ana María (biography and criticism) 87–90, 102–3, 175–7, 188–9
melancholia 144, 150–3
   see also mourning
Meloni, Giorgia 206
memory 1–2, 9–10, 16, 36, 93–4, 107, 110, 121–4, 127–31, 134–9, 144, 158–9, 166, 174, 195
   artefacts of 149, 152–3
   collective 11, 14, 39, 113, 123–4, 129, 154, 177, 203–4
   impersonal 80
   Memory Boom 7, 12
   prosthetic 146–8, 154
   repression of 37
   see also Democratic Memory Law; historical memory; postmemory
mirrors 35, 29, 55, 92–3, 97–8, 102
modernity 3, 7, 11, 16, 44, 76, 82, 85, 102, 109, 144–6, 154, 163, 167, 170, 195
   technology 8, 128
Molino, Sergio del 109, 128–9, 132

monstrosity 9, 29–30, 72, 113, 117–19, 159, 177, 180–4, 187–9
   feminine 19, 32, 34, 90, 179
   racial 42, 45, 49–56, 58–9
Montjüic 191–4, 196–8, 200
Moreno-Nuño, Carmen 11, 108, 115
Morocco, war 88, 90, 94
motherhood 20, 32–4, 64–5, 71–2, 74–5, 85–6, 94–7, 101, 143, 177–9, 182, 184
   see also maternity
mourning 3, 8, 14, 110, 113, 123–4, 128, 132, 137–8, 151
   see also melancholia
mythology 10, 161, 206
   see also folklore

N

National Catholicism 20, 60–1, 63–5, 67, 72, 82, 85, 207, 209
   see also Catholic Church
nationalism 37, 72, 85, 94, 102, 200, 206
nationalists (civil war) 63, 88, 111, 114, 118, 194, 207
nightmares 11, 50, 81, 136, 143, 153, 166, 169, 173, 200
nostalgia 35, 90, 131, 137, 150, 154

O

oblivion 14, 108, 115–16, 121–4, 131, 133–4, 194
   see also amnesia; forgetting; Pact of Forgetting
obsession 2, 34, 61, 63, 73–4, 115, 127, 131, 157, 161, 163, 168, 170, 172

Index

oppression 20, 30, 39, 60, 82, 113, 124, 159, 163, 165, 180, 189, 207, 209
   atmosphere of 32, 47, 78, 97, 103, 183–4
Orbán, Viktor 206
orphanhood 39, 96
otherness 43–4, 50, 53, 58–9

P

Pact of Forgetting 12, 108, 114, 136, 206–7
   see also Amnesty Law
paranoia 83–4
Partido Popular 206
pathetic fallacy 54
patriarchy 15, 19, 24, 27, 32, 37–8, 42, 60, 86, 96–7, 101–2, 182–3
Pérez, Janet 5, 27, 29, 31, 39, 62, 141–4
Perkins Gilman, Charlotte 75
phantoms 41, 51, 55–8, 74, 84, 94, 96, 108, 113, 135, 152–3, 166, 176, 186
   transgenerational 10, 108, 157
   see also ghosts; haunting; hauntology; seance; spectrality; spirits
photographs 78–80, 82–3, 85, 96, 135–7, 144, 147–8
Poe, Edgar Allan 141, 162
poison 163, 169, 171
Portela, Edurne 164–5, 174
postmemory 75, 78–9, 112
Primo de Rivera, José Antonio 63, 205
   see also Falange
Primo de Rivera, Miguel 23, 93
   see also Morocco, war

Primo de Rivera, Pilar 20, 63, 65
   see also Falange; Women's Section
progress 22, 34, 38, 102, 137, 159, 163, 166–8, 170, 172–3, 206
   progression of time 146, 149–50, 154
   see also trauma, of progress
propaganda 10, 20, 63–4, 94, 154, 197
prostitution 21, 53, 64, 69
psychoanalysis 41, 51, 143
   see also Freud, Sigmund
psychosis 11, 61, 136, 152, 163, 171, 198
   see also madness
purity 21, 61, 64
   see also innocence

R

race 8, 43, 45, 50, 53, 58, 200, 207
realism (literary) 5, 7, 11, 24–6, 28, 109, 130, 162, 177
repetition 93, 102, 148, 150, 163, 166, 171–2
   acts 33, 53, 116, 146, 151–2
   narrative technique 30, 46, 80, 130–2, 136, 153–4
Republicans (Spanish civil war) 88, 111–12, 114, 118, 186, 192, 207
Resina, Joan Ramon 10–12, 23–4, 37, 108, 208
revenants 10, 79, 102, 120
   see also living dead; undead; zombies
Rif War *see* Morocco, war
Rodoreda, Mercè (biography and criticism) 23–7
Roma 41–4, 49–50, 53–4, 58–9
romanticism (literary) 28
Royal Spanish Academy 43, 88

Index

Ruiz Zafón, Carlos (biography and criticism) 190–2

S
Sabatini, Anthony 207
Sánchez, Pedro 205
Sánchez Terán, Salvador 121–2
seance 73, 82–3
   see also ghosts; haunting; hauntology; phantoms; spectrality; spirits
Second Republic 180, 182, 186, 207
secrets 32, 48, 50, 81, 107–8, 142, 149, 161, 195, 199, 202–3
   see also unspeakable
Sedgwick, Eve Kosofsky 47, 53, 107
sexuality 12–13, 33, 42, 53, 58, 68, 81, 83, 91, 100, 162, 167, 169, 171
   female 22, 32, 38, 52, 61, 63, 75, 82, 98, 170, 178
   see also Fatal Woman
shadows 20, 54, 56, 119–20, 125, 130, 132–3, 139, 167, 174, 180, 193
silence 37, 107–8, 113, 115, 119–21, 123, 127, 144–5, 154, 158, 207–8
   atmosphere of 69, 74, 89–91, 98, 102, 135–6, 139
   generational 3, 11–12
   silence of loss 132, 138–40
   politics of 6–7, 9–10, 114–15, 122, 124, 134, 200–3
   rural 77, 108–10, 116–17, 129–30, 132–3
   see also censorship; unspeakable
space (physical) 2, 74, 89, 92, 96–7, 113, 126–7, 146, 162, 174, 181, 194
   closed 45–9, 57, 141
   domestic 19–22, 29–30, 34, 38, 66, 72, 76–7, 80, 91, 93, 130, 132
   Heimat 26
   personal 84–6, 99
   threatening 54, 71, 81
Spanishness 44–5, 59, 201
spectrality 35, 102, 107, 152, 154, 180, 184, 192, 199–201, 207–9
   historical trauma 2–4, 7–8, 10, 15, 110, 120, 124, 157–9
   literary function 12
   spectral presences 36, 38, 56, 93–5, 127, 132, 135–9, 150, 166, 178, 188
   see also ghosts; haunting; hauntology; phantoms; seance; spirits
spirits 38, 48, 61–2, 69, 73, 78, 80, 82–3, 93, 150, 161, 166–7, 169
   see also ghosts; haunting; hauntology; phantoms; seance; spectrality
stasis 163, 167–8, 170, 173
subjectivity 147–8, 153–4, 166
sublime 28, 48, 50, 55–8, 81, 84
   see also anxiety; fear; horror; terror
subversion 7, 30, 34, 38, 45, 48, 91, 162, 179, 193
supernatural 25, 27, 29, 35, 38, 41, 48–52, 54, 56–8, 70, 73, 75, 78, 84, 86, 91–3, 143
superstition 51, 161–2, 164, 166–9

T
terror 4, 7, 57, 61, 72, 78, 95, 107, 136, 200, 204, 208
   atmosphere 11, 63, 115, 134, 165, 172, 193–4
   domestic 19, 66, 70, 80–5, 90

politics of 14, 114, 117–19, 197, 202, 207
racial 50, 54, 58
see also anxiety; fear; horror; sublime
testimony 124, 157, 192, 194–203
theatricality 142–3, 147, 151
time (experience of) 36, 77, 79, 109, 116, 137, 139, 144–7, 149–51, 154
see also circularity; linearity
Torok, Maria *see* Abraham, Nicholas and Maria Torok
torture 25, 29, 121, 123, 134, 192, 197–8, 201
tower (structure) 28–9, 41, 48–9, 53–4, 56–7, 144, 147, 164–5, 171–2, 193
tradition 102, 127, 144, 163, 179, 187–8, 206
 cultural 8, 39, 108–9, 112, 129
 literary 42, 73
 national 7, 65, 74, 85, 182
 see also gender, traditional roles
transgression 27, 30, 59, 92, 163, 172, 177, 179, 208
Transition (political era) 3, 5, 7, 9–15, 21, 60, 72, 85–6, 108, 110, 112, 122–4
 see also democracy
trauma 1–4, 37, 41, 110, 120, 136, 138, 140, 157–9, 192, 194, 196, 199–202, 204
 childhood 93, 158, 163–6, 172–4, 178, 188
 collective 3, 7, 10, 115, 117, 133, 139, 178, 203, 207–9
 generational 78, 107–8, 112, 157
 of progress 163, 167, 169, 171
 see also Great Trauma

Trump, Donald 206

U

undead 200
 see also living dead; revenants; zombies
unspeakable 10, 46, 53, 107–8, 141, 154, 157, 193, 195, 203, 208
 see also secrets
urban-rural divide 8, 74, 77, 91, 109, 126, 128, 138, 145, 154
 see also exodus (rural); Great Trauma

V

Valley of the Fallen 2, 4, 205
vampires 9, 119
ventriloquism 151, 153
Vilarós, Teresa 9–10, 15
violence 81, 83, 98, 116–17, 126, 157, 161, 163, 171–4
 children's games 29, 36
 culture of 7, 159, 164–5
 political 113–14, 186–7, 196–8, 202
 sexual 32, 71–2, 75, 84–5
Vox (political party) 206–7, 209

W

war *see* Civil War; Morocco, war
werewolves 113, 117, 119–20
witchcraft 162, 167, 170, 183
Women's Section 20, 61, 63–6, 71–2, 85
 see also Falange; fascism; Primo de Rivera, Pilar

Z

zombies 192
 see also living dead; revenants; undead